DEATH OF A TRANSLATOR

DEATH OF A
TRANSLATOR

Ed Gorman

.

A

Arcadia Books Ltd
139 Highlever Road
London W10 6PH

www.arcadiabooks.co.uk

First published in the United Kingdom 2017
Copyright © Ed Gorman 2017

A catalogue record for this book is available from the British Library.

ISBN 978-1-911350-08-8

Typeset in Sabon by MacGuru Ltd
Printed and bound by TJ International, Padstow PL28 8RW

ARCADIA BOOKS DISTRIBUTORS ARE AS FOLLOWS:

in the UK and elsewhere in Europe:
BookSource
50 Cambuslang Road
Cambuslang
Glasgow G32 8NB

in Australia/New Zealand:
NewSouth Books
University of New South Wales
Sydney NSW 2052

CONTENTS

For Jeanna, Tilou, Florence and Marcus
and in memory of my mother

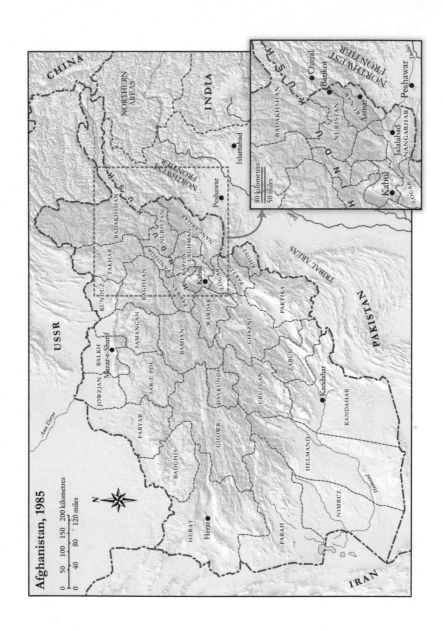

Afghanistan, 1985

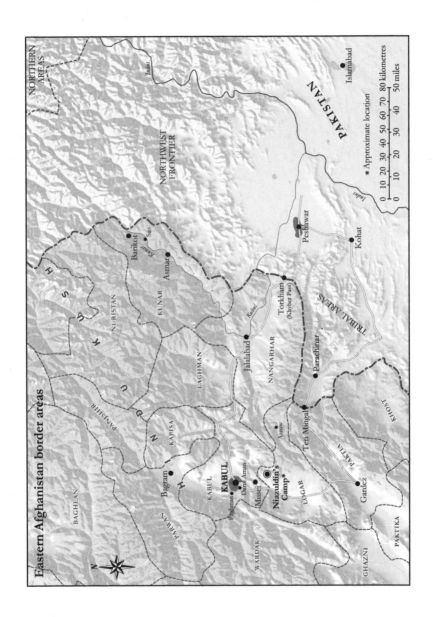

Eastern Afghanistan border areas

AUTHOR'S NOTE

The military force sent into Afghanistan in December 1979 by Leonid Brezhnev is often referred to as 'Russian' whereas it was in fact made up of Russian troops but also soldiers from other parts of the Soviet Union. It should thus be correctly termed the Soviet army. I have used this in the narrative except where I am specifically dealing with Russian soldiers or when Afghans and others have used the term 'Russian' in conversation.

To protect the privacy of certain individuals, some names and biographical details have been changed.

FOREWORD

We had been up since before early morning prayers, getting ready. The rattle and thump of the first helicopter gunships taking off from the nearby Soviet base shook the house every few minutes. Zulmai was his usual bunch of nerves, puffing on one cheap Afghan cigarette after another, as we awaited the arrival of the driver.

Even at this late stage in the plan, we knew that the unexpected intervention of Afghan soldiers conducting house-to-house searches or a visit from the feared KHAD, the Communist government's secret police, could force instant cancellation – and panic. They knew Zulmai was working for the resistance – they were just waiting to catch him and his cell red-handed. Had they arrived unannounced I would have been hustled down – amid frantic whispered instructions – into a hiding hole under the floor, the sort of place where I had already spent hours on other days waiting for the danger to pass.

I shaved for the first time in weeks, hacking at my beard with scissors and then a blunt razor, aided by soap and cold water. Life in the mountains had been spent living and dressing like one of the Mujahidin – the Holy Warriors – and my beard was part of the effect, along with my dark green *shalwar kameez*. Staring into the battered mirror in the primitive bathroom, I saw the whitened frame of my face, my skin stretched taut across it, my eyes dulled.

Dysentery had weakened me but I had no appetite for breakfast that morning in any case. I followed Zulmai's example and smoked instead, running through in my mind the risks I was about to take and what might happen if things went wrong. I just wanted to get it done. I was committed and I owed it to Niazuldin, the commander of the group I was embedded with, and his men who had planned it.

Now Zulmai was telling me to dress – he had presented me with the 'Western' clothes that he imagined might be worn by a young Russian officer on his day off. A brown jacket, fawn trousers, brown leather belt with brass buckle, checked cotton shirt and grey shoes.

I struggled to squeeze my scrawny body into garments made for someone smaller and thinner than I was even then. But I had no choice. I had to inhabit these clothes as if they were my own. I tried to comb my unruly hair. Now Zulmai and one of the others was coming back from the garden. 'He is here, he is here, Mr Edward. Hurry, hurry … you must hurry, Mr Edward – we cannot delay,' he shouted as I grabbed my camera and everyone wished me luck.

'Come, come, come …' I followed him out of the door and across the communal garden where the children stared at this stranger in their midst, dressed as one of their enemies. I had been told to look straight ahead and not make eye contact with anyone on my way to the vehicle.

But I couldn't help myself, smiling at a little girl who stood open-mouthed, as we surged past her towards the door through the high garden wall. I bade farewell to Zulmai. 'God be with you, Zulmai – I will see you soon, *inshallah* …'

It was a fine morning – the first time in Kabul that I had been outside in daylight. Zulmai shook my hand. 'Good luck, Mr Edward,' he said as I stepped out into the street.

PREPARING FOR WAR

My career as a journalist got off on the wrong foot.

I had always dreamed of becoming a foreign correspondent and idolised the leading figures of the 1970s and early 80s. I had eagerly read the memoirs of James Cameron, the celebrated foreign correspondent of the *Daily Express,* and read accounts by reporters and photographers who had covered the Vietnam War. While studying at Cambridge I carried a clipping in my wallet of a column in *The Times* by my then-hero, Robert Fisk. Entitled 'Letter from Sidon', it was a beautifully observed story about a Lebanese family struggling to come to terms with the havoc wrought by the civil war and it summed up everything about being a foreign correspondent I wanted to emulate. I loved the idea of travelling overseas to places of great drama, taking personal risks to report on conflict or human tragedy, and trying to capture what was happening for an audience back home.

On the day that I graduated I read a profile of Mick Jagger in *The Times* in which he said that had he not become a pop star, journalism would have been his thing. It struck me then that perhaps journalism might not have to remain just a dream for me. With a modern history and economics degree under my belt – the economics was a bit of an anomaly since I can barely add let alone tackle long-division or statistics – I thought: 'If it is good enough for Mick, then it will do for me, too.'

But in my chaotic way, I missed the first boat on my own journey to Sidon. I was late applying to the journalism postgraduate programme at City University in east London and I ended up on its periodicals course. This was not a training for newspapers but for magazines and it led, inexorably, not to a job on the *Birmingham Post* or *The Times*, but ... *Satellite & Cable Television News*. After a year of earnestly exploring the imminent revolution in the way television would be delivered to our homes, I graduated to the slightly more mainstream *Broadcast* magazine, the weekly television industry news and gossip organ.

In the spring of 1985 the twenty-four-year-old staff writer of *Broadcast* was sitting like a caged tiger in a second-floor, open-plan office, above the scented precincts of The Body Shop on Carnaby Street in London's West End, ruminating yet again on the central and all-enveloping issue of his working life: 'How do I get out of here and into newspapers where I belong?'

Then the phone rang.

'Hi Ed, it's James.'

It was the confident, clipped voice of James Blount. Although he was a couple of years my senior, I had got to know him pretty well after a mutual friend with whom I was at Cambridge briefly dated one of his sisters. James, who was then working for a small merchant bank in the City, had been at Oxford.

With the upright bearing of a young army officer, he was good-looking and an inveterate women-chaser. The product of a classic English prep school/public school/Oxbridge education, he was the best-informed and most articulate person I knew, with a clinical and exacting intellect. James knew his history and his politics, and in his company I instinctively deferred to his judgement. He also had a reputation as a tenacious climber of any mountain that did not require ropes or crampons and his Notting Hill flat was decorated with the photos of his conquests – the mountains, that is, not the women. Although in many ways a young establishment figure, there was a wild streak in Blount that I understood and warmed to but, even so, what he said next took me completely by surprise.

'I've decided to go to Afghanistan.'

'What?'

'Afghanistan.'

'Oh …' My mind was racing as I tried to remember where Afghanistan actually was. As usual James had wrong-footed me and I struggled to sound on the ball.

'I've had enough of this job,' he continued, 'and I've decided to go to Afghanistan and do some reporting.'

'What … on the mugarharin … the mooja …'

'Yes, the Mujahidin.'

'How on earth are you going to do that? And where are you going to report from?'

'The plan is to travel out to Pakistan,' he continued, sounding like a lieutenant colonel briefing the troops, 'to Peshawar in the North West Frontier Province, and then travel inside Afghanistan with a rebel group and take film and write stories about what they are doing. I'm hoping to sell my first piece to the *Daily Telegraph*.'

It was a classic, no-nonsense delivery of an extraordinary idea.

'Wow, fucking hell, Blounty … Are you really sure you want to do that?'

'Yes, I've made up my mind. If it doesn't work out I can always come back and find another job. Anyway, the point is I was planning to go alone but I've been advised that it is altogether safer and more sensible to go with someone else.'

My mind was already ticking over in anticipation of his next question. Absolutely. Yes. How could I turn down something like this? But I had no money. I had no contacts in Fleet Street. I'd never written a word in a newspaper. And this sounded as if it could be seriously dangerous. What would happen if I got injured? I could be killed doing this. And anyway, what was the war there even about ...?

'Is it something that would interest you, Gorman? You've always said you want to go overseas and write about other people killing each other.' James gave a mischievous chuckle.

When something feels right to me I have never been one to beat around the bush and, in the early spring of 1985 while on a salary of £7,000-a-year and conspicuously *not* working for a newspaper, this looked like an excellent opportunity to leapfrog the yawning gap between *Broadcast* magazine and Fleet Street.

Here was my ticket to a war zone. This was a chance to test myself in a remote and challenging environment and to report – much as my heroes had done – from a romantic-sounding far-flung part of the world. Unlike James's, my education had been about passing exams and if something wasn't in the syllabus, I knew next to nothing about it. The Great Game that had been played out between the British Empire and Imperial Russia in Central Asia was a complete mystery to me and I had a lot of catching up to do. But I loved the sound of it.

I had always imagined that I would go and report on a war. Both my grandfather and my father had just missed their respective call-ups to active service. My grandfather, Jim Gorman, a tough Scot from Edinburgh, who had been the army swimming and boxing champion, was just too old for the First World War and ended up training soldiers for the Front. My father, John, had been too young for active service in the Second World War. But at Marlborough College I had read the poetry of our most celebrated old boy, Siegfried Sassoon, I had studied David Jones's *In Parenthesis* and I had dissected *Dispatches,* Michael Herr's classic on Vietnam, and I wanted to test myself in a war zone.

I already knew that I was never going to write about

education, health policy or even domestic politics – I hated the precision and pernicketiness of home affairs. I wanted a bigger canvas on which to paint my pictures and I couldn't wait to leave London and the claustrophobic world of *Broadcast* magazine behind.

Like James I had a wild streak but I was even more reckless. I had seen my mother die of cancer at fifty when I was a young, impressionable seventeen-year-old and I had fallen out with my father after her death, so I had no adults to report to. I wanted something exciting and altogether otherworldly, and I wanted to make my name. Swapping London, then in thrall to the yuppie-driven boom that pre-dated the 1987 stock market crash, for the wilds of Afghanistan seemed irresistibly attractive.

'I've got no money … but I'm up for it,' I told James.

'I thought you would be,' he said. We both laughed at our grand ambition.

'Let's meet for a beer tonight and start planning,' I suggested before I put the phone down and looked around me. *Broadcast's* editorial office was a hive of activity as my colleagues prepared the weekly edition but my focus had already switched to a distant land.

And so began our own Great Game – two public schoolboys intent on becoming war reporters of a conflict that had already been raging for five years but was receiving little coverage in mainstream newspapers. We knew this was going to be the greatest adventure of our lives.

-◆◆◆◆-

Although I was immediately drawn to James's extravagantly daring idea, I knew next to nothing about what was going on in Afghanistan. The first step was gathering as much information as we could about the war. I learned that a coup in 1978 had brought in a pro-Soviet government against which large sectors of the country had openly rebelled. The then-president asked for Moscow's help and the elderly Russian premier Leonid Brezhnev sent in troops in late 1979 and installed his own man, Babrak Karmal, as Afghan leader.

The Western boycott of the 1980 Olympics in retaliation for the Soviet invasion had made big headlines. But by then, the main news from the war, not that there was much, was based around the narrative of a heroic band of 'freedom fighters' battling a modern-day superpower.

The brave and plucky Afghan Mujahidin or Holy Warriors, it was said, were armed only with ancient weapons, some of which had been used to repel British invaders a century earlier. Now they were up against the might of the Russian bear – more than 100,000 well-armed troops backed by the Communist Afghan army, together with a formidable air force of bombers, jet fighters and helicopter gunships.

In the mid-1980s, the 'freedom fighters' were hailed by the West as heroes taking on what seemed like the evil empire. But at that stage, support for them was mainly rhetorical. There were few weapons finding their way to the exiled leaders of the resistance in Peshawar. The view in Washington was that it was better to have the Mujahidin act as an irritant to the Soviets – to 'bleed' them, as it was put – than give them the firepower to force Moscow to retreat.

As far as Fleet Street and television news was concerned, the five-year-old war was a slow-moving story with little sign of a breakthrough. It was dangerous and expensive to cover, requiring journalists and camera crews to travel inside the country on foot, sometimes for weeks at a time, taking their chances with Mujahidin commanders, some of whom were not to be trusted. There were no mobile phones and only primitive satellite phones so filing stories had to wait until the arduous return journey to Pakistan had been completed.

We talked to journalists who had been 'inside' and they all emphasised that this was not a war that you could report on in the morning, then jump into a cab and view from the comfort of a hotel and the perspective of the bottom of a wine glass in the evening. It was a hard grind. You could spend days 'inside,' eating primitive food, risking illness or injury, and see next to nothing of the conflict on which you hoped to report. For most papers and news programmes Afghanistan was regarded as too risky and time-consuming. Thus, with one or two honourable exceptions – notably Sandy Gall's excellent reporting for ITN – the Soviet war became the province of freelancers. As a result the mixed Russian and Central Asian Soviet occupying force could slaughter Afghans by the thousand and destroy vast tracts of the country largely without the inconvenience of having to answer to the international media.

We spoke at length with a woman called Romey Fullarton, who ran the independent British charity Afghanaid, which had a house in Peshawar and helped thousands of Afghans facing hardship and distress because of the war. Romey knew what we were taking on and she did her best to put us off.

'It's exceptionally tough in there – it's not easy country to move about in and you will be taking risks on all sides,' she warned. 'If the Russians catch you, you will be in big trouble. You will most likely end up being imprisoned and accused of spying. You could be looking at years before you get out.

'And if you get injured or sick in the mountains there will be no one to treat you – you will have to get back to Pakistan somehow. We have seen with the Afghans that even a relatively routine wound can kill, once infection sets in.'

It was sobering stuff. Even if we got out alive we knew that, like other freelancers who had tried their luck in Afghanistan, we would have to hawk our wares around the foreign desks of Fleet Street and accept what were likely to be derisory fees for weeks of work involving hard yomping across tough mountainous terrain and moments of mortal danger.

But I had reached a decision – I was up for this and the

net effect of all the discouragement was to make me more determined than ever. Over pints of bitter and the odd curry off the King's Road, James and I cemented our partnership and eventually selected our date for departure – 7 June 1985.

James's principal interest was in getting film of the war, which he hoped to sell through a small company that dealt almost exclusively with news footage from Afghanistan. My main objective was to write articles for newspapers. Cameras and sound equipment were bafflingly complicated and expensive to my mind and I could not see how we were going to get to grips with the technical aspects of it all in time. But we were in it together, so together we threw ourselves into the business of acquiring Super 8 cameras, Sony Professional sound systems, an Olympus stills camera and film.

I had no money. Luckily James had more than me. We worked out a deal whereby we budgeted the total cost of the trip to be £4,000, including air fares and living expenses, and agreed that he would lend me my half. No interest would be charged but I was to repay it exactly one year after we returned to London and, in addition, I was to forego half of any fees I made on newspaper articles.

'After all,' said James, 'I've got to treat this as an investment, haven't I?'

As the weeks went by we gradually accumulated what we imagined were the necessary belongings. Boots, bivouac bags, emergency medical kits and insurance policies. James took out a policy on my life, applying his strict logic to an unfathomably unpredictable undertaking and concluding that I was hardly likely to be able to pay him back if I was six feet under somewhere in the mountains of Afghanistan. It may sound a little morbid and self-serving but I could see his point.

It was easy to extract myself from my base-camp existence in London. I shared a two-room flat with James Root, a school and university friend, in Baron's Court in the west of the city, where I slept on the sofa and James had the bedroom. Our landlord was a charming South African bachelor who used to pop in every now and again to refresh the paintwork but without going to the trouble of moving our belongings first. A notable casualty was my beautiful Harris Tweed overcoat – the only possession I had inherited from my grandfather – which had white paint splattered on its sleeves.

James and I worked in the day and drank by night, and a succession of girlfriends made their way to our place on Charleville Road. In the early months of 1985 I had been nurturing a hopelessly impractical relationship with a beautiful Californian actress who was working tables in a Manhattan bar.

Kathy and I had met and fallen head over heels in love when I visited New York on my first-ever foreign assignment – for the aforementioned *Satellite & Cable Television News*. My job was to report on how the Americans had pioneered cable television and I concentrated pretty hard on that until the electric moment when I set eyes on Kathy. Tall, with long fair hair and Carly Simon good looks, she was an exotic creature who dreamt of stardom on Broadway. We literally bumped into each other in a SoHo club, our Tanqueray and tonics spilling on the wooden floorboards, and the attraction was irresistible.

Kathy was charmed by my English accent and I by her flower-power Berkeley – or should I say 'Bezerkeley' – background. For months I spent my hard-earned pennies on air fares to New York just to grab a day or two with her at the chaotic brownstone house that she shared with three girlfriends in Brooklyn Heights. It was a romantic and ambitious liaison but all the more intoxicating for it. When I told Kathy of my plans to head to Peshawar, she was stunned but, after reaching for an atlas, agreed that if it was something I wanted to do then I must do it. She would be waiting for me when I got back, whenever that was, and in the meantime testing the efficiency of the Pakistani postal system to its limits with her letters.

I went to see the editor of *Broadcast* at the end of May and told her that I wished to leave in two weeks and explained why.

'You're doing what?' she cried with a look of shock and disbelief. 'What the hell d'you want to do that for? You must be off your rocker, Ed.'

'No, I'm serious. I've loved it here,' I lied, 'but this is an opportunity I really cannot turn down. I want to get into newspapers and the chance to report from Afghanistan is just too good to miss.'

Although it was inconvenient to lose a member of staff at short notice, she was understanding and wished me all the luck in the world.

'You'd better learn to speak Russian,' she said with a wry smile.

Most of the other journalists on the magazine thought I was mad as well. They quickly came to see it as 'typical'.

'That's just Ed. A jumped-up, overgrown public school-boy playing at soldiers in Afghanistan.'

'Yeah, he'll be back like a shot.'

My leaving card was full of good-natured newsroom banter: 'Enjoy your "Boys Own" adventure,' wrote one colleague.

'To DickEd Gorbachev,' wrote Basil Comely, my next-door neighbour in the office, who went on to become an executive editor for Arts at the BBC. 'A bullet in the brain can only improve what's there. Love Basil (I suppose I'll miss you!).'

Someone else tried a little verse:

There was a young dreamer called Ed
With a voice in his head that said:
'If you want to be a man
Go to Afghanistan.'
So he went back to bed instead.

Generally the reaction among friends was one of incredulity. Women friends and my three sisters almost all worried we would get ourselves killed. At that time, for no good reason I could put my finger on, I was quite sure that if either of us did get killed, it would be James, not me. He saw it, quite independently, exactly the other way round.

A young barrister and fellow Cambridge graduate told me one night that he thought Afghanistan was passé.

'Why not go somewhere *really* exciting, Ed?'

'What d'you mean? Afghanistan *is* exciting,' I protested. 'It only seems passé to you because hardly any journalists go there so you never hear about it.'

The lack of established reporters made it a unique opportunity for young guns like James and me who wanted to break into the business of war reporting. An opportunity like that might never come along again. I was irked by my friend's sneering dismissal of my plans and even more determined to go through with it. 'I'll show all those disbelieving fatheads,' I thought to myself.

A recurrent theme bouncing around the bedsits and shared flats of west London was that we should be more wary of the Afghans than the Soviets. My brother-in-law, a cattle farmer from Herefordshire, put this most eloquently: 'They'll cut your goolies off given half the chance, Ed,' he predicted over a large glass of red one evening, laughing uproariously. 'You'd better take a special chit saying "Please Do Not Cut My Balls Off: I Am A Journalist Not A Choirboy."'

This friendly advice reflected more a sense of respect for the Afghans than contempt. The British had failed to subdue them on three separate occasions in the distant past and those bloody encounters lived on in our collective memory – as they did in those of the Afghans.

My father was singularly unimpressed with my plans, which I shared with him over a tense encounter in a London restaurant. He subsequently made his views abundantly clear in the course of a long letter that amounted to a lecture on my considerable failings as a young man: 'I know it sounds, in the history of writing, as if it is jolly good sense to go to Afghanistan and, after all, Hemingway and others have blazed heroic trails,' he wrote. 'But the East and the Near East and South America and Africa are full of youngsters bumming around in the belief that they have got something which other people and the world are dying to hear and, for the most part, it is self-indulgent folly.'

Inspiration indeed.

※

A big item on our agenda was getting fit. James was ahead of me in this area – as in most others – with his experience in the mountains and he had also trekked in many parts of Britain. I had been subsiding over the past two years into a state of lethargy. My rugby-playing days at school and in my first year at university were a distant memory and a diet of sandwiches at lunchtime, alcohol most evenings and a lot of cigarettes had rendered me breathless and overweight.

We began by running three times a week around Wormwood Scrubs, an area of parkland in west London that is best known for the prison at one end. We finished with a trip to the Brecon Beacons on the Welsh border which, we thought, would give us the chance to test our bodies, and our equipment in the field. We set off one Saturday morning and trudged up and down for about seventeen miles, our rucksacks filled with tins of baked beans, corned beef and packets of biscuits. The plan was that we would sleep out in the open for two nights.

On the first night we hitched a lift into Brecon, where we got stuck into a few beers and some Cornish pasties. At closing time we made our way out of the town for about two miles and found a field in which to bed down in our bivi bags.

We were both freezing cold and woke at dawn to find that we had been asleep in sheep shit. Undeterred, smelly and damp, we set off up Pen Y Fan which, at 3,000 feet, is the tallest and toughest of the Beacons. At the top we met a lecturer from a northern polytechnic who offered us chocolate biscuits. We watched a platoon of paratroopers being frogmarched up the side of the mountain towards us.

'Left, right, left, right.'

'Come on, you fuckin' tosser. Get your stupid little arse up. You fuckin' piece of shit. Move … Move …'

The sergeant-major – who, incidentally, carried no pack – was walking alongside a young trooper carrying a huge army rucksack. With his mouth inches from the trooper's ear, the sergeant was bellowing at the poor chap. The young soldier was sweating profusely and was near collapse. James and I thought this was superb. Here were the heroes of Goose Green showing us what they were made of.

The lecturer, undoubtedly a pacifist, looked over in disgust and said simply: 'Cunts.' In the driving wind and rain, we were in no mood to argue.

We stomped off along the next ridge. Or, in my case, hobbled – because within half an hour my left leg had packed up and the best I could do was limp off the mountain down to the nearest village with a call box. From there we phoned my eldest sister Jane, who lived nearby, and we stood shivering in the rain awaiting her arrival. So much for our two nights out. We had proved one thing – that I wasn't fit; and another – that bivi bags alone were not warm enough for the Welsh mountains. But we weren't too worried because we knew that Afghanistan in summer would be hot and there was almost no chance of rain.

Another weekend was spent at James's parents' house in Hertfordshire practising how to identify various Soviet tanks and armoured personnel carriers. We did this using tiny models made by the British army, supplied by James's brother Ollie, a former officer in the Gurkas. When placed in the gravel driveway and viewed through binoculars, the models looked exactly like life-size weapons of war in the distance. I was hopeless at it. I couldn't tell a BMP (infantry fighting vehicle) from a T72 (tank). As usual James was far better at this than me. Such were our preparations for war and the journey of a lifetime.

◆◆◆◆◆

As the date of our departure grew closer, I never had the slightest doubt about what we were doing – only mounting excitement. Afghanistan offered that irresistible combination of adventure and the chance to make my name. Going to war was a challenge Englishmen down the generations had taken on going back hundreds of years. In my case, I was sure it would open my eyes to a real world I had barely touched during my privileged upbringing. I was never going to do something like this in my fifties, I reasoned. Now was the time to seize the opportunity.

2

OUR GREAT GAME BEGINS

James and I set off in early June with our rucksacks packed to the seams with the clothes and gear we thought we would need. We flew the long way to Peshawar on the dirt-cheap Jordanian Airways service from Heathrow via Amman and on to Karachi. Then, equally cheaply and cheerfully, we took the internal flight that stopped at Lahore, then Islamabad, before finally landing in the baking heat of the chaotic capital of the fabled North West Frontier Province.

We arrived exhausted but buzzing with excitement. As our taxi crawled through the hot, dusty streets and narrow alleyways of Sadar Bazaar in downtown Peshawar, we kept the windows wide open to catch a breath of cooling air. For the first time we heard the cry of the muezzin and hooters of the ubiquitous rickshaws weaving their way in and out of the crowds, or racing past horses and carts on the roads. The smells were of freshly cooked chicken tikka and horse manure.

If downtown was an assault on the senses, the suburb of University Town, where James and I found our digs at the home of Afghanaid, was another world. The elegant house on Gulmohar Road, standing in its own garden, overlooked the Khyber Express railway line up to the hills and was set among villas where genteel Pakistani families and their servants lived in relative luxury. All was quiet in University

Town save for the packs of wild dogs that roamed the streets, howling and barking deep into the night.

Not far from the Afghanaid house we found a chatty local barber who wielded a cut-throat razor with panache and followed it with a head-pummelling massage, while setting the North West Frontier to rights in fluent English, all for a handful of rupees. We didn't tell him why we were there but he guessed. 'You boys need to take it carefully,' he warned. 'These Afghans bring us nothing but trouble.'

We wandered the streets during our first days there, in a city that was teeming with Afghan refugees mingling with tribesmen from the frontier. Described by one visiting British journalist at the time as the 'Asian Casablanca', Peshawar was bubbling and boiling with intrigue; there were guns everywhere you looked and the place had the feel of a staging post for a war being fought just across the mountains.

Kipling once described Peshawar as a 'city of evil countenances' peopled by smugglers, soldiers of fortune and spies. Not much had changed by 1985 except that you could add in a new generation of visiting adventurers, a huge drug-smuggling trade and a growing aid community staffed by expats driving around in gleaming new pick-ups. There was also a big American presence – aid workers, diplomats and CIA staffers whose weapons programme for the Mujahidin would become one of its biggest overseas operations since Vietnam. And Peshawar had its own relics of Raj-era Imperial India with a vast cantonment built by the British army. You only needed to be in the city for a few days to realise that you were not the first Briton to venture into this wild and romantic part of the world.

In the exiled Afghan community there was an undercurrent of bitter rivalry that periodically broke out into open fighting, targeted killings or bombings. Leading resistance figures would be blown up in car bombs or shot by agents sent in by the Communist regime in Kabul. Unexplained acts of violence were routinely blamed on Pakistan's unruly neighbour or their Soviet allies.

We had come to Peshawar to present our credentials, such as they were, to the offices of the various Mujahidin resistance groups, most of whom were based in quiet suburban back streets. I had letters of introduction from a couple of papers that barely knew who I was and were certainly not offering any money upfront. But I had managed to talk a couple of assistant foreign editors into signing them. They were short and to the point:

To whom it may concern

Edward Gorman is a journalist from Great Britain. He is planning to travel to Afghanistan to prepare articles for publication on the Soviet war against the Mujahidin. I would be grateful if you could assist him.

Yours faithfully, etc.

I had them beautifully preserved in a plastic folder that would stick to the palms of my hands as we sat in taxis, crawling across town from one backstreet rebel 'office' to another. Those letters were our passports to the war. The most important thing was that they were printed under the newspaper's letterhead – in my case one of these was the *Glasgow Herald* – and this proved enough to impress the front offices of what were then quite primitive political organisations in exile where few people could read English.

The offices were usually residential villas that had been transformed into the unofficial embassies of each rebel group. They were easy to spot because of the large numbers of armed men standing around keeping guard. Climbing the steps of the forecourt, we would take off our shoes and inquire through a translator, whom we had borrowed from

Afghanaid, whether we could meet with the senior figure or the commander. Around us were often scores of refugees from Afghanistan – all men, of course, and dressed in brown *shalwar kameez* – queuing for money, for weapons or for favours from tribal, village or provincial elders.

In those early days we learned to wait like the Afghans. They do it uncomplainingly for hours, either chatting or whispering conspiratorially to each other or just sitting quietly working their way through their prayer beads. James and I got our first lessons in the pace of life in what was then almost a medieval country as we sat in stifling anterooms waiting to be seen, drinking green tea by the gallon. We broke the monotony by exchanging irreverent observations about those around us.

'Elvis is coming back and he's got the Hunchback of Notre Dame with him ... maybe this time we are going to be seen,' I would offer.

'Fucking hell, these people don't seem to want to be helped,' replied James.

'You sure we want to do this? We could just walk away now and check into the Holiday Inn ...'

'Come on ... Surely we have to be next ...'

The trick was to find a way into Afghanistan with one of the more pro-Western groupings that were prepared to assist foreign journalists. After a few days of doing the rounds of the various offices, we were intrigued to be offered a chance to travel into Kunar and Nuristan provinces on Afghanistan's north-eastern border with Pakistan. We would be the guests of an American-educated Afghan professor named Jusef Nuristani, who was associated with the moderate Mahaz-e-Milli Islami or National Islamic Front for Afghanistan.

Jusef was one of the very few highly educated and Westernised Afghans. In poor health, with a pronounced limp, and a committed chain-smoker, he was from an important tribal family within Nuristan, as his name indicated. He had been educated at Kabul University, where he studied history and geography. He had then won a Fulbright scholarship to the University of Arizona at Tucson where he had taken an MA in Oriental Studies and had studied for a PhD. With a voice like tyres on a gravel drive, he spoke fluent English with a strong American accent and enjoyed using his vocabulary of Western swear words to the full.

In Washington Jusef had campaigned for help for his countrymen in the early years of the war and, after twelve years in the States, had come back to see what was happening in his homeland. He felt guilty that he had been living it up in America while his countrymen suffered. But he was remarkably positive about the eventual outcome of the conflict. He predicted that while the Afghans who had supported the Soviet occupation would be locked away after they had gone, a civil war among the resistance groups or between them and those who had thrown in their lot with the pro-Moscow regime, would be avoided by a general pardon. Matters would be helped, he argued, if the West stopped aiding what he called 'the crazy ones' among the more extreme rebel factions.

A beautiful, mountainous region, made famous in Britain by Eric Newby's classic *A Short Walk in the Hindu Kush*, Nuristan was hardly the epicentre of the war. But we thought it might prove a useful introduction to the country and we accepted Jusef's invitation. We were to visit Nuristan and Kunar just a few days after the end of a combined Soviet and Afghan army operation to re-supply a key local garrison at a fort in the town of Barikot that was besieged by Mujahidin fighters. Jusef estimated the tour might take three weeks.

Our trip started at 4.30 a.m. one morning when a pick-up arrived at Afghanaid to take us to a village just eighteen miles from the border. Like Jusef – who had business to attend to and would join us later – we had exchanged our Western dress for local clothes, the better to blend in and avoid detection by the prying eyes of Pakistani police or spies inside Afghanistan. Under 'General Expenses', I recorded in my notebook that I spent 250 rupees (approximately £2) on a dark green set of *shalwar kameez*, 125 rupees (£1) on a fawn Chitrali hat (the soft woollen cap worn by Afghan men of the Chitral region), and a little more on a dark brown *putu*, the blanket Afghans use to sleep under or wrap themselves in against the cold. There were also payments of 2,000 rupees (£17.50) to an interpreter and 4,000 rupees (£35) for our vehicle hire.

I had a crashing hangover after a night in the American Club not far from the house. This was *the* place to go in Peshawar if you could find someone who was a member to sign you in. It was a social club primarily intended for US diplomats and their families and it was like an island of Western decadence in an Islamic desert. The club's bar – where you could buy ice-cold American beers and hamburgers, and throw a few darts – had become the watering hole of choice for journalists heading in and out of Afghanistan. It was where swashbuckling stories were told, where young men chatted up the girls working on aid programmes or as journalists, and where young freelancers preparing to go 'inside' would sit nervously thinking about what was ahead – days or even weeks in the mountains with all the privations and risks that that entailed. After stumbling back from the club to Afghanaid, I spent my last hours before the off frantically packing and re-packing my canvas rucksack – originally blue but now painted green to camouflage it – and writing a long letter to Kathy assuring her that I would be back soon.

James and I left Peshawar in the company of two Afghans, Hashim and his brother Abdul, our translator Hamad, and a Pakistani driver who scared the hell out of us. Not unlike the Pakistani airline pilots whose expansive manoeuvres had helped us on our way north from Karachi on our flight from England, the driver had an over-developed sense of daring and drove as if he would rather be killed than surrender even an inch to oncoming traffic.

Once out of Peshawar, we travelled through a fertile plain with the mountains rising dramatically to our left. The villages appeared to have been unchanged for centuries, with lush vegetation fed by swooshing irrigation canals. Eventually we climbed off the plain up through the mountains and down into a drier valley on the other side. By this stage the driver had exhausted himself and the car started slowing and meandering across the road as he fell asleep at the wheel. I shouted at him and he jumped back to life, but it was time for a break so we stopped and all got out for smoke. There was a look of real excitement on Abdul's face as he pointed out the dark outline of the frontier range in the distance with his fingers crossed: 'Afghanistan – there. Look, Afghanistan,' he said in English.

The rural tranquillity was reminiscent of Egyptian communities on the banks of the Nile that I had visited during my year off between school and university and, as we moved higher up, the flat-roofed mud houses reminded me of villages on the edge of the desert in southern Morocco. We saw few women en route and most of them were in full purdah – mysterious figures peering out of black or bright blue headdresses through narrow blinds around their eyes. I fantasised that under those disguises walked the women of my dreams. Many of the young girls we saw were incredibly beautiful, with long straggly brown hair, deep brown eyes and fine features.

After passing through several refugee camps, where houses were made of mud covered with UNHCR tarpaulins, we turned off the tarmac down a rough track and through a small gate into the courtyard of Hashim's house. The gates were shut behind us with an unmistakable air of secrecy. We unloaded our bags and were shown into a long, dark sitting room that was to be our base. There were Afghan rugs on the floor and flower designs painted on the mud walls under the beam-and-rushes roof. Hashim, a squat, strong-looking individual, was concerned that we remain inconspicuous until our meeting with Jusef the following night.

So we were confined to the room and subjected to an overwhelming amount of food served by young boys. Bread and tea, more sugary tea, then potato stew with rice and salad and more bread. Then watermelon and, by six o'clock, yet more tea. We were not allowed to lift a finger, even to refill our cups. Was this, we wondered, what it felt like to be kidnapped? A few pictures on the wall told in English and Pashto of the war and of the martyrs. On the veranda, cartoons painted on the outside wall of the house depicted Russia as a bear with its head stuck in a honey pot and Babrak Karmal as a two-headed clown.

Waiting there was frustrating. We were getting closer, getting the feel of Afghanistan, but we weren't there yet and James and I were both itching to move on. Why was it taking Jusef so long to get here? Had something gone wrong? Hashim, who told us he commanded 600 men, said he expected to move the next day with fifty of them and they would be taking thirteen sacks of flour with them. The following morning we could hear the local mullah reading from the Koran accompanied by the regular beating sound of the flour mill as, inside our 'prison', we breakfasted on bread with butter and tea. Far from moving on, we stayed exactly where we were.

Idling away the hours, James and I listened to the BBC World Service and discussed the big issues of the day, particularly any news of Afghanistan that we could share with our hosts. At that stage talks were rumbling on in Geneva between representatives of Pakistan and the Communist government in Kabul to try to find an agreed mechanism by which the Soviets could withdraw. But they appeared to have no chance of bridging irreconcilable gaps. The talks were described by a BBC correspondent as 'a useful sharing of views on the problem'.

In another bulletin we heard that twenty Afghan pilots had been executed on the orders of the Afghan prime minster for refusing to carry out orders to bomb populated areas. This followed an attack on an airfield by the Mujahidin in which twenty planes were said to have been destroyed. It all seemed a long way from this lonely outpost on the Afghan border with Pakistan; these titbits only heightened our impatience to get going.

Hashim told us he had been an education administrator before the war in the provincial town of Kundus. Now thirty-eight, he had left Afghanistan in 1980 with his eight brothers and lived on land leased to the Pakistan government by private landowners. We discussed with him the possibility, then widely mooted, of a negotiated settlement with the Soviets.

'I am not interested in talks in Washington or Moscow unless a withdrawal of the Russian army is on the agenda,' he told us through our interpreter. He said he believed that economic and political pressure would not move Moscow and only the ceaseless and continued prosecution of the Holy War would force them out. 'It is by jihad that we will succeed,' he said in a mantra we would hear almost daily. 'At one time, the Russians were our friends but no more and they will never be forgiven for what they have done to us,' he added.

With a twinkle in his eye, he explained that he was educating his little children about the war and explaining to them what had happened to the Afghans, always reminding them where their homeland was. And he was insistent that Afghanistan had been betrayed by the West. Like many Afghans he believed that the Soviet Union had invaded because it wanted access to warm-water ports – even if Afghanistan was only a step in the right direction on that score.

'I am disappointed,' he said. 'We rose up against the Russians on our own and the West was happy to stand by and do nothing.'

All James and I could do was nod in agreement and remind him that we were there to try and draw attention to their struggle.

After another day of waiting in the heat, Jusef finally arrived along with some men carrying Chinese AK47 assault rifle replicas, the ubiquitous killing machine used in countless Third World wars.

'How ya doin', guys,' he said by way of a greeting in his American drawl. 'Sorry for the delay. Not long now before we get going.'

We went out to inspect a new weapon, just delivered from Peshawar: a water-cooled heavy machine gun made in 1918 in Berlin. Not only was it hopelessly outdated, enormously heavy and cumbersome, but it didn't work. Abdullah, a tough twenty-five-year-old Nuristani of European appearance, whom we nicknamed 'Franz' after the German footballer Franz Beckenbauer, valiantly, but with a hint that he understood the foregone futility of the exercise, took the machine to pieces and cleaned it.

After about two hours of patient fiddling, the gun was finally assembled and set up with its full might pointing at a hillside on which a cow casually grazed. We waited for the primeval roar of this old man but every time we crowded round, fingers in ears, we were greeted with an anticlimactic 'click' as the side-loading bullet belt failed to engage. 'These good people deserve more than this,' I thought. Suddenly the old gun succeeded in regurgitating one shot with a deafening boom that echoed around the forested mountains. It was the exception that proved the rule: the old beast remained stubborn in its silence for the rest of the day.

These Mujahidin carried a wide variety of weapons, from old 303 rifles – Russian-made and stamped '1917,' or British from 1934 – to replicas of the Kalashnikov. Our group was not heavily armed but carried two RPG7 rocket launchers.

'You quickly get used to having loaded guns with the safety catch off pointed straight at you or left lying unattended on the floor,' I wrote in the black notebook that accompanied me everywhere.

As I sat minding my own business, one of Hashim's men, a gnarled-looking fellow with a scowl in his eyes, cheerfully loaded his ancient rifle, took the safety catch off and pointed it at me. I didn't have time to react before he calmly pulled the trigger.

'Shit,' I muttered, pushing the word slowly out through clenched teeth, my heart thumping.

The man was laughing as I swallowed hard, trying not to show how much he had frightened me.

'You should take a photograph of that thing,' he said, gesturing with contempt at the 1918 German machine gun. 'Then the West will know what aid they are giving us.'

Getting killed accidentally by the Mujahidin was high on our list of things to avoid, as was being murdered by the very people we had trusted to take us into the country. I had read news reports – and listened intently to stories in the American Club bar – about Western journalists who had died in both circumstances. Among the worst cases during those years was an Italian cameraman who was run over and killed in Kandahar by an Afghan driving a captured Soviet tank, and a British cameraman who was killed and robbed in Nuristan by Mujahidin who dropped a rock on his head while he slept. In another incident a freelancer, who had gone in with a Mujahidin group, was promptly handed over to the government in exchange for a release of prisoners. In this case I would have been the victim of little more than ill-disciplined bravado – another characteristic trait of Mujahidin guerrillas.

The next day we finally got going. We breakfasted at Hashim's and, after collecting ten of his men, set off, eighteen all together, in two Toyotas that climbed about 6,000 feet to the border. For about two hours we drove higher, leaving the hot plains of Pakistan far behind us in the haze and driving up into the cool air of the pine forests in the mountains. Finally we reached the uppermost ridge, where Hashim ordered us out. We had reached the frontier.

So as to avoid the police checkpoint, where James and I could have been apprehended for crossing illegally into Afghanistan, we climbed the last hundred yards at a sprint across rough ground alongside the road, where we could not be seen. The pick-ups then passed through, meeting us five minutes later on the other side.

Finally we were in Afghanistan. 'Here we go, Jimmy,' I said, wild-eyed with excitement. 'This is it.'

3

'INSIDE' FOR THE FIRST TIME

A mile further on, and within sight of some rather scrawny camels, we unloaded and prepared for what I thought would be a testing climb. To my disappointment, we only walked as far as the next valley, where we were ordered to rest until the following day. We bedded down on the roof of a little one-room house with a panoramic view. The temperature was much cooler than on the plains and it rained and thundered for two hours after our arrival.

It was an extraordinarily beautiful alpine setting: jagged mountains with fir trees and, far to the north, the high snow-capped peaks of Chitral. The area had been summer grazing land for the Afghans before the war but by 1985 it had become their permanent home as they sought refuge from the fighting. Wheat grew in terraced fields. Across the valley we could hear a baby crying, birds in song, cockerels calling and the occasional sound of distant gunfire echoing in the hills. That evening James and I added to the echoing reports as we took turns firing rifles with our new companions.

Up at 3 a.m. the next day, we set off in the dark, finding our way by torchlight. We were now in a party of around thirty. We climbed along tough rocky mountain paths until 7 a.m. when we reached the top of the range and were greeted by a breathtaking panorama: snow-capped peaks stretching away into the distance, like an enormous natural fortress.

Kunar province lay before us and, in the distance, Nuristan in all its rugged beauty.

In *A Short Walk in the Hindu Kush,* Newby quotes the Chief Survey Officer of the Indian Section during the Raj who wrote of this area in 1908: 'Who will unravel the secrets of this inhabited outland, which appears at present to be more impracticable to the explorer than either of the poles?' By 1958, when Newby wrote of his own travels in Nuristan, he reckoned little had changed: 'Neither the aeroplane nor the motor-car has made the slightest difference. To get there you still have to walk.'

In 1985 when James and I stood gasping for breath at the top of that ridge, staggering under the weight of our back-packs, the same sentence could have been written. Nuristan and Kunar were still beautiful backwaters. They had been pummelled from the air by Soviet MiG jets and helicopters but many of the villages and small valleys were still inaccessible to vehicles and could only be reached on foot. And the war meant that the easiest routes were to be avoided. As James and I discovered, this was going to be tough.

After stopping for breakfast of tea, bread and goat meat, we began what turned out to be an agonising descent to the Kunar River thousands of feet below. All around the valley lay evidence of the battle ten days ago. From high up on the pass, we could see timber-and-stone houses that had been destroyed by rocket fire and, lower down, fields that had been burnt before harvest and were scarred with bomb craters. We saw herds of dead cows, stinking fiercely, that had been killed, we were told, by fire from a helicopter.

On finally reaching Kunar, about which I had read so much, I was struck by how barren, uninhabited and remote this valley was. Steep-sided and covered in holly oaks and firs at the top, it had plenty of scree and bare rock too; we scrambled down, slipping on loose stones.

We made it to the village of Sao, about forty miles from

the Soviet garrison at Barikot. Looking to our right up the valley, we could see the corrie at the other end where the beleaguered fort was situated. Plumes of smoke rose lazily from the mountains where Soviet mortars had set the hillsides alight.

Sao had been surrounded at the beginning of the Barikot operation a week earlier. One Soviet and two Afghan units had landed on the hilltops and begun pounding the village below. As we approached we could see that only about one-fifth of the buildings remained standing and most of those were damaged by fire. The immense power of the explosives had left craters twenty feet wide and mountains of rubble. The flimsy wattle-and-daub houses had crumbled and were contorted by the massive destructive forces launched on them.

Jusef told us that after two days the Mujahidin had managed to slip out by night. We never discovered how many were killed but their escape must have been a remarkable one. A little further down the valley, we were told, five men lay where they were shot, now smelling and decomposing, the ground around their bodies littered with mines.

On our way into Sao we met groups of migrating Afghans who had given up and decided, like millions of others, to seek refuge in Pakistan. One family was carrying all they had: a teapot and some plastic cups. One of the men had a live chicken under each arm. In this family there was only the father, his brother and a young girl who looked exhausted from her climb. What had become of the remainder, we never found out.

In its heyday before the war, Sao had been, at 700 families, a veritable metropolis by Afghan standards. Now there was no one left except about thirty dirty, emaciated and exhausted men. I had never seen anything like this and was full of admiration for their determination to stay, whatever fate awaited them. They had been reduced to mere squatters in their own village, their clothes covered in grime, their faces sunken and pallid from undernourishment. A terrible, instantaneous moment of destruction – wrought by firepower from another century – had destroyed their lives.

'Look what the Russians have done to this place,' snarled Jusef in disgust.

The men proudly showed us around, pointing out the remains of the mosque with religious paintings visible on the one wall still standing, despite being scarred by fire. Bombs had been dropped by parachute and had exploded horizontally to maximise the destruction; a parachute from one hung from a tree amid the rubble. The village had been sprayed with small landmines that, together with several unexploded munitions, posed a lasting hazard.

One of the men pointed to a lump of grey plastic, shaped like a butterfly, and mimed an explosion. When I didn't initially comprehend, he picked up a handful of stones and lobbed them one by one at the object until it ignited with a dull thud. The charge was powerful enough to blow off a hand or a foot, but not to kill outright. These mines maimed hundreds of thousands of Afghans, many of them children who picked them up thinking they were toys. They didn't detonate when you stood on them but only when you lifted your foot off. I tried to imagine that agonising instant when you realised that you had already condemned your body to terrible trauma and there was no way to avoid it.

My informant spread his arms to indicate that they were all around us, probably dropped from Soviet helicopters to float to the ground and lie in wait for ignorant or careless Afghans – or visiting journalists from west London – walking along the Mujahidin supply routes through the mountains. At six inches across, with little winglets on either side of the explosive charge, they wouldn't be too hard to spot if you kept your eyes firmly on the path ahead. But we had also been told about more sophisticated anti-personnel mines buried underground by the Soviets and there was no way of spotting them. Thinking it all through, I felt a creeping sensation in my flesh. One wrong step and I could go home without a foot – or worse.

Food was scarce here. The generosity of the poorest of these people stretched only to a couple of scraps of bread, a few mulberries and a cup of tea. In many places the intricate terraces on the hillsides had been bombed but they were still determined to bring in whatever remained of the year's harvest.

We left Sao and walked on to the village of Marait. From afar it looked undamaged, but as we got closer we realised that there was a deathly hush in the air. Once a prosperous place of eighty families, almost every house had been destroyed when on two consecutive days Soviet bombers came at sunrise. There was twisted bark where fully grown oaks had been ripped apart, the sweet, sickly smell of freshly burnt timber filling the air; other trees that remained standing were little more than charred outlines. A few donkeys were sleeping in the shells of houses that once belonged to their masters. In some cases there were giant craters and no sign of the houses that had been swallowed by them. The survivors hadn't yet made the decision to leave, but there was resignation in the air.

We met a local community leader, one Ayanulah Nuristani, who had been the headmaster of the school in Kunar before the war and had a history degree from Kabul University. Dressed in dark green *shalwar kameez* with a fawn woollen waistcoat and sporting a long beard, he spoke wistfully of the past, before the fighting started, and of a relatively peaceful and self-sufficient community. But he had no plans to be driven from his homeland.

'We lived quietly according to our custom, we never had any argument with Kabul, but now our homes have been destroyed,' he told me. 'The natural instinct of everyone here is to stay. I would prefer us all to stay together. Once our children and women are gone it adds to our problems. We will not leave our land to someone else,' he added. 'What's the use of a Holy War if you leave the country? What's the sense of fighting from Pakistan for a few days as a visitor? You have to stay, be ready and resolve to fight.'

That was going to be the problem for the Soviets, I realised: they could capture Kabul and some other towns but they could never control the countryside without the most absurd influx of troops. Most of Afghanistan is rural, populated by a semi-feudal people, and could never be said to be conquered until the battle for the countryside is won. The motorised weapons of war brought in by the invader were entirely inappropriate for a country that was by and large without roads. The Soviet army would have to get out and walk to win – and its soldiers had shown no inclination to do that.

On we trekked in tough country through one ruined village after another as we crossed the provincial border into Nuristan with people eking out an existence in what remained of their homes, trying to decide whether to leave for exile in Pakistan. Some had resolved to fashion a life of sorts among the rocks or under the trees rather than risk returning to buildings that could be targeted again.

The defiance was what impressed me. We came across a farmer who had stopped on a high pass with his herd of goats, their bells ringing in the still mountain air.

'Our resolve has not diminished at all,' he said. 'We are ready to fight until the end. But there will be times when we might not survive if they kill all our animals and burn all our villages. Then we will have to go. As long as we can tend our herds then we will stay.'

Despite the misery and hopelessness of their situation, everywhere we went James, Jusef and I were accorded the highest honour by the people of Kunar and Nuristan. We stayed in elegant farmhouses that had escaped the bombing, offering a glimpse of a relatively comfortable life before the war. Animals paid the price as everything from chickens to goats were slaughtered and served up to mark our visit. At one dinner James was required to eat the grilled rectum of a goat killed at the top of a pass. This was a great honour that I managed to side-step by vociferously explaining that James was 'my commander'.

'You bastard, Gorman,' was his response as he smiled politely at his hosts before taking a mouthful. 'I'll get you back for this.'

We did some of the toughest walking James or I had ever done, sometimes fifteen hours up to the snow line and back to the heat of the valley as we made our way in and out of Nuristan. My knee, which had complained so painfully in the Brecon Beacons, seemed to have settled down but walking with full packs on our backs was hard. On one ridge I was sick at the summit, my body protesting at the altitude. Both of us struggled with the sheer effort of climbs that went on forever, our morale not improved by walking with Afghans often shod in flimsy plastic sandals, who seemed to have unending energy for the task. Water was a constant preoccupation as we sought out streams whenever we could to fill our bottles. And all the time we were watching out for mines.

We also learnt more about waiting, for hours and hours, while decisions were made as to where it was safe for us to go next and when. Bursting to get on and still thinking in a Western timeframe, I was tortured by the frequent and often apparently inexplicable delays in a distant part of the world where life was conducted at a snail's pace.

At one point Jusef disappeared and we were left in a small farmhouse with some men with whom we could barely communicate. The place had very poor sanitary arrangements – just a flea-infested, excretia-covered open courtyard at the back without so much as a pit. Stuck there, we whiled away the hours playing Hangman or Battleships in the back of our notebooks while listening to the Test match or the arid impartiality of the news on the BBC World Service.

We had fun trying out our Walkmans on astonished boys and young men who had never seen such contraptions let alone listened to strange Western music. Through us they experienced a little vicious Tom Waits, a taste of the Stones' 'Sympathy For The Devil', boogie courtesy of Glenn Miller, and Dvorak's 'Sixth Symphony'.

We moved on the next morning but my notebook entry for Day 7 of the trip offers a flavour of my growing impatience at the frequent delays. 'Set out from doing nothing. Walked down the valley. Said goodbye to Hashim. Both contracted the shits. Wandered aimlessly and depressingly slowly up the valley – both really f***** off.'

The following day was back to hard yomping. 'Up at 4 a.m., we walked for fifteen hours down one side of the valley and then straight up the next to a lodge on the tree line. Incredibly exhausting – pack carried by me all the way – both still ill and eating very little.'

James decided he'd had enough: 'Over there ...' He pointed in the rough direction of Kunar and the frontier. 'We want to go back to Pakistan.'

'Pakistan – we want to go to Pakistan,' I shouted allowing my temper to get the better of me, but we were met by incomprehension – or, perhaps, indifference.

We were hungry and started dreaming about what we would do when we got back to Peshawar. Under the heading 'Pakistan,' I listed my preferences on the inside cover of my notebook. 'Coca-Cola, Cigarettes, Chocolate, Food and Fun.'

My diary shows that in the closing days of that trip we were handed from one commander to another – Hashim to Abdul Remi, Abdul Remi to Mohammad Amin, Mohammad Amin to Sheir Ahmad – as we gradually retraced our steps towards the border.

That two-week tour was a dramatic and testing introduction to a land at war but my overwhelming sense when we got back to Peshawar – and this was something that would heavily influence what I did next – was that James and I had misfired on this initial outing. We had gone to the wrong part of the country, too far from the centre, and both of us were determined to see some action in this elusive war. We had proved we could put up with the hardship of trekking through mountains and uncertain food supplies. We'd seen the impact that Soviet bombing had had on peaceful rural communities and we had come across mines and weaponry for the first time. Now we wanted to get some real stories.

As we retraced our steps to the frontier and, after two weeks' absence, fell on the delights of Peshawar's American Club, we were already planning a way to get to the heart of the war.

'Next time it has to be Kabul province,' James said. 'We could waste months on the periphery.'

I agreed. In my diary I summarised our experience of Afghanistan to date: 'Wrong turning from Peshawar.'

Despite all that we had seen in Kunar and Nuristan I managed, in my first article published in a newspaper – the *Glasgow Herald* of 4 July 1985 – to offer only a general strategic analysis of the war under the headline 'Where cave dwellings are preferred to Russian rule'. My first sentence in my first-ever despatch for a newspaper was a very long one:

The war in Afghanistan between the Soviet-backed Karmal regime and the anti-Communist Mujahidin or freedom-fighters is now halfway through its sixth year, and the indications are that there is no end in sight, no chance of a military victory for either side nor much faith in the negotiations held recently at the UN in Geneva between the Karmal regime and the Pakistan government.

And so I continued in a report that I filed to copy-takers in Glasgow over a landline from Peshawar on a baking hot afternoon when the daily power cut had intervened to shut down the air conditioning at the Afghanaid house. Dripping with sweat, I read it out, word for word. For my troubles, and two weeks of hard labour in the mountains of Kunar and Nuristan, I was paid £90, half of which went to James.

In that report, published in the 'World News' section of the paper, I did not offer the good citizens of Glasgow details of any of the places we had been or the remarkable people we had met. All the interviews I had conducted with farmers, refugees and fighters remained stillborn in my notebook apart from the one with Ayanulah Nuristani in Marait, whose defiant sentiments about staying on to fight the 'jihad' I used as the coda to the piece. Although I had been impressed by the fortitude of the people I had met, I didn't believe I had seen anything of note.

I had set the bar very high for this expedition, something that shaped my next trip inside, which we embarked on only a couple of weeks after we got back to the safety of Gulmohar Road.

4

INTO THE LION'S DEN

Determined to get to the heart of the war on our next trip into Afghanistan, James and I sought out one of the main resistance groups, Harakat-e-Inqilab-i-Islami, also known as the Islamic Revolutionary Movement, which we had heard was involved at the sharp end around the Afghan capital, Kabul.

At their offices on Charsadda Road in Peshawar, we were introduced to a man called Niazuldin, one of ten Harakat commanders from the Kabul area, and straight away I was bewitched by him. Wild-eyed, immaculately dressed, his long jet-black curls and beard well groomed, his giant hands gripped me like the paws of a tiger and his face lit up with a dazzling smile. Not particularly tall but solidly built, he was a classic-looking Pathan with a Rasputin air about him, the kind of man you would not want to meet coming at you with a knife on a dark Afghan night.

'You want to go to Afghanistan?' he bellowed through our new interpreter, an easygoing heavy-set individual called Shams-ul-Haq, who had known Niazuldin for years. 'You want me to show you this war? If you come with me I will take you right to the centre of the occupation of our country by the infidels, but you must write and tell the world what you have seen.'

'You can tell Niazuldin that that is exactly why I am here,' I informed Shams.

On hearing this Niazuldin laughed and shook my hand again.

'Looks like we might have hit the target here, James,' I said, watching Niazuldin watching me.

Compared with the men we had met in Nuristan, this guy felt like he *was* the war. He had the weapons, he told us; he had a guerrilla base high in the mountains in Logar province south-east of the capital; and he boasted a record of daring hit-and-run attacks that he and his men had pulled off against Soviet and Afghan government targets in Kabul. I asked about his background and learned that he used to be a shopkeeper who sold clothes in downtown Kabul but that he had taken to the hills to fight after the Soviet invasion, leaving his wife and four children in a refugee camp in Pakistan. He had climbed the ranks of his guerrilla band to reach the status of commander as others had faded or been injured or killed. When I met him, he was thirty-two and in his prime.

For a man of such humble origins Niazuldin had a ready understanding of the unwritten contract between us: I was prepared to risk my life to report what he was doing. It would be his job to ensure that I would get out alive. It was not a case of him just being a gracious host; Niazuldin could see that getting journalists killed was not the way to promote his aims. He saw the chance to take us inside as an opportunity to show the world how he and his brave Mujahidin were taking on the might of the Soviet army and also as a way of impressing his own party leadership. Good coverage in the Western media, and perhaps a special story to tell, would bolster his case against rival commanders when it came to handing out new weapons. At that stage the Mujahidin were getting some weapons from the CIA via the Pakistani military and there was intense competition between commanders for the best of what was available. Niazuldin was up against other proven leaders in other parts of the country fighting for Harakat, so anything that he could do to raise his profile would help.

Right from the start Niazuldin and I got on fabulously well. It is hard to explain the intensity of a relationship that was largely conducted, initially at least, through an interpreter. I was an English public schoolboy with rock music on my Walkman and a cigarette always at hand; he was the good-looking, charismatic commander of a Mujahidin force who had sold jeans for a living in downtown Kabul. But we hit it off immediately.

Six days after my story from Kunar and Nuristan was published in the *Glasgow Herald*, James and I were off on our second trip into Afghanistan. As before, our departure came after a mad final night getting drunk in the American Club in traditional fashion and then dashing off another long letter to Kathy in faraway Brooklyn – who was doing her best to understand what on earth I was up to. We were accompanied this time by Lawrence Walsh, an American journalist in his forties who we met in the Club. Lawrence had covered the Vietnam War and was curious to see how the 'Russian Vietnam' was going, five and a half years after Soviet tanks rolled into Kabul.

My diary entry on Wednesday, 10 July 1985 records that I spent 600 Pakistani rupees (£5.30) for the coach trip from Peshawar to the border and then 10,500 Afghanis hiring a horse. (This could be as much as £120 but we exchanged our dollars for Afghanis on the black market in Peshawar and the real price was probably much lower.) Niazuldin had suggested horses, thinking we Westerners would not be able to cope with the rigours of the trail.

'We left with about fifty men,' I wrote in my diary, 'three horses – one for me, one for Shams, one for Lawrence – carrying our rucksacks in fertiliser bags, sewn up for disguise.' James had wisely declined the option of hiring a horse; as it turned out, I rarely rode mine, preferring to walk through the hills into Kabul province – hills that were far less testing than the jagged peaks of Kunar and Nuristan.

The early stages of this trip had a much more intense feel compared with the leisurely pace of our adventure with Jusef. We made quick progress to a staging post near the border and on only our second day out of Peshawar we reached one of the main crossing points into Afghanistan for guerrillas operating around Kabul. The plan was that we would link up with Niazuldin later at his mountain lair; for now we were accompanied by his right-hand man, a softly spoken, bearded mullah named Fazil-Jan who spoke no English but was close to our translator, Shams. At forty years old, Fazil-Jan had a quiet authority about him and I never heard any of the men question his judgement. The group had an altogether more professional feel about them than the men who had taken us into Nuristan.

At the border crossing point at Teri Mingal hundreds of fighters were preparing to go in or heading past us on their way out for time off with their families in Pakistan. Reached across a vast and desolate plateau, Teri Mingal was a one-street village scratched into the hillside with tea houses and shops selling basic provisions: clothes, boots, sweets and biscuits, medicines, weapons and ammunition, and cheap Afghan cigarettes. The place was a marshalling yard for a resistance army and it had been bombed not long before we got there, as several wrecked buildings testified.

In my notebook I wrote – rather incongruously – that Teri Mingal had the feel of *M*A*S*H**:

There are hundreds of horses standing on the terraces, their heads deep in nosebags, their tails constantly swishing against the flies. The Muj are everywhere, unpacking lorries full to the top with brand new weapons in their heavy wooden casing and ammunition boxes. There are several groups preparing to go in, loading up camels with impossible amounts of stuff. We are shown into a tent with rugs and cushions. Outside stands a Dashaka heavy machine gun. The air is punctuated by the sound of gunfire as the men test their weapons – Kalashnikovs, Dashakas and rifles. The reports register with tremendous echoes in the surrounding mountains.

After a delicious lunch of lamb and rice with tomatoes we set off once again for Afghanistan. Fazil-Jan had waited for a large group of border police to come down to buy their lunch, so that the coast was clear.

I wrote in my diary:

> After a short climb we reached the frontier post that amounted to two bored-looking Pakistani soldiers sitting on a jeep casually eyeing our progress. Me in a turban sweating profusely, head down, hardly aware we had reached the frontier. Once we were safely out of range, Fazil-Jan called the men together and they prayed for the success of the war. 'Other Mujahidin fight between them-selves,' he reminded them, adding that they should forget their quarrels. 'Be together and fight together.'

So off we went into the heartland of what seemed a futile war pitting mainly illiterate peasants farmers, increasingly coming to rely on their religion for inspiration, in an unequal fight with the brutal tactics of the Soviet military machine. We were heading once again into scorched-earth land but this time the destruction was more comprehensive. The Soviet army had taken to heart Mao's dictum: in order to kill the fishes, first you must drain the sea.

On that first day out from Teri Mingal we encountered our first wrecked Soviet armoured vehicles, lying rusting by the side of the track, remnants of long-gone battles in the earliest days of the war. We came across groups of dead horses and camels, stinking in the heat, covered in flies and with maggots exploding from their insides – evidence of recent airborne raids by Soviet helicopters on this, the most important re-supply route for the resistance around Kabul. One dappled grey lay with its head blown off.

Dead horses were followed by our first encounter with Mujahidin wounded, a haunting and arresting sight that reminded me of the risks I was taking. You could get hit in a way that might be entirely manageable if good medical attention was to hand but, as Romey Fullarton had warned us, in this war there was precious little medical equipment or expertise available. Once injured, you could be days from the border facing a dreadful journey back, either walking or, like these men, slumped on the backs of horses.

There were two animals bearing their desperate-looking charges. The men seemed delirious, their bodies lying awk-wardly, their heads slumped forward next to the horses' manes, their complexions grey with blood loss. You could see brown iodine stains on their clothes and we stood in silence as the animals were led past, the wounded gently groaning with each bump in the path. At least we knew, even if they did not, that they were close to some sort of help. But whether it had come too late we would never find out. The man leading them confirmed that they were members of Harakat and had been shot during a battle in Paghman, north-west of the capital. I watched them pass by with a feeling of dread in the pit of my stomach: could this be me on our return journey?

We marched through several villages that had been bombed early in the war and several times since. Some of the buildings gave us a glimpse of life in these parts before the arrival of scorched earth. There was some surprisingly elaborate architecture, houses sporting gables and balconies.

Our first night was spent at a Harakat house belonging to relations of Fazil-Jan. We got there after hours of walking, tended to our feet and prepared for dinner, taken sitting down with the men. First we washed our hands from a jug carried round by one of the youngest in the group. Then rice and mutton in a weak gravy was set before us on big platters from which we ate together, using our right hands only. We drank water with the food and then tea. In the evening the men took part in a lengthy praying session, a feature of life with the Mujahidin – the Holy Warriors fighting a Holy War – that I quickly got used to.

That night Fazil-Jan took his chance to convey to us what the war was all about. Speaking through Shams, this mild-mannered individual talked of his visceral hatred not for the Soviets, a term that encompassed a wide variety of ethnic groups, but for the Russians who tended to dominate the combat units of the occupying force.

'We will never forget what they have done to us, and one day we will take our revenge,' he said. 'We all used to live at home – we were good family boys – now we have lost our youth and we live badly in the mountains. But the Afghan people will fight to the end. We are one people and we will fight against the Russians. Even the small kids are fighting in the villages. They make small groups – one pretending to be Russian, one Mujahidin – and they make ambush sites and fight each other. They make wooden Kalashnikovs and rocket launchers and once they even killed one of the "Russian" boys. This shows our anger at the Russians and our determination to take revenge.'

He argued that Russian Communists were not just his enemies but were the enemies of humanity. 'They will surely come to Western Europe too,' he warned. 'We will fight to the end. But the promises of the free world do not materialise into weapons – we do not get enough.'

Then he predicted an eventual victory for the Mujahidin. 'Our country will be free one day but we will remember who helped us in this crucial time, and who did not,' he warned.

That evening we also talked to Lawrence, our bearded American fellow traveller, who seemed ill at ease – angry even

– at his own decision to head back to war. Perhaps, I thought, he was searching for his lost youth. Lawrence was immediately irritated by the privations we were suffering – the poor food, the discomforts of sleeping on the hoof – and he was more concerned about the possible dangers of this trip than I was. He was also less impressed with Niazuldin and his band than I had become. The Mujahidin had a certain natural indiscipline about them that I loved but to Lawrence, who had been tested in combat, these were worrying signs.

'I dunno about these guys – they're all over the place,' he said as we talked after supper. 'I'm not sure I would want to be in the trenches with them when the shit hits the fan.'

Lawrence was gathering material for a book on guerrilla warfare. Rather than use a notebook he preferred to pace up and down, talking his observations into a little tape recorder. I admired his professionalism, was jealous of his experience in Vietnam, and was impressed that he was working on a book, something I regarded as way beyond my compass. But after we had been chatting together on the trail, he made a prediction that stayed with me: 'You will also write a book about this one day,' he said.

The next morning we were woken at 2.30 a.m. by the men. It was freezing cold in the hills. I lay for a few seconds watching the stars, shivering in my sleeping bag that was proving woefully inadequate. We were moving early to be safe. The Mujahidin had long since worked out that they needed to make the best of the hours of darkness and take the toughest routes to try and avoid ambush.

That day we overtook horse trains loaded with ammunition, rockets, ground-to-ground missiles and Dashakas. We stopped at little tea houses or *chaikhanas*, at one of which we were given our first lesson in inter-resistance rivalry. The seven main rebel groups, each of which had their headquarters in Peshawar, were notoriously quarrelsome, fighting over the leadership of the war, access to weapons supplied by the

West, and the degree to which they followed the true calling of the Koran. The squabbles often boiled over into violence. At one *chaikhana* stop, we holed up at a Harakat place while across the track we were eyed by rival fighters from Jamiat [the Islamic Society]. There was no communication between the two groups; the men just watched each other with undisguised contempt.

It was a day that also brought home to me the danger of spies in the camp, something I had not considered before. Fazil-Jan announced to everyone that we were going to wait in the village of Babur for three days, at which James and I protested vociferously. We'd done plenty of waiting on our last trip and this time we were expecting steady progress.

'Why do we have to wait?' I asked Shams. 'Why can't we carry on now?'

He glanced around, turning to look over his shoulder before he replied: 'We are going in an hour, but don't say anything.'

I looked at him blankly. 'But why ...'

He explained to us that every camp had their spies, which was why Fazil-Jan often tried to mislead the men about their movements. The Communist-led Afghan government of Babrak Karmal put a great deal of effort into infiltrating the resistance, exploiting family or tribal feuds and sending agents into Pakistan to mingle with fighters before they set off. The Soviets and the Afghan government did not want publicity in the West and groups taking journalists would be targeted for that reason alone. We were slowly beginning to realise the added risk Niazuldin and Fazil-Jan were taking by smuggling three foreigners into the lion's den of the war.

Every day Fazil-Jan played games with his own men about our movements and he was perpetually concerned that Soviet soldiers or their Afghan allies might be waiting for us over the next pass. I was grateful for his caution and happy to trust his judgement.

After Babur we came across the royalty of the re-supply operation: some of the best-kept horses I'd seen anywhere in Pakistan or Afghanistan. I wrote in my diary:

> Sitting under walnut and apricot trees, the tranquillity of the afternoon is disturbed by the arrival of twenty-five horses – greys, chestnuts and browns of all shades. These animals are in magnificent condition, their shiny coats glistening in the dying sun. There's a wild instinct to them – unkempt manes and tails on creatures that have never been broken by man. They are work animals first and foremost, responding to the stick and the leather whip. They come clattering over the rocks, trotting freely, coming to rest under the trees. Then, one by one, they are relieved of their loads, a bag of hay is hung over their ears and a stake is driven into the ground, to which they are tethered. The horses eat, their noses pushing hay into their mouths. There's a lot of loud neighing and then rolling in the dust. These beasts know this route well and travel easily at night.

At the village of Buzurghana near Azrow we chatted to Mohammad Sharif, who was dressed in grubby khaki-green *shalwar kameez*. What struck me was his explanation of his age – he reckoned he was approximately forty-five, telling me how he estimated his date of birth: 'When I was born it was the harvest season and it was not raining.' It was a revealing insight into the world that we had entered. He was a former sheep farmer, who was now growing marijuana for hash that he sent to Pakistan, and his hatred of the 'infidel' Russians was all too clear. 'I am thirsty for Russian blood,' he growled after describing how his village had been destroyed.

Then we met an old man who spoke in a croaky voice and with a lisp through missing teeth. On his head he wore a white turban. He sat cross-legged on the ground before us and did not get up. His shirt was thick with dirt and sweat. We listened in stunned silence as he told us that a month earlier he had lost twenty-five members of his family, including his wife, all five of his children and many of his grandchildren, in the village of Chakerie near Kabul. He was heading for Pakistan. There was nothing we could say.

On our fourth day we were again woken at 2.30 a.m. and set off half an hour later, walking by the light of the moon over a high ridge where we stopped for breakfast. For the first time we saw Soviet MiG jet fighters high above us flying, according to our companions, towards the southern city of Kandahar. We also heard the distant engines of transport and spotter planes – a high-altitude, slowly modulating, groaning sound that would haunt me for years. Who was up there? What could they see? Was this a prelude to terror on the ground? It was an eerie sensation listening to that noise and imagining the firepower that could be unleashed in its wake. The Mujahidin told us about the 'Black Tulip', a name given to the Soviet transport planes that flew their dead back to Russia and elsewhere. Listening to a distant engine, I imagined an aircraft hold full of body bags making its way slowly back to the Motherland.

The country we were moving through was almost completely barren, with little vegetation, few trees and no cultivation. The villages were deserted except for small garrisons camping out in the ruins, just as we had seen in Kunar and Nuristan. Before the war there had been beautifully ordered tribal structures in these areas dating back to medieval times. Life had been the same for generation after generation of Afghans. These were highly sociable people and Shams told me it was common for Afghans to walk twenty miles just to have tea with friends or relatives. But now, modern war and modern weaponry was destroying this fragile culture, and accentuating rivalries between the various ethnic groups.

That day we came across our first big gravesite. Seven fighters, who had been ambushed two months before, were buried where they had fallen as an enduring reminder of what Shams called their 'heroic action'. The site was surrounded by a low stone wall and set under trees. Each of the graves was marked by a stone at head and foot and standing above each was a tall stake with green, purple, blue and brown prayer flags, fluttering and fading together. On the graves, the possessions of each man had been lovingly arranged by their fellow fighters: waistcoats, combs, cufflinks and buttons, a wallet and, on one, a metal watch strap. At the foot of each grave, the men's socks had been clamped under stones. Next to one lay a combat jacket offering a vivid picture of how he had died: the arms and chest of the jacket were torn by twenty or thirty bullet holes, the fabric beginning to fray at the edges. There was a terrible and pervading sadness about the place, the colours speaking of lives violently lost.

As we approached, the men accompanying us fell silent, each opening his arms as if to embrace the dead and muttering words of prayer to comrades they regarded as martyrs. Afterwards, with many gestures, they explained to James, Lawrence and me that these seven Mujahidin had been caught in the open by a helicopter gunship.

We were keenly aware that we too could be ambushed at any time and, as we moved through deep gulleys that, we were told, had been favourite killing grounds, increasingly elaborate precautions were taken. Fazil-Jan would send men forward while we waited to hear the reports of their Kalashnikovs indicating the all-clear. We were also coming across increasing numbers of mines, especially the green or grey butterfly-shaped anti-personnel mines dropped by helicopters or Soviet infantry that we had encountered in Kunar. I was always eagle-eyed for them knowing that something as innocent as heading a few feet off the track in the dark to attend to the call of nature could be my undoing. I'd vowed on our first trip never to lead a group when walking in the hills because of the danger of mines, but now I found myself taking the risk because I preferred being out in front.

It was not all tension and nerves though. There were moments of hilarity, moments when relationships with the most talkative and inquisitive of the men started to develop. In my notebook I described a little scene involving some shooting, for example. It was the first and only time I fired a Kalashnikov.

Suddenly we stop for no apparent reason. There is a chorus of clicks as the men cock their weapons. Had they seen some movement higher up? Perhaps we would be ambushed. The leader of the group broke away, moving deftly through the rocks up the side of the hill. He waited. We waited. Then, to my great relief, a scrawny old hare ran out from under a rock. He fired twice and missed as it ran higher, only its rear now presenting itself to the guns. Now it was everyone else's turn and soon the hillside was alive with the sound of gunfire as each man took a pot shot – and missed. How, I asked, jokingly, could they hit a Russian if seven of them couldn't even hit a hare? I had not realised how difficult it would be to hit a tiny animal with a high-velocity bullet. Later we saw some partridge moving in the rocks. Now it was my turn. A Kalashnikov was thrust into my hands, safety catch off, ready to fire. '*Zu, zu,*' (go, go) whispered the men urgently. I fired at a bird sitting on top of a large rock and missed. I fired at another and missed that one too and then, more improbably, I had a go at one flying, which I missed as well. '*Bas, bas,*' (enough, enough) they shouted. Red-faced I handed the weapon back to its owner amid the roars and laughter of the men. I guessed they were telling me 'You see, it's more difficult than you think.'

After trekking for hours through dry, barren and enclosed mountains, we finally emerged over a ridge and saw before us a huge plain with single peaks rising dramatically above it. We approached a village nestled between two low undulating ridges. Having travelled through one deserted village after another, I was looking forward to seeing a place that bore signs of life.

A young girl was walking slowly up to the houses with a pot of water on her head and a dog was barking fiercely from a rooftop. A wisp of smoke rose above one house. But once again appearances from afar were deceptive and, as we came close, we could see that the depressingly monotonous pattern was repeated. Many of the roofs in the little village of Darban had caved in and several houses were destroyed, the remains of their four walls standing but broken and eroded by the rains. The place had last been bombed in December, by which time most of its inhabitants had already fled.

By then we had walked for around fifty or sixty miles from the border on a trajectory that, if continued, would have taken us straight into Kabul. We had come through much barren land, but we had not seen a single village that was not either deserted or bombed. I was struck by how empty the countryside was so close to the capital but also by how sparsely populated it would have been even without the war. We had walked across vast plains with no trees and no settlements, just miles and miles of scrub running abruptly up to mountains rising steeply above them.

After tea in the remains of Darban we continued for another two hours until we reached one of Fazil-Jan's staging posts on the plain. We were now only five hours' walk from the outlying districts of Kabul and security was all-important. The men pointed out a Soviet post across the plain on a small hill. The house where we stopped consisted of three rooms around a bomb-damaged courtyard, with a little shop running off it. At that, the first shop we had seen in Afghanistan, we found batteries, biscuits, sugary sweets that the Afghans eat as a dessert with tea, and cigarettes. I stocked up while I could, buying several packets of Red & White ciggies – a rough local brand, favoured by the Muj, that I came to rely on.

We slept on a roof that was completely exposed to air attack and surveillance, and were warned not to use our torches. I lay awake in my sleeping bag and under my *putu* blanket staring again at the vast amphitheatre of the clear night sky, completely untainted by artificial light. I tracked a satellite moving steadily at thousands of miles an hour above us, a reminder of a modern world that seemed so remote when viewed from the ruins of a building in a ruined village that was supplied by neither electricity nor a road. I could hear the men on guard duty talking and laughing quietly as they smoked the night away. I wondered what had happened to the family that had lived in this house and where they might be now. There seemed only two possibilities: either dead and buried in the ground around us or living in the agony of exile in Pakistan. And in the stillness of the black hours, I wondered if death was to be my fate out there.

Although James and I had faced danger before, it was the proximity of the Soviet stronghold of Kabul that brought home to me for the first time that there was a chance I wouldn't come out of this alive. I decided that if that was what was going to happen then so be it; at least, I thought, I would have died doing something exciting and something worthwhile, rather than being stuck in a desk job back in London.

―◆◆◆◆◆―

The next day we were up at 4 a.m. We were told that we would go to a 'safe house' over the next ridge where we would spend time resting. Most of the men were going straight up to Niazuldin's mountain base.

51

'Why can't we go to the camp now?' Lawrence demanded angrily.

James, Lawrence and I had tried in vain to hold Fazil-Jan to a Western-style schedule, emphasising the importance of arriving on time and getting on with our mission. Fazil-Jan whispered conspiratorially with Shams, who then whispered to us, in a long-winded conversation that was broken off whenever anyone he did not trust came within earshot. The upshot appeared to be that we must spend a day at this place before we could proceed.

But it turned out to be another example of Fazil-Jan's meticulous campaign of misinformation because at 3.30 p.m. that same afternoon we were told it was time for us to set off for the mountains.

The day was hot and I was sweating under my rucksack as we climbed towards the ridge. We were not allowed to go first in the group and at one point we had to wait for a sign from the men ahead, in the form of a single rifle shot at the pass, before we continued. Then we made our way up a steep and heavily bouldered ravine, twisting and turning with the course of a stream until we reached a point where we were within earshot of the sentries. The men shouted a greeting and we awaited the expected reply. The voices echoed. All was clear and, five days after leaving Peshawar, we made our way at last into Niazuldin's camp in the hills above Kabul.

5

AT THE CAMP

I was immediately impressed by Niazuldin's lair. This was a proper guerrilla operations base set in a place the Soviets or the Afghan army would have to think hard about taking on. Nestled high up in the mountain but several hundred feet below the highest ridges, it was a cockpit of the war with a commanding strategic position. In peacetime this was land beyond use, left to wild animals and the birds of prey that circled silently above, but in war it had become the nerve centre for a group of men who were determined to liberate their country.

'I can see why they chose this spot,' James said, gazing around. 'It would be difficult for helicopter gunships to target this place. They'd have to fly down below the ridge line, making them vulnerable to heavy machine-gun and RPG fire from all sides.'

Looking at the deep, twisting ravine I agreed with him. We would certainly be safer here than we had been walking through the hills and over the passes from the Pakistani border.

Shams showed us round the camp. The heart of it consisted of little more than two single-room huts made of mud, stone and timber set under mulberry trees next to a stream running down from the higher ground. The two structures, which would have been almost impossible to pick out from an aircraft, were separated by a flat terraced area where men were sitting talking among themselves. Alongside the terrace ran the main pathway, which led downhill to the narrow gully where the sentries guarded the entrance and uphill to the ridge, half an hour's climb away, from where you could see Kabul in the distance. Shams told us that five Dashaka machine guns were permanently placed at strategic points on the ridge.

The men had installed a clever sluice system on the stream that regulated its flow and enabled them to store water in two small ponds that were used for washing and laundry. Every now and again the sluices would be opened and the whole area would be drenched with clean water cascading over the terrace and down the path. A couple of caves that were used as ammunition stores had big rocks stacked in front of them to protect them from air attack. There was a cooking area where a bread oven had been dug out of the ground. The hillsides were littered with rocks, and pathways to vantage points meandered among them. There were a few trees clinging to life and plenty of lavender bushes that were harvested for burning at the base of the bread oven.

'Is Niazuldin here?' I asked. Since we arrived I'd been glancing around hoping to see his friendly face.

'Not yet. Soon,' was all that Shams would say.

We had dinner of rice and potatoes then lay down on our *putus* under the stars. Although I was exhausted, I couldn't sleep. At last I was in a proper Mujahidin camp and the enemy was only a few miles away. Occasionally I heard the sound of a helicopter – the rhythmic pulse of its rotors ebbing and flowing as it made its way through the night. Thinking logically, I realised that the only way the Soviet army could attack this place would be to land special forces some way away on the plain below at night, who would then have to walk for several hours before climbing up through the boulders along the stream bed. They would have to kill the guards

– there were usually two – with knives. Assuming they had achieved this without giving themselves away, they would have to creep up to a point where they had a field of vision across the terrace before opening fire. Then they would have to deal with the men in the huts. That scenario played on my mind. I had read accounts of mainly Russian Spetsnaz special forces troops conducting exactly these sorts of operations. Careful planning followed by a stealthy approach and then the advantage of surprise could lead to a rout of unwary guerrillas. Unlike the Americans in Vietnam, the Soviets did not have the media to answer to and could kill at will, whatever the circumstances.

The camp had its own pattern of life dictated by prayers that the men performed five times a day, starting at sunrise and ending at sunset. They would stand in lines on the terrace, their weapons on their *putus* on the ground in front of them, with Fazil-Jan or one of the younger mullahs leading. It was a ritual that impressed me – disciplined, spiritual – the well-spring of their inspiration in a Holy War that demanded enormous sacrifices. They would spend months in the camp, either based there or using it to prepare for attacks in Kabul, and not see their wives or children in exile in Pakistan sometimes for more than a year.

The camp could accommodate more than a hundred people and there was always movement in and out as fighters headed off on missions into the city, returning days later with their wounded and stories of battle. Men heading back to Pakistan from other Harakat camps would stop by, as would young Afghans who had been released from the notorious Pul-e-Charkhi prison in Kabul, where inmates were routinely tortured and beaten by officers of the feared KHAD, the Afghan secret police. Others came in with stories that sparked suspicion: young men who said they had deserted from the Afghan army and wanted to join the resistance. Were they spies? Had they come to report back on numbers

Niazuldin's camp

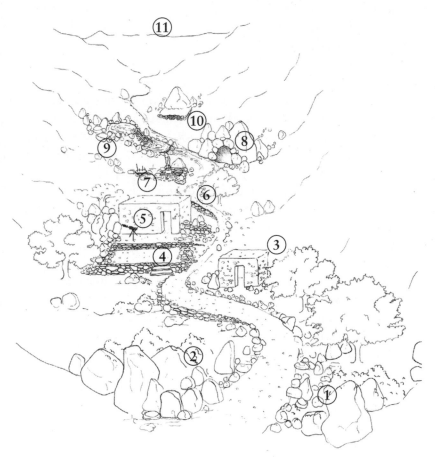

1	Sentry post	7	Bread oven/cooking fire
2	Sentry post	8	Cave/ammunition store
3	Lower hut	9	Pools for washing/water
4	Main terrace	10	Big rock for meetings
5	Heavy gun	11	Top ridge
6	Upper hut		

and weaponry and the presence of foreigners? I never saw a woman or a child there. This was a fighting base in a chauvinistic society.

The men kept to a strict routine. Communal meals were taken like clockwork. Breakfast – usually old scraps of bread and tea – was taken early; lunch was at 12 p.m. on the dot – often rice with potatoes; and dinner in the early evening – again rice and potatoes, occasionally with some meat. Almost all the food had to be brought in from Pakistan on the backs of donkeys or horses, a testament to the effectiveness of the Soviet scorched earth policy, so there was never more than a minimum to go round. None of the men had an ounce of extra weight on them and I quickly shed pounds on the 'Afghan-plan' diet, despite the fact that the cooks always made sure that James, Lawrence and I – honoured guests – got a little extra. Onions were a treat – I used to eat them raw – and the arrival of a goat was a sign that a big dinner was on the way.

On the day after our arrival some men turned up with a calf. Its eyes sparkled with fear and panic as it lay on the ground with two men holding it down. A third sharpened his blunt knife before sawing away at the animal's neck, its blood oozing out into the gravel and dust as it expired. There were no wild animals to speak of, though my notebook records that at one point, on a little walk up into the ravine, I killed a poisonous-looking silvery snake by smashing it with a rock. But there were songbirds in those mountains, some of them brave enough to take scraps of bread from the terrace.

The morning after our arrival, James went off with Lawrence to do some filming while I began a series of interviews, using Shams as translator and taking notes in my notebook. I wanted to get a flavour of who these men were and learn a little about their life stories.

All of them spoke of their defiance, their determination to fight to the last and their belief that one day they would prevail. They hated the Russians in particular, people they regarded as infidels and cowards who were rarely prepared to get out of their armoured personnel carriers, tanks or helicopters and fight on the ground. By that stage most of the men had lost members of their families and those left were living in miserable exile on the red-hot plains of Pakistan. Often very young, no more than eighteen or twenty, ill-educated and illiterate, they were happy to die a martyr's death and happy to submit themselves to the disciplined existence of life in Niazuldin's ranks.

Abdul Manan, at twenty-two, spoke of his early and lost ambition to be a doctor. He had been brought up in Kabul and had studied until he was eighteen, learning Pashto, geography, history, English, maths, physics and chemistry. When the Soviets arrived his teachers had tried to force him to join a small class of pupils who were to be re-educated as Communists – students Abdul Manan knew would later be deployed as informers and spies.

'They taught us that the Mujahidin were bandits who were blowing up bridges and mosques and spending American dollars and Pakistani rupees,' he explained. 'We were told that outside Afghanistan our enemies were America, China, Pakistan, Egypt and "all the imperialists". They said the Communist revolution was going to win and the Mujahidin would lose their game. They were teaching us that we would have a new Afghanistan, but I never believed that.'

Abdul Manan's refusal to join the Communist class placed him under suspicion and he was arrested one morning and taken to prison, where he was beaten and tortured with electric shock treatment administered through his toes. After finally convincing his captors that he had nothing to do with the resistance, he was released four months later and promptly headed straight to Peshawar to join up.

I asked why he had joined Harakat and not one of the other rebel groups.

'All my relatives are with Harakat,' he said, 'and I know they are fighting better than the other parties. I liked Harakat and I requested my relatives to admit me to the party. My whole life will be devoted to the jihad for Harakat,' he added.

Eighteen-year-old Sherulah had a similar story. During ten months in jail, he was whipped by women officers of the KHAD and held in a cell for four days with the lights on and Indian music blaring in his ears. It all happened, fittingly in this war that set Communist against Holy Warrior, in a cell overlooked by a portrait of Lenin. His brother was still in jail as he spoke.

'I was in prison because I was a Mujahid,' he said. 'My brother was too. I used to give lectures against the Russians to my friends at school. I used to inform the Mujahidin about new government posts on the edge of the city and new military activities. And I used to go to ambush sites and tell the Mujahidin when the Russians would attack.'

Sherulah said he did not break under torture. He refused to divulge information that would have been of use to the regime but he made a play of denouncing the Mujahidin. When he was eventually released he could hardly walk after being held in a cramped cell with twenty other political prisoners. But now, after a year of training in Niazuldin's band, Sherulah had been presented with his first Kalashnikov and had taken part in his first attack on an outpost on the edge of Kabul. 'The Russians must leave Afghanistan because they are causing misery to the poor Afghan Muslim people,' he said.

One man scared me from the moment I met him. Abdul Khalil had a shock of black hair under his turban, an Asterix moustache and dark eyes that seemed to see straight through me.

'You are my enemy,' he said bluntly, with an embarrassed Shams translating.

Abdul Khalil refused to shake my hand, telling me he

wanted to avenge the deaths of his forefathers in the wars against the British in the nineteenth century. He made it clear that he would kill me if given the chance. 'I know the history. I read the books in school. You also invaded Afghanistan like the Russians,' he said.

I tried to laugh it off but I was concerned. Was he serious? Perhaps he would kill me in my sleep – there were plenty of rocks around that could do the job – or just shoot me in cold blood in front of everyone in a dramatic and ultimate gesture.

'Don't worry, he won't do anything,' Shams said afterwards. But I always kept a wary eye out for Abdul Khalil.

Throughout our stay at the camp I was continually to misjudge the ages of the men, always assuming they were much older than they were. Partly this can be put down to the almost universal practice of wearing beards but, even so, men of twenty-four often looked ten years older. Shams explained that the war and its privations had affected the health of many of them and the requirement to fight from sixteen onwards had enforced a premature maturity upon them. Typically they would spend up to nine months in the hills and on operations without seeing their families. 'They are still children,' said Shams, 'but they have lost their youth because of this war.'

A common misconception among the men was that James, Lawrence and I were part of some high-level government delegation and that we had come laden with heavy weapons, money, medical supplies and food. If that was not the case, we were to tell our respective governments to get on with supplying the brave Mujahidin with what they needed to fight.

'Tell your Queen what we need,' was a common instruction. They could not understand the subtleties of the superpower game being played out over Afghanistan. Why couldn't the Americans and British just give the Mujahidin everything they needed directly, instead of dealing through the mendacious Pakistanis, who were making their own choices about who got what weapons and were creaming off money and munitions for their own uses? And they could not accept that we were not Muslims and never ceased trying to persuade us to pray with them. 'Muslim man!' they would say pointing at me and threatening me with the deadly consequences of being a 'kafir' or unbeliever.

A couple of days after we got there, Niazuldin arrived. Dressed immaculately in laundered grey *shalwar kameez* with a white and purple scarf draped over his shoulders, he greeted Fazil-Jan and his other senior lieutenants and then sought out his visitors. He hugged me, first to one side then the other, with a gleam in his eyes, saying 'Welcome, welcome, my friend.' The atmosphere in the camp changed instantly on his arrival. Niazuldin was a natural leader to whom everyone gravitated, with abundant self-confidence, huge energy and an infectious laugh. Wherever you went, you could hear his voice, and he sat in a central position at every meal.

It was great to see him again, this time inside Afghanistan, and over dinner that night I asked him more about his early life, before the chaos and disruption of the war. He said that back in the 70s, when he was selling jeans in Kabul, he used to wear Western clothes – not everyone would admit to that by then – and, even more surprisingly, he told me he had no religious convictions, which was a bold admission even by 1985. Almost as soon as the Soviets arrived in 1979, he left the city with his family and headed to Pakistan before returning to fight. He said he had been working under another commander who had been 'martyred' and his men selected him to take over.

'Everyone knew I had to be a commander,' he intoned in his deep, sonorous voice. 'They told me "You are the only one who could be our commander."' His face was transformed by a huge smile revealing a set of brilliant white teeth.

Niazuldin explained that he had been instructed by his dying predecessor to go and attack a particular Soviet position so that the enemy would not think they had inflicted a decisive blow by killing his colleague. 'I did it successfully,' he said without a trace of modesty. 'He was quite happy and told me "I know you can do the work well after me."'

Then Niazuldin spoke of his methods in Kabul. The translation by Shams gave his words a slightly abrupt feel but he still sounded like a man speaking from the heart. 'We always take risks with our lives,' he explained. 'We go to a house, we change our clothes, we wait for the tanks, we lie down in the road and wait for them. When I hit a tank it gives me great satisfaction. I see the Russians burning and the tanks destroyed. Then I feel happy and satisfied. That is a great moment for me. But when I see my Mujahids get hurt or martyred and, at the same time, I can't help them and I can't hit the Russians back, that is the time I feel very unhappy. The thing that annoys me most is the bombardment by aircraft when I can't hit them back because we have no anti-aircraft missiles.'

He claimed he had once attacked the Soviet embassy and killed scores of soldiers in the process, including four jeeploads of men who happened to be passing. 'I wanted to kill all of them, not just the ambassador,' he said. He showed us the Soviet army boots he said he had taken from a dead soldier and the bullet belts he wore across his chest like an old Mexican fighter. He also had a Kalashnikov captured from a Russian with a bayonet that, he was at pains to point out, he had used to cut a Russian throat.

Later that evening James and I sat smoking under the stars. He was sceptical about Niazuldin's war record.

'How do we know he's not just a big talker?' he asked. 'I've never heard of an attack on the Soviet embassy. You've got to remember that these guys want weapons and they are going to say whatever they think will impress us.'

'Yeah, I know. You're probably right,' I replied. But I liked Niazuldin – I liked his confidence and his no-nonsense approach. 'I just feel he's the real deal,' I said. 'There's something about this guy ...'

'If he is so accomplished then why does he not have the best weapons available already? He's not one of the most renowned commanders of the resistance, is he?' countered James.

'Yes, but would he really go into that amount of detail about individual operations within earshot of his men if it was all bullshit?'

It was an exchange that highlighted the strong and immediate bond I had formed with this Harakat commander of the Kabul Mujahidin, a bond that was forged at an instinctive level. It was a relationship that crossed vast cultural, linguistic and geographical chasms but I never regarded Niazuldin as 'foreign'. He was like a big brother who just happened not to speak English; from the beginning he and I always understood what we were saying to each other.

Niazuldin ruled the camp with a rod of iron, something we found out early the next day when there was a disagreement over sentry duty. One young fighter had refused to go on watch for the night. When he discovered this insubordination, Niazuldin exploded with ferocious violence, tearing into the poor chap, thumping him and dragging him along the stone path through the camp. It was physical abuse and psychological humiliation all at once. Niazuldin was roaring at him and would have left him with serious injuries had not others intervened to restrain him. The message was clear: you disobeyed Niazuldin at your peril. The object of his anger was sent up the mountain to keep lookout at midnight and for the next four days was barely able to sleep as he was made to pay for his misdemeanour.

Niazuldin was unapologetic about the treatment he had meted out. 'If discipline is not there, how can we fight the Russians?' he asked. All his men would be heading for disaster without discipline, he explained. 'If they are not good professionals, how can we fight a superpower army and their tanks on the roadside?'

I later discovered from Shams that not long before this episode, another of his men had turned his gun on his commander but had frozen in his moment of betrayal. Niazuldin had been sleeping by the stream and when he turned and looked him in the eye, the young would-be traitor, who had been paid by the government to assassinate Niazuldin, had pulled the trigger and missed.

'I investigated him and then I shot him with thirty bullets,' Niazuldin recalled when I asked him about it, going through the motions of wiping his hands of the memory.

Did he enjoy exacting his revenge, I enquired through the good offices of Shams.

Niazuldin grabbed me by the neck and attempted to throttle me with his huge hands. 'Of course I did,' he roared. 'If you had been there, you would have fainted,' he said.

From very early on I felt I could trust Niazuldin and he and I developed little jokes with each other. If he saw me smoking he would wave a disapproving finger and tell me that it was bad for my health. I'd motion to his Kalashnikov and tell 'Niazuldina' – as I sometimes called him – that that was also bad for his health and he'd laugh heartily. There was a bond we both felt, and I suppose that's why he made me an offer that he did not extend to James or Lawrence.

There had been much discussion about what else we could see now that we were within a few miles of Kabul. None of us wanted to go back to Pakistan at that stage – we had come to report on the war and we had barely started. One option was to stay in the camp for a while interviewing the men as they came and went from combat missions, but that seemed rather limited. Another was to do a tour around the outside of Kabul, visiting the various Mujahidin positions without going into the city, and then returning to Pakistan.

'But what about actually going in?' I suggested to Shams after supper one night.

'Going in where?' replied Shams.

'Kabul ... into the city. What would be involved in actually getting inside the city itself? Has anyone done that?'

'Mr Edward, these men do that all the time but you are a journalist and no one has tried that before. They go in to fight ... it's dangerous and very risky. You could easily be killed or captured.'

'I know, I know. I was just wondering about the idea of joining them and seeing first-hand what they get up to. It would be a fantastic story – a report from the real heart of this war and with the men who are taking the Russians on right in the centre of the occupation.'

There was a pause, as we listened to the distant rattle of another Soviet army helicopter, flying way down the valley somewhere.

'Why don't you just ask him ... see what he says?'

'OK ... but I don't think this will be possible. Even Niazuldin has his limits.'

It was a ludicrous idea but when Shams talked it through with Niazuldin I was not surprised to see him nodding and smiling. They chatted for some minutes. Then Niazuldin beckoned for Fazil-Jan to join them and they talked some more. 'My commander' *was* taking it seriously.

It seemed both Niazuldin and Fazil-Jan could see the impact a story of that kind could have and the prestige that would accrue to them if they pulled it off.

'It would show the world how strong the resistance is if we can take a journalist into the city under the noses of the Russian occupiers,' Niazuldin said grandly when I first discussed it with him.

I didn't know of any other Western journalists who had done this. To my ambitious mind it was an enticing prospect, giving me a unique chance to see what was going on, even if the risks were sky-high.

In those early discussions the focus quickly switched from not just going into Kabul but to how I could get a chance to see the city. This was the nerve centre of the occupation and a place that was largely a mystery to the West in a country that had become enveloped by Soviet-era secrecy. If the initial idea was already ambitious, now a new and even greater level of risk was being added.

Niazuldin ran through some options from a playbook hitherto only used by the Mujahidin on the most daring of combat missions. I could travel around the city with an old man in the back of a truck, dressed as his daughter who would be too sick to speak if we were stopped. I didn't like that idea. Or I could go dressed as a soldier in the official Afghan militia. I would be accompanied by two Mujahids in similar attire, and we would tour the city in an Afghan army jeep. We dismissed that one because physically I was never going to be able to pass myself off as an Afghan. I had grown a beard but it was brown with blonde streaks, which wouldn't convince anyone.

And then Niazuldin suggested a third option. I could pose as a young Russian officer on an errand into the centre of the city in his jeep, a ludicrously dangerous idea but one that just might work. He said he knew how this could be done. There was an Afghan army driver they could use who worked for the Soviets and he could take me on a tour of central Kabul. Niazuldin reckoned I could be got up to look exactly like a Russian and started joking with me that I was a Russian in any case.

'*Shuravi, shuravi* ...' he said, pronouncing the word the Afghans used for 'Soviet' and poking me with his finger.

But then he grew deadly serious. He warned me that this was a high-wire operation and the risks were huge. I didn't need to be told again what those were. He also warned me that it would take between ten and twenty days to set up and I would have to wait at his base until we could proceed. Could I handle the wait? With little real idea about what might be involved, I said I thought I could.

'I will arrange it for you,' Niazuldin announced triumphantly. 'You will be driven by the Afghan chauffeur of a Russian army officer whose brothers are fighting with the resistance. It will be your own personal Kabul taxi. What do you think of that?'

This was far more ambitious and dangerous than simply getting into the city and then getting out again, but it intrigued me. It seemed logical that if I got into the city I would need to actually see something of it and not remain in hiding the entire time and what a coup if we could pull it off. Here was a chance to get an amazing story, to break in as it were to the heart of the Soviet occupation and report on the way in which the Mujahidin were conducting a war of national liberation within Kabul. I'd surely make a name for myself in the world of foreign news reporting with a story like that, I thought to myself.

At sunset on the following night I went with Niazuldin, Fazil-Jan and Shams for another secret meeting. A great show was made of finding a place concealed from anyone else in the camp. First we walked down the hill a little, but that location was found to be inadequate. Then we went up above the camp and sat under a big rock. Two men sleeping there were given their marching orders. I wanted to ask many questions about the trip and how it would work. This was out of the question, said Niazuldin, flashing his teeth, his big face lit up with that smile. It all had to be kept secret. He confined himself to telling me that I would be taken to a safe house on the edge of the city. If the jeep plan was going to work, I would know in three days. Otherwise they would smuggle me around on foot and probably at night. He would show me the old Royal Palace at Darul Aman, the Soviet military

camps and Babrak Karmal's house. We might, he suggested
with a twinkle in his eye, stop at the InterContinental Hotel
for a cup of tea.

I was not allowed to tell James and Lawrence about
these early discussions but on the fifth night in the camp we
brought them into the debate about what we would do next.
Fazil-Jan suggested that they might like to take up the chance
to complete a tour through the countryside occupied by the
Mujahidin around the outside of Kabul and then head back
to Peshawar. That was an interesting prospect, which would
involve crossing the Salang Highway that ran north from the
city. This was a main supply artery for the Soviet army and
was the scene of regular rebel attacks. The trip would involve
coming close to many Soviet and Afghan positions during a
journey in which several different commanders would have
responsibility for their safety.

'How long would it take?' James wanted to know.

Fazil-Jan could only guess but suggested they could be
moving for up to three weeks.

I had the option of going with them but by this time my
mind was set on getting inside the city and the Russian officer
adventure.

'It's a huge risk to take, Ed,' said James, when I explained
it to him. 'If you get caught the Russians will not see the
funny side of it.'

'But do you think I should do it? Would you do it?'

'I can see the attraction – you could get an amazing story,'
James replied, sucking air through his teeth. 'I don't know.
The stakes are incredibly high and if something goes wrong
you will be on your own.'

'But would you do it?' I persisted.

'Maybe if there was room for two.'

But Niazuldin had made it clear there was only room for
one and I had already grabbed the slot.

'If you go on your boy-scout adventure to Kabul, Lawrence

and I should get to take Shams with us,' James argued. 'We'll need a translator to communicate with everyone.'

Lawrence agreed. It was only fair, he said, since I was the one who was breaking away from the group, and I could see their point. I convinced myself that I could rely for translation on a shy young mullah called Abdullah-Jan who spoke limited English and was close to Niazuldin. So long as Abdullah was around, I had a way of communicating beyond the body language, jokes and general joshing we had got used to in the camp.

'I might be the one who's short-changed here,' I told them. 'I'll be in and out of the city in a couple of days and back kicking my heels in Peshawar long before you get out.'

'Either that or you'll be rotting in a Russian jail,' James suggested helpfully.

We talked long into the night trying to war-game scenarios about events that were impossible to predict. One thing was clear: if we did split up there was no chance of James going back on his early decision about Shams. I would have to make do without him.

We agreed that between the two of us we were going to get some of the best access to this elusive and secret war that anyone had had in the last five years. We had certainly moved from the periphery to the centre in the space of our two trips inside.

Over a couple of evenings a decision was reached and we prepared to split up. There is no indication in my notebook that I knew I was setting out on a crazy adventure. I was just taking one of the options we had discussed. I could see that, in any normal world-view, even what James and Lawrence were going to attempt was highly dangerous and fraught with risk. In my case, once I had chosen my course of action and preparations began for my trip to the city, I felt that I had to stick to it, come what may. It had been agreed by Niazuldin, Fazil-Jan and Abdullah-Jan and their senior advisers were all in on it.

My determination in that respect was partly pride, partly a

sense of responsibility to the men who, within days, would risk their lives to arrange my passage, and partly a character feature (or flaw). I had been brought up never to shirk a challenge and to stick to my guns, whatever the cost. There was also the distorting effect of war. I had a devil-may-care attitude and my personal safety was low on my list of priorities. I was certainly prepared to take a risk with Niazuldin. We were taking risks every day just by being there, and I was up for more.

The following night Niazuldin and Shams took me to a quiet spot and asked me to sign a note saying that the idea for the trip was entirely my own and that I alone would be responsible for my actions. It was remarkable that they requested such a thing. Niazuldin & Co. did not want to be sued for this, I guessed.

I hesitated over the paper, asking myself whether this was beyond my reach, whether I could cope with the waiting beforehand and whether I could survive without Shams. Knowing this was my last chance to ask questions before Shams left the following day, I made one final attempt to find out how long I would have to wait. The estimate of ten-to-twenty days was too vague. But it was futile. I was trying to impose a schedule on people who didn't think in terms of deadlines about unknown future events. The answer came back – five, ten, fifteen, twenty days or even a month. I almost wished I hadn't asked.

I was reassured by one thing Niazuldin said: 'I will never have planned anything so carefully in my life. Don't worry. You are my son now and my conscience until it is done.'

'What is the chance of being captured?' I asked.

'Probably fifty-fifty,' he replied bluntly.

'And what would happen to me if I was captured? Would I go to jail?'

Niazuldin hesitated before answering: 'You might be shot, you might not. If it turns out badly, my advice is – you must smile when you die.'

6

WAITING

On 17 July 1985, Day 8 of our trip, James, Lawrence and I made our final preparations before the split. I asked Shams to teach me a few sentences in Pashto that might come in handy after he left, including 'Now I want to go to Peshawar!' I was plagued by a nagging anxiety about whether I could handle what lay ahead but I kept my fears to myself. I had decided to take my chance to go into Kabul and I was going to stick to it.

It was agreed that I could accompany James and Lawrence on the first stages of their journey so we all left the camp together, alongside Niazuldin and a posse of Mujahidin, and headed down on to the plain below to the village of Musei, that lay between the mountains and the capital. When we got there we made our way through the narrow alleyways between the houses, many of which were still intact, making Musei a first for us after all the battered villages we had seen in Nuristan and Kunar and on our way into Niazuldin's camp. In typical Afghan style the houses were built around large courtyards with sixteen-foot-high mud walls and huge wooden doors with big, cast-iron door knobs.

We passed through the centre of the village where small shops in alcoves were selling American and Russian cigarettes, warm Coca-Cola, Russian toffees and watermelon. There was a tailor going about his business and for the first time in Afghanistan we saw women and children on the narrow streets dressed in brilliant colours – reds, greens, yellows and blues. Musei was set out along a river and the banks were thick with mulberry, apricot and plum trees. All around the village were neat fields planted with potatoes, onions, cucumbers, wheat, barley and marijuana. There were apple tree orchards and hollyhocks growing in abundance, fed by a neat irrigation system. Lines of poplars ran horizontally from the outermost houses, forming windbreaks. The village was a scene of beauty and simplicity that day, the tranquillity broken only by the constant drone of helicopters and bombers high above.

Our destination was the home of a cheerful mullah called Ajab Gul, a man whom I soon learned was never seen outside without his Bren gun. We knocked on his door and were quickly ushered behind the high mud walls of a comfortable – even Westernised – house with fruit trees in the garden and a gurgling stream running alongside the pathway outside the front door.

That day I wrote:

We are now just one hour's bicycle ride from Kabul. Helicopters overflew us high above on our way here, dropping magnesium flares to deter possible missile or rocket attacks and forming huge lingering question marks in the sky. We heard mortar fire much closer. The rest of the day has featured almost constant aircraft noises, especially helicopters, and tonight we can hear the sound of continuous explosions coming from the city.

I had intended to make the twenty-five-hour walk to Paghman with James and Lawrence but Niazuldin insisted I stay here at Ajab Gul's. James and Lawrence did not set off until 9 p.m. – they were not allowed to talk or use their torches. Their route skirts Russian posts and takes them even closer to Kabul. I accompanied them to the edge of the village where we said an emotional farewell with handshakes in the English way. 'Good luck, mate,' James offered as he turned to go, shouldering his rucksack. I bid Lawrence goodbye and offered them both the best of luck. I felt intense loneliness for a few minutes that gradually subsided into anxiety about what lies ahead and the long wait. For the first time I am confronting my decision head-on.

Following James and Lawrence's departure Niazuldin left for Kabul to make the arrangements for my trip, telling me that in the meantime I would not be allowed out of Ajab Gul's house. I hadn't been there on my own for long before I realised I had seriously compromised my ability to communicate by letting Shams go with the others. It was now just me and Niazuldin's men and I was reliant on the limited English of the good-natured but not very fluent Abdullah-Jan, which left me feeling isolated and generally unable to control my own destiny. This was manageable while life remained reasonably peaceful but it would ramp up the pressure when it did not.

The following day at Ajab Gul's I had more to say in my notebook on this watershed moment:

After bidding James and Lawrence goodbye, I returned to Ajab Gul's as a Mujahid – my turban is always on and I carry an AK47. I was not allowed to speak any words of English on the journey back to the house. We are so close to Kabul and very aware of the ever-present danger of informers, maybe among the children, or are they among the men in disguise? My return to the camp, it seems, will be cloaked in secrecy. At one point I 'leave' to fool the locals into thinking I had gone and in any case all our routes are reconnoitered first, which means long delays.

Before I would ever see the streets of Kabul I was to endure a lengthy and, at times, seemingly unending wait, as preparations were made, arrangements cancelled and then reinstated. My notebook tells the story of doing nothing in a war, when everything from daily routine to ambitious plans to move in and out of the city were governed by the vicissitudes of the Mujahidin struggle with the Soviets. The entries are etched in for each day as July meandered into August.

Later on my second day in Musei – 18 July – I was told that we were leaving the village and heading back to Niazuldin's camp. All that day the skies had been busy with helicopters so we waited for a quiet moment and set off at around 4.15 p.m., taking a mountain route, perhaps to avoid being seen again in the village after my earlier pretend departure.

Our return journey was uneventful and before long I was back in the familiar surroundings of Niazuldin's mountain camp but it felt different now. After the first night on my own, I got through a day without James or Lawrence for company and returned to my notebook that evening:

The camp is quiet with only a few of the men here. Some are in Musei and others with Niazuldin and Ajab Gul in Chihil Sutoon, a neighbourhood of Kabul. Occasionally we hear pairs of MiGs overhead. Breakfast this morning was not up to previous standards. I suspect a big show was put on for us earlier. Now we eat off a dirty tablecloth with all the scraps from the night before and the new bread is divided into small hunks between us. During the morning the younger boys are given a long lecture on the mechanics of the Kalashnikov, supervised from afar by Fazil-Jan.

Manan is a shy and gentle creature with long wavy hair and Christ-like features. Occasionally he wears a 50s-style plastic 'leather' jacket with extravagant lapels. 'Made in Korea,' he tells me proudly. He is a softly spoken chap with a stillness and resignation in him. Cherulah has a round face, which is unusual here, and a suggestion of Tibetan in his eyes. [He was probably a Tajik.] Niazuldin is expected the day after tomorrow I am told. Fazil-Jan and I talked briefly of Kabul. We agreed my trip is still a secret from the men. For lunch we had rice with potato and then bread-dunking for supper [this was my expression for the standard dish of bread served with a bowl of grease – normally stewed old lamb bones which were cooked over and over again]. There was also very sour yoghurt.

At this point I had finished reading *In Evil Hour* by Gabriel Garcia Marquez, one of only two books I had brought with me. The other was Marquez's classic *One Hundred Years of Solitude*. I was already worried about running out of reading matter and out of paper in my only notebook. On my Walkman I had a good selection of music, including my favourites – The Doors, The Stones, Neil Young, Bob Marley and Joni Mitchell. The albums that would come to dominate my listening were John Martyn's classics, *Solid Air* and *Bless the Weather*. Occasionally I would try them out on my companions, as I had in Nuristan. The Afghans generally reacted with bafflement on hearing the great Scottish troubadour mumbling along with his echo-track guitar.

Another detail: I had stupidly – ludicrously – decided in Peshawar not to bring a toothbrush *to save weight*, which meant that I quickly picked up the Afghan habit of using pieces of wood to clean my teeth. We did our ablutions in private places behind rocks on the hillside and used stones and then water – left hand only – to clean ourselves.

On 20 July, Day 11, I wrote:

I get up later at 5.30 a.m. after a fitful sleep. There always seem to be things eating me at night. I had weird dreams.

There are big preparations in the camp today: everyone is armed and new RPG ammunition is brought out from the caves. I thought this could be in preparation for an operation and prepared to leave. In fact Fazil-Jan was going down to Musei to meet his brother. These were the elaborate precautions taken for the protection of Nia-zuldin's right-hand man – he is expected back tonight for supper. Six new Mujahids arrive in the camp. They are young-looking, some with a little English. There is more rifle-cleaning with MiGs and drones [a reference to the hum of spotter planes and Soviet transport aircraft] overhead. Last night there were big rumbling explosions coming from Kabul. My boots are about to fall to pieces. Tonight the explosions sound much closer than last night. Two more Muj have arrived from Kabul. One is a thirty-two-year-old geography teacher who spent four years in Pul-e-Charkhi [the much-dreaded prison] and speaks pretty good English, which offered an already welcome opportunity for me to converse in my own language. I washed my clothes and took refuge in John Martyn and *One Hundred Years*.

Day 12 – 21 July

The camp is very quiet. The sentries are on duty as always but there are only around ten men here. Over the past few days I have given up trying to get any of them to pronounce 'Edward'. They just can't seem to do it. What comes out is RedWhite – their way of saying the cigarette brand Red & White – and so from now I agree to take that name. RedWhite is ready and waiting... Yesterday they opened the sluice gates to the pools and the water came thundering down, sweeping the rubbish further down the valley and giving us the chance to wet everything. There were some rumbles from Kabul this morning and no torches are allowed at night. Abdullah-Jan [the translator] is ill.

Today is Sunday – perhaps Niazuldin will return tomorrow night, though I doubt it. No one has a radio here. I managed to sleep until 8 a.m., which is pretty amazing and knocks four hours off the day at least. I wonder when this thing will happen, how it will happen and if I will survive it. I can't envisage my return to Peshawar at all but it doesn't enter my mind that I might get caught or killed. Dreams of newspaper stories and flying to England and seeing Kathy. The men have no idea what on earth I am doing sitting with them day after day.

They have taken the opportunity, with Fazil-Jan gone, to ask me when I will return to Peshawar. I say I don't know but that I don't expect to be with them for more than a month. Jacub-Jan, my friend and Mujahid Extraordinaire, exclaims, 'Wery, wery good!' – his only two words of English. Jacub serves us most meals and supervises the kitchen. He always makes a special effort to provide me with the best food, which is embarrassing. At lunch, which generally consists of huge plates of rice topped with not very much potato in a peppery sauce, I am always given a separate bowl with an extra and generous portion of the prized potato. I am yet to discover a method of eating rice with my fingers without covering myself with it.

Abdul Rahman, the thirty-two-year-old from Kabul who had spent four years in Pul-e-Charkhi, asked me whether I was a member of the CIA. 'No,' I replied firmly, 'I am not.' But is the CIA good or bad, he countered? 'Sometimes good, sometimes bad,' I answered vaguely. Talking to him about my stay and how long I would be here and so on, I catch the watchful gaze of Abdullah-Jan, warning me with a quick gesture of the hand to keep my mouth shut. Abdullah is the only one here who knows what I am doing and I am sure we have established '*Islamabad*' as our call sign to refer to the Kabul trip. I like him and trust him. There is a quiet authority about him. There are loud explosions in the next valley and three choppers pass close by. We watch them carefully. But there is still no Fazil-Jan. He is at Ajab Gul's – maybe. Let's hope they are working on my case.

Day 13 – 22 July

I found a huge spider next to me this morning. I made a futile attempt to sleep until 9 a.m. but there is too much noise and general tea-drinking to do that. What will happen when I finish *100 Years*? Niazuldin is expected today but Fazil-Jan hasn't returned yet and somehow I don't expect Niazuldin tonight. I need a radio. The camp is quieter than ever – people have left this morning too, leaving only a handful of us. Everyday life for these men is so boring. How they survive, or don't go mad or start taking it out on each other, I don't know. As I write two MiGs fly high above me, heading south. Fazil-Jan returned at lunch and suddenly the camp is overflowing with familiar faces. Fazil-Jan has been at his 'planning desk' under the rock all afternoon with Abdullah-Jan and the other mullah. I watched Sherin making the bread using the lavender for burning at the base of the oven. The bread is so much better hot than cold.

Everything takes a long time here. I am living in a society without telephones, cars, television or radio. Even the simplest tasks require a messenger sent one way and then his return. Plans are committed to precarious scraps of paper of doubtful value since often their recipients either cannot read or write or do so with great difficulty. Then there is the suffocating insistence on, and intensity of, their religion. This war is not capable of being understood if it is not appreciated that the notion of a Holy War and a war of national liberation are indivisible in the minds of these men. It is inconceivable to be a Mujahid without being a strict Muslim. Hence the concept of martyrdom. On some nights the men don't just pray together – they spend hours chanting lines from the Koran inside the huts, working themselves up into a frenzy of howling and shrieking. When I first heard it – an Englishman with precious little in the way of religious faith – I could barely believe my ears.

Day 14 – 23 July

Little seems to have happened today; an arrival here, a departure there. The UN chauffeur [an Afghan whose official role was to drive cars for UN dignitaries visiting Kabul – he was related to one of the men in the camp and he served as a useful conduit for gossip and information on the comings and going in the city] went back this afternoon after a prolonged conference with Fazil-Jan. Could he be part of plan *Islamabad*? Fazil-Jan and Abdullah have been deep in discussion all day on the rock. I like to think they are working on me but I suspect it is all up to Niazuldin. One of the boys has malaria, another appears to be a diabetic. One who is passing through is a boy who deserted from the Afghan army two months ago. He had been in Panjshir and now he is on his way to Massoud [Ahmed Shar Massoud, the legendary resistance commander in the Panjshir valley] via Peshawar.

The most astounding event so far was that there was no rice for lunch. Instead we had bread and onions, which was a bit of a let-down. I tried, through Abdul Rahman, to ask Fazil-Jan if I could join in with some of the tasks. I don't think he understood. He seemed to say none of it is for me. Rahman thinks there may be a radio coming tomorrow, especially for me. I am totally committed to the trip – only the boredom of the mornings kills me. I have finished *100 Years* but I was not touched by it much. I buried it ceremoniously after finishing it. This lot are a happy, intelligent and friendly bunch.

Day 15 – 24 July

I slept outside, which was much more comfortable, and had a full shower with soap! Our food is all at sixes and sevens. Last night we had potato stew. This morning around twenty-five men from a neighbouring camp arrived on their way to a base between here and Kabul. A group went off yesterday to get more food from Kabul. Fazil-Jan won't let Rahman leave – he has to formally bid him farewell before he can go and Rahman is getting annoyed. He's been here for four days. Does Fazil-Jan think he is dubious? Perhaps I shouldn't have given him my letters. [I had written two letters for Abdul Rahman to post to Kathy in Brooklyn. He was supposed to send them in Peshawar. They never arrived.] Maybe Fazil-Jan wants to wait until Niazuldin returns and I am safely out of the way. Now to re-start *In Evil Hour*.

The donkeys are here. Looks like the food has arrived. I feel happier today – somehow reaching a week [since James and Lawrence left] is an important milestone and every day on top is building on strong foundations – every day is one day nearer the trip and a return to Peshawar. Everyone will eat together tonight. There are problems with the reservoir – Jacub-Jan comes to the rescue.

Day 16 – 25 July

Breakfast is at 5.30 a.m. Khalil and his three men have come back from Paghman and Abdul Rahman and his trio have left for Peshawar. Fazil-Jan explains that I will be here for six months. I think he is joking. Is this only 25 per cent war and fighting and 75 per cent something else? What the hell does Abdullah-Jan mean by *ascari karmali* and a cutting-of-the-throat motion? Are we infested with informers? Three Muj passed through yesterday on their way to attack the Russian HQ on the edge of Kabul at the Darul Aman Palace. Khalil says Niazuldin will be away for another ten days. I feel depressed. Time for a fag and cup of tea. The men display a prodigious appetite for conversation and are capable of talking their way through hour after hour of inertia. It feels like they are wasting their lives. I'm asking and posing more questions than writing down answers. Could it be 75 per cent chat and 25 per cent war? Another unanswered question.

Day 17 – 26 July

Last night we heard explosions very near. Fazil-Jan says it was the Khalis Mujahidin [a rival group] on an operation. I managed to sleep until 8 a.m. Over the last two days I have helped pass the time by peeling the potatoes and onions. Jacub-Jan thinks this is hilarious and calls me 'Commander *Katcheloo*' – Commander Potato. Fazil-Jan says Niazuldin is coming in five days, which makes it Tuesday or Wednesday. We live in hope. Lunch has slumped in the past two days to just rice, though the potatoes do appear at dunking time. Last night I could hear more weird fundamentalist wailing from the camp below. [There was a Khalis camp a little further down the valley. It was one of many under the control of the famed commander Abdul Haq who was eventually tortured and then shot by the Taleban in 2001.] It sounded like a portent of the end of the world. In a surprising upturn, I played noughts and crosses with Abdullah and Sherin this afternoon. This evening, for the first time, I heard MiGs overflying us at night.

Day 18 – 27 July

I feel very much encouraged after a chat with Fazil-Jan and a young mullah from Kabul who works with Niazuldin. The jeep trip is still the plan and Niazuldin is expected to be here in five or six days. My stomach is not too happy. There is some cloud about. In fact it is quite cool today. Back to tatties and rice for lunch. I spent most of the morning and early afternoon washing my clothes and hair. The day has gone really fast – maybe I should wash my clothes every day. A mullah and three men arrived from Fazil-Jan's place in Peshawar. I discovered that one of them is deaf and lip-reads.

Day 19 – 28 July
I slept in various places until 8.30 a.m. Then I did the potatoes. There were a couple of arrivals but nothing of consequence. I write in utter ignorance. Something has bitten me on the eyelid in the night and now I have one eye open and one closed. It's almost time for me to take my weekly malaria pill. As I write, the old mullah has arrived with lots of ammunition and a heavy gun of some kind. Abdullah-Jan whispered after supper that the 'jeep in Kabul' is still on – he seemed to say that I would leave in two days.

The boredom and tedium emanates from these pages as I waited, my spirits starting to seesaw between moments of hope and despair. At this point three men turned up with stories of a big battle in Lalandar, south-west of Kabul, in which four men had been injured. I got the impression that Niazuldin had been involved, something that did not reassure me about his priorities. Had I been forgotten? How much longer would I have to endure the stultifying boredom of the camp?

Day 20 – 29 July
At lunchtime Abdullah-Baran arrives. He is exhausted after two days without food and his ears are damaged by bomb blasts. We hear more about the operation in Lalandar. There are three men here with bullet and shrapnel wounds. One in the foot only, one in the arm and leg,

With my mother in 1976, two years before she died.

During a visit to Howard and Celia Root in Rome,
in my university years. (James Root)

Left: The author fully kitted out in *shalwar kameez* and Chitrali hat ready for the brutal challenge of the mountains. (James Blount)

Below: James Blount: every bit the Nuristan tribesman.

Kunar: a beautiful backwater but tough country to walk
in when the easiest routes are out of bounds.

A camp fire in a mountain-top refuge: time to drink more green tea.

Fulbright scholar – and our host – Jusef Nuristani enjoys a break from the trail as we make our way deeper into his homeland.

Logar province: heading into the heart of the war with Niazuldin's band. I am partially obscured in the back row, seven from the left, with James Blount in front.

Commander Niazuldin: Mr Charisma, a natural leader
to whom everyone gravitated – including me.

Niazuldin in discussion with his right-hand man Fazil-Jan
at the camp in the mountains south-east of Kabul. A heavy
machine gun sits behind them covered in sacking.

A smile that could brighten up even the most frustrating day.

A team photo of Niazuldin's boys ready to make martyrs of themselves in the war against the *shuravi* (Soviets).

Still waiting for the trip into Kabul: I am inside one of the two mud and timber buildings at Niazuldin's camp.

Abdullah-Jan, the shy young mullah who became my translator, looking towards the camera just a couple of days before he was killed.

Farzad aka 'Mr Noisy' (on the right). He seemed to think that if he shouted at me in Pashto I would have a better chance of understanding him.

At the camp: the entrance to the lower of the two buildings is visible between the trees that provided excellent camouflage from Soviet air threats.

Abdul Haq at his base lower down the mountain. A famous Mujahidin commander who was a great help to me, he was murdered by the Taliban in 2001.

I think, and another I'm not sure about. Fazil-Jan seems to say they will not go to Peshawar but will recover here. I have seen no doctor here and I wonder about their safety from infection. Lots of people have arrived in the camp – many of them Niazuldin's men. Abdullah-Baran says Niazuldin will come tomorrow. Jacub and the rest have come back from Musei with supplies – Russian soap, cigs, tea (green and black), rice, flour and batteries. Jacub has been given his first Kalashnikov, albeit with a broken handle. It's a proud moment for him.

So many old faces have returned that I feel sure Niazuldin will be back soon. I pray the plan is still going to work – it better – after all this waiting. I'm prepared for any risk. Mr Noisy – my name for Farzad – seems to think that if he shouts at me in Pashto I will have a better chance of understanding him. He is an ebullient character with a ripe sense of humour, who is always amusing the men with his long and increasingly hysterical stories. His delivery veers between a whisper and sharp gutturals flying off the tip of his tongue.

The wounded bring home to me the reality of the war – this *is* war – and that when the men go out on regular patrols or on an operation, they are risking their lives. The boy lying under the shade of a mulberry tree is screaming in pain as the 'paramedic' picks the shrapnel out of his shattered thigh. He says he is a doctor but I am not sure what training he has had because his treatment seems woefully inadequate – just enough to prevent infection perhaps but not a proper recovery. This guy should go to Peshawar. I don't see why not.

Day 21 – 30 July
I awake to find Fazil-Jan in a bad mood about something. I think a gun has gone missing. Several people left the camp this morning for Musei, including the Jamiat

commander who has been with us for the past two days. Last night we had beef soup and meat which was excellent [the day before the men had killed a calf]. One of Niazuldin's men has a radio. It's only a tiny little thing but I found the World Service clear as a bell. I sat up until 10.45 p.m. listening avidly to *My Music*, *Sports Round-up* and *Newsdesk*. There has been a coup in Uganda, Reagan is still ruling the roost in the White House, a naval officer has been assassinated in Madrid and the Russians are proposing a one-year ban on nuclear testing. At about 2 p.m. there was a small earth tremor. The men joked that it was President Karmal shaking in his grave but on the news I heard that a major earthquake had hit Soviet Central Asia and Pakistan and two people had been killed in Chitral. Today I confidently expect Niazuldin. He had better come.

Day 22 – 31 July

On the news last night there were reports of heavy fighting around Maidan airport last week. It was said to be the heaviest of the war with the Mujahidin using rockets and the Soviets responding with helicopters. There is still no sign of Niazuldin, which is depressing, though I am sure he is working on my trip now. There seems, according to Baran, to be some problem with the camp in Kabul where the jeep is delivered or kept. The whole thing is a huge security risk. I should not be so impatient though it has been two weeks now since James and Lawrence left. I feel less the expected sense of achievement and more a kind of dull ache of loneliness and desperation. I keep losing sight of why I am here. Last night, in the middle of prayers, Fazil-Jan made a long speech that provoked lively discussion. Sherin was reprimanded – it seemed to be some disciplinary matter to do with the running of the camp.

This morning the four wounded men left for Peshawar on horses. They will be treated by the Austrian

Relief Committee [another of the many charities based in Peshawar that helped displaced Afghans]. We had a thunderstorm this afternoon and some rain. Niazuldin's brother arrived at 2 p.m. The man himself, however, remains elusive.

Much to my joy and surprise, after a day of mind-bending frustration and hopelessness that had me feeling tired and lethargic, Niazuldin turned up that evening with about twenty-five men. I felt totally embarrassed greeting him, like a child running into his father's arms. He hugged me on both sides. '*Salaam alaikum*, may God be with you, RedWhite,' he thundered and thumped me playfully on the shoulder. It was wonderful to see him again, but difficult to communicate with him in any meaningful way without Shams around. I think he felt frustrated too. I was desperate to know how the planning was going and with Abdullah-Jan we had a brief discussion that seemed to indicate progress was being made. I clung to my belief that, now that he was back, things would start to happen.

Day 23 – 1 August
Last night a Kabul commander arrived with around twenty men. I reckon there were around eighty to ninety in the camp by then. During pre-prandial prayers the thunderstorm, brewing all day, burst on us. Everything got soaked, including my sleeping bag and my *putu* blanket. We all crowded into the two rooms and ate our bread dipped in grease by torch and oil lamp. It was a revealing insight into this war in winter. There would be room for fewer people in the camp. With everyone having to sleep inside, the conditions would be far less good, cooking would be difficult and the weapons would always have to be kept dry. And it would be cold. I reckon it gets bloody cold here. I ended up sleeping in a damp sleeping bag outside.

This morning the commander departed and Niazuldin sent a whole troop off somewhere. He and his lieutenants and Fazil-Jan and Abdullah have been in discussion on the 'new rock' this morning. I am sure they are talking about me. One of Niazuldin's men whispered to me 'Kabul-jeep' and signalled 'two days'. The men have been building a stone terrace outside the ammunition store. 'Noisy' got his finger trapped under a huge rock and shattered the end of it. It was a gruesome sight. For a moment, I thought I was being called upon to play doctor but luckily the ever-reliable Abdullah stepped in.

Day 24 – 2 August
It rained again last night. We had supper inside, which was very stuffy. I am restless for solitude and slept outside on the damp terrace with the radio. England dismissed Australia for 257 on the first day of the fourth Test. Desmond Tutu is clearly going for martyrdom, spurred on by his newfound newsworthiness as a result of his Nobel. I was very encouraged by discussions yesterday. It appears we leave tomorrow and then walk to Chihil Sutoon via Musei. The following day, during daytime, I would spend three hours touring the city in the jeep and then return the day after that. If I am understanding Abdullah-Jan [who translated for me] correctly, it sounds incredible.

I had a very amusing 'chat' with Niazuldin, who wants my little camera and seems to say that he will come to Peshawar with me afterwards, which would be tremendous. Abdullah-Jan has turned out to be the brightest of the men by miles, and also the most sensitive and understanding. Even he couldn't resist a smile of excitement when he explained to me the plan and the timetable. I just pray the 'war' doesn't break out between now and when my trip is completed – it would be awful if, after this long wait, some last-minute factor was to intervene. Yesterday

I had chips [I had shown Sherin and Jacub how to cut them].

This morning Fazil-Jan and his lieutenants appear to be discussing or planning an operation. There is mention of 'posts', rockets, Kalashnikovs and approaches. We were woken by a very low overfly of a MiG. There is some bombing going on. It sounds like Musei again. This has been the first clear day for flying for two days. When we talk about my trip, the big joke is that I am going to have tea at the Kabul InterContinental. I hope nothing gets in the way. I am totally committed. Somehow the thought of getting injured or killed, arrested or tortured, doesn't enter my real thinking. I have total confidence in this madman Niazuldin. I think the jeep will be driven by a regular Afghan soldier who is not a 'double' – not a Muj dressed up. Who knows? I can't believe this could be the last day of genuine waiting.

Day 25 – 3 August
One young fighter arrived with the news that three others had been shot. Two of them were seriously wounded and Nabi was killed by Muj from another group in Musei. There is no better demonstration of the problems that exist between the groups. Fazil-Jan's men tried to tell me it was the Russians who were responsible but I already knew that wasn't the case.

Day 26 – 4 August
Last night a chopper circled in the Musei valley. When we woke this morning, we realised that it had been preparing for the arrival of a Russian armoured group today. They took up positions along the river at the foot of the hills between Musei and Kabul. The main armaments were about half a mile from the village but four tanks were less than half that distance away. There were twelve

tanks, support vehicles, armoured personnel carriers with guns on top and mortars – Abdullah reckons 40mm. We watched the bombardment from the ridge above the camp.

The Russians picked out one or two specific areas of the village [of Musei] and hit them continually, the bombs and shells producing huge plumes of smoke and dust and starting one or two fires in the ripe cornfields. There was a more or less continual accompaniment of machine-gun fire that indicates that the Muj were retaliating but with little or no success. The Russians were too far away and perfectly protected by the open ground between them and the village. At 3 p.m. the Russians abruptly moved off, leaving clouds of smoke as the tracked vehicles tore through the dust. They made elaborate looping movements in the approach valley to protect themselves from ambush.

My impression was that the Russians could have been having a day of firing practice for all they cared. They had taken up their position casually, in full view of the village early in the morning – the soldiers were walking about openly – and then, when they had prepared themselves, in their own time, they set about the destruction of the village. The Muj retaliation was pathetic and ineffective. It was puzzling that no helicopters were used on a stormy but clear day, which would have been an effective way of flushing the fighters out from the lines of trees running along the forward edge of the village. Abdullah says the Mujahidin were from three or four groups but I'm not sure how many there were or who they were.

Why did the Russians choose today and Musei for this treatment? Why do they leave some areas intact? What is it about some places that have a right to survive and others not? Why hasn't all of Musei been flattened years ago? It is ironic that only three weeks ago I was writing about the preserved splendour of Musei and now it should be

subjected to the destruction and violence suffered by every
other village I have seen in Afghanistan.

Meanwhile, there was no sign of departure. Just as we had
relied on Shams before him, Abdullah was now my lifeline.
Like Niazuldin I trusted him unquestionably though he could
hardly have been more different from his commander. Where
Niaz was the epitome of self-confident leadership from the
front, Abdullah was a careful, meticulous and measured
individual with gentle, bearded features and an easy smile.
He was a proven fighter and he commanded respect among
his peers. His English was self-taught and I started helping
him with a few new words to add to his vocabulary.

Niazuldin appeared to hate waiting even more than I did.
He looked bored and irritated by the delays. When I asked
through Abdullah how much longer before we could go to
Kabul, he lifted two fingers but I wasn't sure whether to
believe him or not. Besides it could have meant two days,
two weeks or two months. I'd been told one thing then the
other over the last eighteen days since James and Lawrence
had left. The only way I would know for sure was when we
were actually packed up and walking out of the camp – and
even then it could just be a feint to mislead informers.

I was totally in the hands of this larger-than-life, charismatic, unpredictable figure, and during the long hours of
sitting in the camp waiting to make my way into Kabul, I
began to analyse what had brought me, a classically English,
middle-class public schoolboy, to the hills of south-east
Kabul, about to take part in an escapade that could easily
see me dead before I reached my twenty-fifth birthday.

7

DIVORCING YOUR CHILDREN

My upbringing was very stable to start with. The third of four children, I have two older sisters, Jane and Kate, and one younger, Fiona, and we were brought up in a largely happy home. My mother, Avril, was the daughter of a God-fearing Dubliner. My grandmother, Florence Kiernan, was a strong-featured girl from what she regarded as the wrong side of the tracks. One of the thirteen children of an Irish policeman, many of whom died in infancy, she married an up-and-coming young Englishman, Howard Penfold, whom she met when he visited the Irish capital to train with his new employer, Guinness. Thus began that side of my family's headlong rush to social betterment.

My father, John, was from an equally transformational background. His father Jim, with whom he fell out at an early age, had started life after the army as a bookie – not that this was ever acknowledged in his lifetime in our family. He built up a big business in his native Scotland, becoming a millionaire with all the trappings: a mansion in Edinburgh, a flat in Belgravia, a house in the south of France, a string of race horses and a custom Rolls. Jim married a slight, elegant but rather cold woman called Marjorie and sent his two sons to boarding school, the Roman Catholic outpost of Stony-hurst in Lancashire run by the Jesuits. My father became a barrister while my uncle went on to become an accountant and was for some time the financial director of the *Financial Times* – which was about the only connection any of us had to newspapers.

Rather gloriously, I always thought, Jim spent most of his money enjoying the fruits of his labours. But there was enough left over after he died for Marjorie to chain-smoke and read her way to her ninety-eighth year in an elegant Victorian terrace in the golfing village of Gullane on the shores of the Firth of Forth. When we visited her on family holidays, I would stare longingly out of the window at the waters of the Firth and the ships at anchor. On those holidays I got my first boat – a model yacht that I would sail on the beachside pool at North Berwick. Jim also bequeathed his Rolls, that stood in all its immaculate glory in the garage, until Marjorie sold it one day for £400 to a man who came to the door suggesting he would do her a favour by taking it off her hands.

In my early childhood, we lived outside Birmingham where my father practised criminal law, and we were a busy family at the centre of the Warwickshire social scene. Unlike her husband, whom she met in the socially ambitious environment of Edgbaston tennis club, my mother was a gregarious soul who was forever entertaining and organising get-togethers with family friends. She inherited my grandmother's hard-wired Catholic faith and was something of a saint in her own right. In her twenties she had been determined to become a nun but she abandoned that idea and, somewhat ahead of her time, studied at Nottingham University.

After graduating she worked for Cadbury's for a while before practising as a social worker in Rugby, in which capacity she visited patients in mental asylums and was a prison visitor. Her commitment to helping others often seemed to me to come at the cost of her attention to myself and my sisters. But we learnt to live with telephone calls from suicidal people on Christmas morning or the arrival for a two-week stay of a disabled person from France to whom my mother offered our home as a chance for a change of scene.

From my mixed Celtic and English background I inherited a determination to get on in life, to do everything properly, to push myself to the limit, and a clear sense that I could not let my parents down. Our family was always on the edge financially. We lived in a spacious Queen Anne-era home in the Warwickshire village of Ufton and my sisters and I all went to fee-paying schools. But the cost of this meant everything else was cut to the bone and all of us felt the pressure not to waste the opportunity we had been given. I am sure she didn't intend it but there was pressure from my mother. She was ambitious in every way and would regularly remind me of the sacrifices she and my father were making to send me first to Emscote Lawn preparatory school in Warwick and then Marlborough College in Wiltshire.

At prep school I duly got stuck in, playing all the sports on offer and learning the trumpet and other musical instruments at a frantic rate and trying to be head of this and head of that. Very early on I learnt to do things with unbridled intensity. 'If you are going to do it, do it properly,' as my father would say. Playing the trumpet was a classic example. I showed some early promise, having started the cornet at the age of ten, but it developed into an obsession and by my early teens I was not only a music scholar at Marlborough but I was practising for four or five hours a day during the holidays. It got me to the heady heights of the National Youth Orchestra, an experience that cut me off at the knees musically. At that point I realised I was no musician; just a slogger trying to please my school and my parents.

Out of school I worked with my father in the garden where we grew all our own vegetables. I caddied for him at the golf club and I went beagling with him on cold winter mornings when I would much rather have stayed in bed. There was no choice in this. If he was going to spend his day running

across acres of dismal plough in Worcestershire or wherever, then I was going too. I walked most of the Pennine Way
with him when I was just ten, 200 miles of it in three weeks,
including thirty-five miles over the Cheviot Hills on the final
day. I learnt to sail on summer holidays in Cornwall when
my father would shout in panic as we approached a jetty. 'We
can't afford to make a fool of ourselves here,' he would hiss
as we brought our heavy Fairey Falcon dinghy crashing into
the dock at Restronguet. He taught me how to distinguish
between classical, romantic and modern composers and how
to run a garden. There was great emphasis on achievement
and matching up to his exacting standards.

Despite trying to meet those standards, it was a generally
happy childhood. My sisters rode horses, I rode bicycles. We
used to go exploring in the old gravel pits near our home,
or spend days lounging around in the garden playing with
our terrier, Jester, or go to the local farm and do some
wild-oat picking in the cornfields for pocket money. I made
model ships and planes, supported my local team, Coven-
try City, and listened earnestly to classical music (but was
then stunned when I heard T-Rex and Pink Floyd for the first
time). We went on camping holidays to Pembrokeshire or
Argyll; we walked in the Cotswolds and Suffolk and we travelled to London to hear concerts at the Royal Festival Hall.
I imagined that, when I grew up, I would become a lawyer
like my father.

But then things started to unravel. The glue that was
holding our life together was my mother, something none of
us realised until her grip began to weaken. It started when
I was still at prep school, aged ten years old. I was boarding by that stage, even though Warwick was only down the
road. My mother had sent me there full-time because I was
driving her mad around the house. I could be a noisy and
disruptive child, given to breaking things, shouting a lot and
then having to wait for my father's return of an evening when

punishment would be handed out. This was a pattern that did wonders to sow enmity between him and me.

I suppose I always pushed things that one step too far. I hated being trammelled by adult authority; I wanted control of my life from an early age. On one occasion I drove my mother past even her limits and she came for me with a broom and whacked me over the head with it, causing a wound that required stitches. These days she would have been prosecuted for it, but what an injustice that would have been. I was the guilty one and I knew it. Bedtime was always the worst. I hated being sent up earlier than my older sisters and would fight all the way up the stairs. My mother's finest hour in this respect came when she walked into the garden where I was playing cricket with my village friends one summer's evening and sent me to bed in front of them, thus combining an early bed with a very public humiliation.

Prep school and boarding with other boys seemed to do the trick and I loved it. Then came the day when the head-master told me that my mother wanted to speak to me on the phone. It was a weekday evening and this was unprecedented. There were normally no calls allowed and I could not understand why she would want to speak to me. 'I love you, darling,' she said. 'Are you OK?' I put the phone down none the wiser. What on earth was she doing? It was only later that I discovered that she was calling from her hospital bed where she had undergone a mastectomy after being diagnosed with breast cancer. Following that operation, my mother could never bear to look at herself in the mirror again.

At first I did not realise the seriousness of her condition but as the disease took its course over the next seven years, it become all too obvious that she was fighting for her life. My mother was tough and determined but the cancer wore her down. After chemotherapy, she suffered the indignity of losing her hair and wore a wig. She died in her fiftieth year in 1978, when I was seventeen.

My father was attentive to her but, unbeknown to us, he had started an affair at about the same time that my mother got ill. By then a QC, he had moved his work to chambers in London and had a flat nearby where he spent most of the week. I have no idea when my mother found out about his affair but she certainly knew it long before we did and it contaminated the final years of her life.

A few days before she died, I spent my last agonising hours with her in her bedroom that was infested with the pungent smell of decay and dying. She asked me whether I thought she could recover and I lied and told her she would. 'Of course you will, Mummy,' I promised, as she lay ravaged by the disease. And she knew I was lying because when I looked at her my expression told her all she needed to know. Soon after that she entered the half-world between the living and the dead, drifting in and out of consciousness for a few days, and I never spoke to her again.

By the time she died my relationship with my father had dramatically deteriorated. At that stage I had no idea about his affair but he was riddled with guilt about his deception and he and I were locking horns at every opportunity. Even before my mother's death, under the influence of the new woman in his life, my father was regularly telling us that he regretted the middle-class values and lifestyle he had brought us up with, the schools he had sent us to and the privileges we had enjoyed. I was a typical teenage public schoolboy, finding out about girls, drink and partying and he was not impressed.

But little did we know what lay in store after my mother left us one cold January morning. I think I was the only member of the family who did not venture in to see her still body – I couldn't face it – and I never properly mourned her. Instead I went downstairs and played the piano – until, that is, my father tore into the room and screamed at me for not showing respect to the dead.

With my mother gone, my father set about dismantling our previous life. I do not think either my sisters or I have much to complain about when compared with the extreme hardships suffered by some children, but I have always believed these things are relative. If you have never known what happy family life is like, you are not likely to miss it. If, however, you have been brought up with the certainty and security of a stable home, then its sudden removal, even at the age of seventeen, can be a destabilising shock. It felt as if the rug was being pulled from under us.

Within six months of my mother's death my father revealed that he was getting married to a fellow barrister, a woman with whom I could find very little in common and who had a very different value system to ours. Suddenly I understood where all the radical new thinking about 'privilege' that my father had sought to impose on us had come from. Events moved fast: not only did he marry her in short order, but he also put our house on the market and cleared our bedrooms of our possessions. There are some of mine I still long for to this day. He did this while I was at school, making all four of us effectively homeless. My father then bought a new home in Somerset with his new wife, which I went to only once. It was made clear that this would not be our home; we could visit only if we were invited and we would have no rooms of our own. I was subsequently informed that I could no longer even telephone my father there for fear of upsetting the new Mrs Gorman.

From then on all four of us were dependent on the kindness of the parents of our friends; the three youngest among us were each informally adopted by other families. I was welcomed by the parents of James Root, my best friend from Marlborough, with whom I would go on to share a flat in London after Cambridge. Howard and Celia's home in Winchester, with its thousands of books, was a haven for me, just a stone's throw from the cathedral where Howard, formerly Professor of Theology at Southampton University, was a canon.

My father and I had one of our final clashes at the beginning of my year off between school and university, when we nearly came to physical blows. I felt I needed to stand up for my sisters and for my mother's memory and these confrontations had become increasingly traumatic. I left him in December 1980 with a cheque for £400 in my pocket and headed off to see something of the world, spending four months in Israel and Egypt.

There is no doubt that the battle with my father and what I saw as the loss of so much that my mother stood for marked me deeply. In many ways I still loved him – as I do today. But I was angry, although I did not recognise it at the time, self-destructive and rootless, always looking for somewhere to hang my hat. I tended to lunge for things and I lost the natural rhythm of my life.

My relationship with my father got no better; in some ways it got worse. I arrived at Cambridge with a place to read law. But I had grown allergic to him and the law and barristers were *his* world. I immediately tried to switch to history, something that Pembroke College was not prepared for. Only after I had gone on strike for six weeks of my first term did the college agree to allow me to change. But I would have to endure economics for Part I of my degree before I was allowed to change to modern history for my Part II.

My father marked my twenty-first birthday by driving to Cambridge with the few possessions of mine that had found their way to his new home. He must have waited for me to leave my digs because I discovered them piled on the floor when I got back after popping out for a few hours. Apart from what was left of my worldly goods, there was a watercolour by Edward Wesson of Skiddaw in the Lake District, the sort of peak my father and I might have climbed together when I was younger. It was left by way of a present, accompanied by the briefest of messages scrawled in fading black felt tip on the notepaper of the Post House Hotel in Birmingham.

Dear Edward

A birthday greeting on your 21st and good luck for the future.

Your
Father

The main impact was the feeling that he had washed his hands of me. Over the years since then I have come to the conclusion that, had my mother lived, my father would have divorced her. When she did not, he divorced his children instead.

Despite the loss of my mother and the break-up with my father I was still an ebullient and ambitious young man but there was an element of recklessness in me, a restlessness of spirit, and I was free to indulge that. With no one to care for me, I had stopped caring for myself. I simply didn't regard my life as all that valuable and was prepared to take extravagant risks – risks such as travelling into Soviet-occupied Kabul with a group of Mujahidin at the height of that brutal war.

8

ACTION

After three weeks of waiting around since James and Lawrence's departure, weeks that had driven me close to despair at times, events were about to speed up. On 5 August, the morning after the Musei attack – about which the Mujahidin initially made ludicrous claims, including that forty Soviet soldiers had been killed – I was woken with the news that it was my time to go.

The evening before I had made it clear to Niazuldin and Fazil-Jan, in a rather depressed and angry manner, that I could wait only one more week and would have to consider heading back to Peshawar if a move into the city was further postponed. So after a quick breakfast I gathered my stuff together for my trip into Kabul.

I was allowed to take only a few things with me and I prioritised my two small cameras, some film and batteries. Goodness knows what I thought I was going to get with them. Then at 9.15 a.m. we set off and headed to the lake below the camp where Niazuldin was waiting with seven hand-picked men who were all briefed about the plan; among them was a friendly young man known to all as the 'doctor' for his work on the wounded, although I don't think he had any medical training.

Niazuldin was a bag of nerves that morning. He was not coming with us but was anxious to make sure the men knew exactly what they were doing. The plan was simple, as far as I understood it. We would make our way to Musei, wait there for dusk and then start the hour-long walk across no-man's-land into the outskirts of the city. Once inside, we would head for one of the safe houses used by Niazuldin's fighters, from where I would make my little journey in the jeep. Once that was completed, assuming we had not been rumbled, we would head out again the next night and make our way back to the camp to a hero's welcome, and from there to Peshawar and a cold beer.

In contrast to Niazuldin, I wasn't particularly nervous. Mostly I was overwhelmed with relief that at last something was happening. It seemed an age since we had first discussed the plan and all my instincts had been to get on with it, whereas one delay had followed another. Now I was buzzing again with the sort of excitement I felt when we first arrived at Teri Mingal. This was what I had come for and I was ready for whatever was coming my way.

We each hugged the commander and said goodbye. 'So long, and see you in two days, *inshallah*,' I was thinking as we set off on our three-hour trek to Musei, making our way past the sentries and down the gully towards the plain.

We walked in single file. I was in the middle of the group. All of the men were armed, most with AKs but two carrying RPGs. For some reason, I was not allowed to wear my boots, possibly because the brand and style – they were modern mountaineering boots – would have given me away as a foreigner. So I was wearing my trainers, which quickly resulted in blisters. I carried a small rucksack over which my brown Afghan blanket was draped, and I was not allowed to speak.

We made our way into Musei and then went by a back route to Ajab Gul's house, which we reached at midday. Although I did not know all of the men in the group, and none of them spoke more than a few words of English, there was a feeling of close camaraderie among us and a sense that they had been chosen for a special operation. For them, my safe deliverance back to Niazuldin was the one and only measure of success. I was more concerned that none of them was hurt or captured. We had rice, potatoes and melon for lunch at Ajab Gul's and all was looking good for our mission as we set off for the outskirts of Kabul at 6 p.m., turning left at the far end of the village an hour later.

Then all our plans and our hopes were dashed when we ran straight into the Soviet army. A large detachment of armour was trundling down the road towards us about a quarter of a mile in front. We crouched by the side of the wall of the last house on the edge of the village, watching scores of tanks, armoured cars, jeeps, and armoured personnel carriers come down the valley, their lights glaring in the long column of dust. We watched them for half an hour in the gloom. I counted three groups of twenty vehicles and they were still coming. Instead of continuing on to Kabul, they stopped, forming a big circle on the flat ground alongside the road, their engines revving as the soldiers positioned their vehicles in the best arrangement to defend against attack.

So here at last were the Soviets, the *shuravi* – the 'infidel' occupiers of Afghanistan about whom I had heard so many dreadful stories. After weeks in the mountains moving on foot, it was a shock to the system to see mechanised weaponry and soldiers in uniform running around organising themselves with the strict discipline of a modern – albeit Soviet – army. I watched them impassively, not connecting the sounds of the engines and shapes of the tanks and howitzers with the terror those machines could produce in an instant. Mainly I focused on the biting realisation that the trip was off.

We all knew it was impossible for us to continue and there was no choice but to retrace our steps. We set off again, single-file, heading back to Ajab Gul's house. Flares lit up the sky above Musei and on the way we met some fighters who told us that the soldiers were expected to move into the village the next day and that all the Muj were leaving, heading for the safety of the hills, so we should do the same. It was turning into a long day and I was starting to wonder what the true impact of this abrupt intervention might be.

After a brief stop at Ajab Gul's we set out again for the country, marching swiftly through the fields and up into the clear and undulating ground above. We were on a route back to Niazuldin's camp that was different from either of the two previous ones we had used. Eventually we scaled a ridge and, at midnight, exhausted, we arrived at a burnt-out village on the plain. As we approached we were greeted by a chorus of snarling and barking dogs. But we were friends, not foe, and the other Mujahidin there paid little attention as we filed into the ruins of the mosque where we prepared to spend the night.

One of the men went off to find food and came back with some hunks of cheese that he had bought off a wizened old man, who seemed to be the only resident of the place. The men prayed in the darkness and then we tried to get some sleep. I was exhausted – as we all were – and deflated. The trip had gone to the four winds. The plan, so far as I understood it, was that if the Soviets left the next day, we were to return to Musei; if not, we would head back to the camp.

The bombardment began at 2 a.m. I woke to sudden, ear-splitting explosions and leapt to my feet instantly. The ground was shaking and loose rubble was falling from the damaged roof of the mosque. My heart was pounding as I tried to work out how close the artillery was and which direction the shells were coming from. It was impossible to tell in the noise and the dust and the disorienting effect of the blasts, which were coming thick and fast. Using sign language, the men indicated to me that we should run for the mountains, so I grabbed my gear and followed them.

Straight away, I realised we were heading into open ground under a clearing sky and a full moon – and into increasingly heavy and well-directed shellfire. I was thinking at a million miles an hour, trying to scour my memory for clues about what was happening. I had nothing to go on except war films and I quickly came to the conclusion that the Soviet soldiers could see us. They must have moved up on to the ridge behind us and were directing fire down onto our trail. It was so clear that night that our bodies were leaving shadows on the moonscape all around us. All they needed was one direct hit and we would be shredded. 'Fuck this,' I shouted to myself as we ran wildly in the hope of finding some cover. For once in Afghanistan I couldn't give a stuff about where I was placing my feet; in the order of battle, mines were now very low down my list of priorities.

Perhaps someone in Musei had informed on us; maybe someone had been forced to say what they had seen of our departure. Either way, there was no doubt we were being targeted, because there was nothing else to aim at. The sense of vulnerability was chilling. We were running across a great open sweep of land, gently rising up to a ridge behind us from where we could hear the whooshing sound as the shells flew in pairs through the still night air, momentarily lighting up the sky with a bright red glow, before crashing and exploding in the dust around us. I followed the example of the men and each time a round came in, I dived to the ground. With no military training I instinctively landed on my back and then rolled over – taking precious extra seconds to protect myself and cursing my stupidity each time I did it. We could smell the munitions, hear them and feel them.

When we reached the junction of the valleys, the shelling was closer than before, but by then I had realised they were not large rounds because the spread of the shrapnel was limited. Then I saw something that to me, with my Western sense of self-preservation, was hard to comprehend. Under fire, some of the men turned and began shouting at their oppressors. I couldn't understand any of the words but the tone was one of fierce defiance as they shook their fists in the direction of the enemy. I realised that some of them were hoping to get hit, hoping that they would be chosen for a glorious death and then be remembered as martyrs in their Holy War. Watching this playing out on that plain, as they stood around me, apparently oblivious to the danger, sent more than just a shiver down my spine. I shouted and screamed at them to hit the ground and then run for a series of undulations ahead of us where we might at least get out of the line of fire. But they merely walked. After weeks of indolence in the camp, I was gasping for breath by the time we made it to relatively safe ground.

We reached the camp at 5 a.m. and, as we made our way up through the rocks to shout at the sentries, the earth was shaking with huge explosions on the other side of the ridge. The Soviets were firing artillery shells up from Musei and at 6 a.m. sharp the bombardment of our camp and the immediate surrounding hills began. It was to last two hours. The Soviets were throwing everything at it apart, thank God, from getting out and coming up to find us on foot. We all scrambled up to a vantage point halfway up the ridge and watched as six helicopter gunships, working in pairs and dropping bright white flares, made their way along the hillside, their rotors thumping. As they circled around their targets, we could hear the growl of their Gatling heavy machine guns – weapons that fire up to 5,000 rounds a minute – and the percussive boom of their rockets.

'MiGs in pairs screaming across the sky,' I scribbled in my notebook. 'Diving low, dropping bombs on the hillsides and reconnaissance planes droning high above throughout. Several bombs landed close to the camp but no one was hurt. Artillery raining fire on the ridge above. At 12 p.m. the MiGs returned, dropping phosphorous flares and bombing our valley – huge detonations shaking the ground – with bombs landing immediately above and below the camp.'

It was a dazzling display of pyrotechnics. The men on the ridge were also casual about their safety, some standing up and laughing defiantly while we were under fire. I was beginning to realise that all the praying – not to mention those strange evenings when the Muj would work themselves into a frenzy for hours at a time – had created a level of fanaticism that made them dangerous to be with in battle. And this was only 1985 and Harakat was considered one of the more moderate of the seven main resistance groups.

I sought shelter under the mulberry trees – as if they could have protected us – with Niazuldin and Fazil-Jan. It felt reassuring to be alongside them as the MiGs flew past at low level. Niazuldin had nothing to use against the jets and we just had to wait it out. I remembered Shams translating one night when Niazuldin was talking angrily about the poor state of his weaponry, particularly against airborne threats. Now I understood a little better what he had meant when he said: 'We have nothing to fight them with – our Kalashnikovs and RPGs – nothing else except *Khoda* [God].'

I wondered why the Soviets had come to this area. Was it a punishment for Sunday's fighting around Musei? Not only had I seen a graphic illustration of the mismatch of forces in the war but also the futility of much of what the Russian-led army was doing. They were expending millions of roubles-worth of shells and air-time for helicopters, jets and surveillance planes with, it appeared, little success. The helicopters and planes seemed to be bombing the hillsides at random with no sense of a target. Perhaps it was intended to intimidate the Mujahidin into leaving – but that was never going to happen. Only a concerted ground offensive involving thousands of paratroopers at great expense in life could have flushed them out, and only briefly at that. If the Soviets had been wasting ammunition that day, the Mujahidin, for their part, were totally ill-equipped to reply and did not, except for a couple of rockets. The dilemma for them was that engaging their enemy with heavy machine guns from the high ground would give the camp's precise location away and might lead to its destruction.

That night the bombing resumed at about 11 p.m. and continued until 2.30 a.m. It seemed more accurate than during the day, with some munitions landing with a resounding crash very close to the camp. The deep ravine and the surrounding steep hillsides made it a perfect sound stage for explosions that shook the ground and rocked our ears. In the lulls between the detonations, the valley echoed to the calls of the men, shouting across to each other from neighbouring hilltops. Their morale was strong in the most perilous of circumstances – even if some of them were inviting death wherever they could find it – and I was impressed by their fortitude. It seemed they would rather die fighting for this camp and its surrounding mountains than leave.

The following day the gunships and tanks attacked the hills on three sides of the camp. It was getting quite intense and continued all day, although this time there were no MiGs involved. As previously, all the men dispersed from the main centre of the camp – the two buildings and the terraced area – and scrambled up the hillsides leading to the ridge from where Musei and Kabul were visible. There was no one around to give me instructions and I was left to fend for myself. Taking my cue from what everyone else was doing, I made my way a short distance up the hill, above the pools, and found an old, shallow fox hole that was just big enough for me to crawl inside, protecting most of my body from shrapnel. I had not found a particularly good spot – it was nothing more than a concave dent scratched into the hillside – but there was nothing I could do to improve it with no tools at hand, apart from piling up some loose rocks along the front. Abdullah had raced up to the top to man one of the machine guns, and I spent the morning alone, listening to the crashes and explosions and the shouts of the men in between.

In the afternoon a lone Mi-24 Hind helicopter gunship appeared in our valley, a truly horrible sight as I lay cowering on the hillside with no protection to speak of and easily within its pilot's line of sight. It came growling and thumping along, green camouflaged, with its two pilots clearly visible in their glass pods, like a giant, nasty fly buzzing towards me. It was remarkably close because it had come in under the ridge line and was flying – with some courage on the part of the pilots – with hostile ground close on all sides (it was doing exactly what James had long ago predicted would not happen). I watched it out of the corner of one eye, frozen in my little dip in the ground, wishing I had made more effort to cover myself up. The 'flying tank' steadied for a second, its tail rotor up and its nose down, its main rotor slicing the air. The pilots were scanning the hillside for a target. It fired a burst from its heavy machine gun. Then the pilots unleashed a rocket that delivered a muffled explosion on the ridge above me, where I knew some of the men would be manning the Dashakas.

As quickly as it had arrived, the helicopter turned tail and disappeared. After all the noise, the quiet of the hills returned. I breathed a giant sigh of relief but, as I crawled out of my fox hole, I sensed immediately that something was wrong. The men were coming off the hill in silence – there was no chatter or shouting. Someone answered my expression of concern with the words 'Abdullah-Jan' and *shaeed*, which means 'martyred'. I asked again and they repeated the words.

This came as a terrible shock. Abdullah was one of the best in the camp, a kind and thoughtful young man with a family waiting for him in Pakistan. He had become my eyes and ears after Shams had left and he was one of Fazil-Jan's best friends and most valued counsellors. Although his English was poor he had done his best to help me when he knew I was struggling to understand what was going on.

I pieced together what had happened from the others' sign language and the odd words in Pashto that I understood: the young mullah had been spotted by the pilots, perhaps after opening fire with his Dashaka. The explosion that followed tore into his upper legs, severing arteries, causing damage from which he had no hope of surviving and prompting a heart attack that killed him within minutes.

With everyone else I waited on the terrace for Abdullah's body to be brought down. I was shaking with nerves after hours of bombing, and trying to quell my edginess with cigarettes, which only made me feel sick.

After a long delay, just as dusk was falling, one of the strongest men brought Abdullah into the camp on piggyback. His lifeless features seemed to move as if animated as his head lolled backwards and forwards with each step. Slowly the man carrying him made his way past the big boulder where we had sat together only days before, then past the pools and the ammunition store and then laid him gently down on the terrace. We all stood to receive him. The tenderness the men showed their fallen comrade was underlined by Fazil-Jan, who was distraught at the loss of his trusted lieutenant. I had imagined that the commanders would not show emotion in front of their men but Fazil-Jan was weeping openly as they stood and prayed around the body.

From the waist down, Abdullah was soaked in blood. Carefully they took all of his possessions from his pockets, to be returned to his family, and detached the buttons from his jacket, which were handed round as keepsakes. There was a half-finished packet of cigarettes in one pocket and someone handed them to me. Then they brought a bed – a crude wooden structure with rope webbing – from one of the huts and wrapped him up on it in a sheet ready for burial.

I spent the evening chain-smoking Abdullah's cigarettes and looking at the lifeless body of the man who had been so good to me after Shams left. As I lit the last one it struck me that I had been smoking a dead man's tobacco before he was even buried. It seemed a callous thing to have done, disrespectful somehow, and it haunted me.

Later that night, under another perilously bright moon, we set off down the ravine in silence with four men carrying Abdullah's corpse on the bed to the graveyard at the bottom of the valley. At the place where others from the camp had been buried not many weeks before, they dug his grave under a mulberry tree and then stood in a line to pray for him and to say goodbye.

I watched from the side and said my own farewell to Abdullah, thanking him for helping me and protecting me from my own naivety during the weeks I had been in the camp.

I was trapped. I'd had no sleep and no food, my nerves were on edge with the shock of the bombing and then the tragedy of Abdullah's death. I had no control over my own destiny and there was no prospect of escape from this place. In my diary I managed one line: 'Thoughts: shit-scared, hated all of it. Under fire the Muj seem incredibly casual about their own safety, laughing it off literally, which made me feel sick.'

9

BREAKING INTO KABUL

After Abdullah's burial the bombing started again with MiGs overhead and we headed off from the cemetery towards a broken village not far from the camp. Fazil-Jan was worried that the camp might be attacked by paratroopers coming up the valley on foot. Our route took us close to an Afghan army outpost and yet again the men were impressively ill-disciplined close to the enemy, walking past chatting as if they were taking a stroll in the park.

We spread out among the ruined buildings, some of the men wrapped up in their blankets trying to get a little sleep while others sat in small groups talking and smoking. I huddled up in my *putu* in a corner, mulling over the events of the past few days. Sleep was beyond my compass that night. At 5 a.m., helicopters and reconnaissance planes began overflying us again. By then I had grown sick to death of the whole thing. I wrote in my notebook: 'That painful, nightmarish aspect has returned. No sleep, nerves on edge, cigarettes and heartbeat racing with the shock of the bombing. Abdullah looked so life-like being carried into the camp and it was so hard to accept that this friendly young man was dead. A haunting aspect to it all – great fear in me.'

After kicking around in that village all that day – Day 31 of my trip – at dusk we marched back to the camp. On the way we stopped at the Khalis camp, whose occupants

enjoyed relatively cordial relations with their Harakat neighbours and where Abdul Haq – a fluent English speaker – was
in residence. This was a huge bonus for me. He explained to
me what had been going on over the last few days, saying that
the first time the Soviets had come to Musei, they had been
looking for Mujahidin and weapons. They found none but
took some old men, women and children prisoner instead.
The search was interrupted by Haq's guerrillas who attacked
the Soviets, destroying three tanks but losing at least twelve
of their own men in the process. This sounded reasonably
likely. Abdul Haq was a man whose reputation as a fighter
was legendary and there was no need for him to exaggerate.
He reckoned the Soviets returned two days later – the day we
had tried to head for Kabul – as a direct consequence of that
first action by the Muj. He couldn't say for sure how many
tanks and other armaments there were but he believed there
were around 200 altogether, including tanks, APCs, support
vehicles and trucks.

'The bombardment is typical,' he said. 'It happens all
the time here. The accuracy of it, however, depends on the
"information" available to the Russians concerning the exact
location of the guerrilla bases. In this case, the information
was not particularly good.'

Back at our camp that evening, I was devastated to be told
that the Kabul trip had to be postponed for another couple
of days. After seventy-two hours of bombardment and now
this, I'd had enough. The following morning I wrote in my
notebook: 'The Kabul plan has been instantly abandoned by
me. I don't want to take risks with these men for the sake of
a "good story". And especially not after the death of Abdullah who helped plan the operation and who offered welcome
encouragement. I am losing patience and want to go. Fazil-
Jan seems annoyed with my apparently sudden desperation.
Jets were flying too low this morning.'

I had reached the point where I felt I needed to make a

stand. I packed my rucksack in a boiling fury, got my boots and made as if to head out of the camp. I was on my way to Teri Mingal on the border whether anyone was coming with me or not. I was saying, in effect, either we do this now or I am out of here.

Someone must have come running after me because within fifteen minutes a meeting had been arranged between Niazuldin, Fazil-Jan and Abdul Haq, who came up to the camp to act as interpreter and adviser. It proved a great opportunity to clear the air after three weeks of frustration and mangled communication.

I explained that I was not sure if the trip could, or should, go ahead after Abdullah's death.

Niazuldin, for his part, was determined that it should still happen: 'This will demonstrate that I can do whatever I want in Kabul. And it will show the West that we are strong even in the centre of the Russian occupation,' he said.

'I don't want everyone to take these risks just for the sake of a good story,' I replied. 'It's not fair on them.'

'Let me decide what risks the men take,' Niazuldin said. 'You will leave for Kabul tomorrow and the trip will take no more than three days. When you return we will not keep you at the camp for a minute longer than necessary.'

This prospect appeased me somewhat. I think my sudden 'wobble' must have alarmed Niazuldin, who saw his prize possibly slipping away, because that afternoon he decided it was time to go. The trip was on at last and, as I prepared, the excitement and anticipation of what lay ahead quickly overwhelmed my bad temper and nerves. As before, I was glad to be doing something and not facing further days of inertia in the hills, with or without the accompaniment of Soviet artillery.

Invested with a new confidence after the clarity of our talk-through with Abdul Haq, I said my goodbyes to Niazuldin and everyone else and set off at 3 p.m. It was almost the same group of eight, but this time we were led by a stocky twenty-one-year-old fighter called Asil who wore a gold turban in the shape of a mitre over his long black locks and who knew only a few words of English. Yet another quiet and softly spoken individual, he was nevertheless authoritative; I'd heard he was being groomed as a future commander.

On that first day we walked for nine hours, stopping only for the men to pray. Once again we made our way down to Musei and then through the village, at 7 p.m. reaching the point where we had been forced to turn back on the first attempt. From there, we struck out across the open desert in the darkness. We were in single file with a fighter carrying a machine gun on a tripod at the front and RedWhite walking in the middle between two men carrying RPGs. We walked briskly and in silence, watching for hand movements from Asil to direct us.

After about half a mile we found one of the few tarmac roads then in existence in Afghanistan – a spur of the Kabul to Gardez road that was heavily used by the Soviets and their allies in the Afghan army. We walked for some minutes on the tarmac, the distance marked by telegraph poles, the smooth surface a sudden contrast to weeks of rough terrain in the hills. Then we cut out again to the left into the open desert to avoid Soviet and Afghan security posts on the road.

Even at this early stage in the journey, I was beginning to realise that getting into Kabul was not going to be straightforward; it was akin to breaking into a giant prison or army camp. The city was the jewel in the crown of the occupation and the Soviet army had put considerable effort into protecting it from infiltration by insurgents.

A prowling helicopter flew slowly above us, making a hell of a noise but remaining invisible to the eye, save for a series of bright flares that it dropped almost immediately overhead. They were like nine stars lighting up the sky with a menacing orange glow and picking us out against the flat terrain. To my surprise and consternation – was this the 'living martyrs' syndrome again? – we did not crouch down or stop but continued, seemingly oblivious. I was convinced that the pilots must have seen us and my body was pulsing with adrenaline in anticipation of a sudden explosion of violence all around us. All they had to do was press a button. We probably would not even hear the fusillade of shots that killed us.

But on we went as the flares died away and the helicopter faded and my heartbeat steadied. After another hour we reached a tree line that seemed to mark the far eastern perimeter of Kabul: at last, I assumed, I was at the edge of the city but really I had no idea where we were. At that point we were on the cusp of a ridge and, as we moved between the trees, Asil motioned for us to crouch low. I couldn't see where the threat was coming from but before long we were able to continue without incident through a series of villages, where it appeared much of Kabul's food was grown. We maintained strict silence but our progress was signalled loudly by dogs as we passed one walled encampment after another. I kept thinking 'If these people support the resistance, why don't they get rid of their dogs?' But then again dogs were, and still are, important guards in Afghanistan. That night I, a dog-lover, would have willingly strung them all up.

The helicopters became our constant companions, lighting up the sky and droning slowly above us as, during the last hour, we made what would be our final entrance into the city. We left the villages and the main routes behind to avoid the guard posts strung out like beads around the perimeter, then proceeded across open ground and began to climb the first of two ridges overlooking Kabul. Suddenly there it was in all its glory, the city sitting like a giant spaceship, lighting up the night sky ahead of us. After weeks in the hills, it was a shock to the senses to see and hear the place, humming gently on a still night. The quiet was broken every now and again by the sharp crackle of gunfire in the distance and by the percussive popping of yellow and orange flares sent up from the guard posts. With Asil leading, we were attempting to pass between two posts – one Soviet (*shuravi*, the men called it), the other Afghan army – located about a quarter of a mile apart on the crests of adjoining hills.

We walked steadily up, almost to the top of the ridge, then Asil motioned for us to stop and get down. I was baffled by this. What the hell was he thinking of, leaving us sitting in completely open ground with helicopters above us and our position clearly visible to the guard posts should they send up a flare? I wished there were fewer of us because we were so conspicuous. I was probably the edgiest of the group. It was hard to judge distances in the dark so I wasn't sure how close we were to the enemy. My protestations, which were along the lines of 'Why the f*** have we stopped here?' nearly ruined it for all of us. Suddenly there was a shout – we were being hailed from the post. The voice piercing the darkness hit me like a bolt in the chest. Shit! We were going to be caught and it would be all my fault.

Asil motioned for us to go back down the slope and we got up and scampered, running bent-double, kicking stones and stumbling as we did so, all the time waiting for the mortars and machine-gun fire.

I threw myself to the ground in a gully with the others, remembering how blithely James and I had decided in Nuristan that we needed to get closer to the heart of the action. 'Well f*** – is this close enough for you?' I muttered under my breath. Nuristan felt a world away and so did London and Kathy in New York. How on earth could I ever explain this to her or anyone else when – if – I ever got back?

As we cowered on the ground, a helicopter thumped overhead and soon the entire area was picked out in bright orange light. We remained motionless, our faces pressed against the rocks. I would have buried myself there if I could have found a way, as my heart hammered in my chest. It seemed to last forever, as we waited for the flares to die down and for the onslaught that never came. In my notebook a few hours later, I wrote that it was eight minutes, but *never* have eight minutes seemed so long.

The adrenaline finally ebbing, we regrouped and I was told, quite rightly, and in no uncertain terms, to keep my mouth shut. We crept back down the ridge and further along the little undulating valley, crouching low every now and again to avoid the wide white beam of a searchlight that was scanning the hillsides for intruders. At this point I was thinking of *Colditz* and films set in the Second World War about escapes from prisoner of war camps. I had never expected this and no one had warned me. Searchlights changed the whole dynamic. We had to watch them and move after they moved, then lie down as they passed over us, and then move again. I was dying for a cigarette to ease my nerves but that was out of the question. I could have throttled Niazuldin.

About a quarter of a mile further on we made our second approach, creeping quietly up the scree, crouching, stopping and lying flat. Finally we reached the top and I got a full view of Kabul's lights before the men hustled me down the slope on the other side.

But still we had not made it. We followed a gentle gully running down to the edge of the first houses and stepped gingerly across a wire sound detector – the men gesturing for me not to touch it and pointing to their ears. Then, in the final few hundred yards, we tiptoed between two posts, at one point walking with our backs pressed against the wall of the first house in an attempt to avoid the searchlights trained directly on us. When the beams caught us, my companions insisted on staring straight at them, one even shaking his fist in defiance, leaving me to assume that the man in charge that night was either blind or stoned.

Now we had made it. We were out of the rough country and walking through the refreshing cool of the city, protected by the houses around us, the air pierced every now and again by the pungent smell of open sewers. We walked for five minutes past mostly deserted and, in some cases, damaged buildings and then stopped in a square for a smoke. We hugged each other in spontaneous celebration. The first part of Niazuldin's audacious plan had gone – just about – without a hitch.

When I looked up I could see the lights in someone's dining room or sitting room, with its beamed ceiling and deep red curtains. The window was open and I could hear the warming sound of cheerful conversation, the sound of people enjoying a genial evening in a city lit with electricity. I felt so envious. It was like a glimpse of my old life that seemed so distant after weeks with the men in the mountains. It was a vision of security, comfort and even happiness that seemed beyond my grasp as I stood sucking on my cheap Afghan cigarette, celebrating our safe arrival.

So far, so good. We had made it into the city. I already had more than enough for the best story of my career. But the way I was thinking then, what had happened so far was only a means to a bigger prize. Now we had to get to one of the various safe houses used by Niazuldin's men without being detected. At the square we split up and divided into pairs. I went with Asil, and we walked through deserted streets for twenty minutes until we came to a garden door where we knocked. It was well past midnight by the time an individual I initially referred to in my notebook only as 'X' came to let us in.

'Welcome, Mr Edward, you will be safe here,' he said rather formally in English.

His name was Zulmai and he was one of Niazuldin's cousins. He was a tall, wiry man in his early thirties who looked ten years older and was living on his nerves and cigarettes. He had been employed as a teacher but was also allowing his house to be used as one of Niazuldin's main bases in the city. Since he was already under suspicion, the government had stopped him from working. Married and with two young children, Zulmai was taking huge risks and was constantly on edge from the moment I met him.

Wearing jeans and a T-shirt – clothing that was a novelty to my eye – Zulmai invited us into his home and ushered us into a sitting room covered in rugs and cushions but also with some simple wooden furniture – chairs and a table. He brought delicious tea with warm milk and pastries. I was exhausted but ecstatic to have arrived finally. It was such a relief to have made it in one piece and now to be in the relative comfort of a Kabul house.

After half an hour Asil left for another safe house in the neighbourhood. We embraced and I thanked him in broken Pashto for looking after me on the way in, apologising again for nearly having blown it for all of us. He waved my entreaties aside, promised to see me in a few days' time for our return journey and then vanished into the night.

I had made it into the heart of the Afghan capital at war. Now I was a guest of the clandestine world of the Mujahidin resistance network inside Kabul – a fighting unit operating right under the noses of the Soviet and Afghan Communist forces.

10

FAKE RUSSIAN

'Mr Edward, quickly. Come quickly. Very many Russian soldiers are coming here,' shouted Zulmai.

It was 4 a.m. on my first morning in Kabul. I had managed only a couple of hours of sleep, lying on cushions on the floor of the sitting room. I shook myself awake to discover that informers had warned Zulmai that Soviet troops and men from the feared KHAD, the Afghan secret police, were searching the area. He made clear with hand gestures that if he was caught harbouring guerrillas, the police would cut his throat. The consequences for me were harder to predict but equally unappetising.

I leapt to my feet, scooped up my stuff and followed Zulmai out of the house. We scampered barefoot across the small walled garden to a hut hidden among some apple trees. As I watched, bleary-eyed, Zulmai worked frantically, muttering 'quickly, quickly' under his breath. He was pulling up layers of sacking then lumps of dry mud and piling them into one corner. Soon he had cleared enough space to reveal an opening that was just wide enough for me to crawl through headfirst and into a small dark chamber, hidden under the floor.

My host piled the mud back into place, extinguishing almost all access to natural light as he did so, and replaced the sacking. Then all was silent amid the smell of damp earth. So this was the life of a resistance fighter, I thought. A gloomy cavern dug into the ground with a small ventilation shaft at one end. I could just about stretch out and change position but this was a claustrophobic space and I tried to stay calm, convincing myself it would not be long before Zulmai came to get me. I was sure Niazuldin would have been in there a few times but there was no evidence as to who the previous inmates might have been.

In fact I spent nine hours scrunched up in there, punctuated by the briefest of visits to the outside lavatory, when Zulmai nervously accompanied me there and back and then confined me again. I could see that he was taking no chances and I was fast getting used to the idea that this was going to be a very nervy few days in Kabul. In the event Zulmai told me that Afghan army troops – not Soviet soldiers – passed through the garden that day but did not come into the house or the hut where I was hiding.

When it was safe for me to come back into the house I returned to the curtained sitting room, hidden as much from Zulmai's wife, as is the Islamic custom, as from the prying eyes of anyone who might betray us. I ate everything I could get my hands on – more pastries, salads, fruit and chicken – and was immediately rewarded with the first onset of dysentery. The cramps when they came were agony and I soon reached the point when I couldn't care who was in the garden when it was time to dash outside for the lavatory.

On my second night in Kabul, despite the fact that I was almost too ill to stand, Zulmai took me to see the huge Soviet army base at Darul Aman. We crept along the back streets and paths in between the high walls of the mud and timber houses and sat at dusk within a hundred yards of the heavy perimeter fence. I could see blue and white Nissen-type accommodation huts and APCs moving along the perimeter while in the background we could hear the constant hum of generators. As we watched, two Slavic-featured soldiers sauntered lazily towards the wire in front of us to buy hash from two Afghan boys. We also saw the huge artillery guns mounted above the camp blasting out into the valleys through which we had come two days before.

All day long this part of the city, close to the old Royal Palace, rattled to the sound of helicopter gunships coming in, one after another, to land or take off. In the evenings the house shook as long-range artillery burst into life. We would sit listening to the sharp crackle of automatic gunfire, the 'whoosh' of RPGs and the rattle of Soviet heavy machine guns as the Mujahidin launched attacks on guard posts and other targets further into the city.

After two days at Zulmai's I moved with him to another safe house about half an hour's walk away. We set off after midnight, stopping at every path or road junction to check for government or Soviet troops before moving on. I was still suffering the effects of my stomach bug although Lomotil tablets that James and I had put on our 'things for Afghanistan' list had begun to ease the worst of the symptoms.

The new place housed five brothers, four of whom were Afghan army soldiers who were working covertly for the Mujahidin. The fifth was listed officially by the government as 'dead', but he was actually part of Niazuldin's group and could only visit the family at considerable risk to both them and him. It seemed that a friend of one of the brothers was the driver for a Russian officer and it was he who would take me on the long-planned trip around the centre of the city. 'No wonder this had taken some time to arrange,' I thought, as I pieced it all together in a series of broken conversations with Zulmai.

The day I had been waiting for had finally come. With a pair of scissors and a blunt razor, I hacked off my beard which, with its blond patches, made me look more Scandanavian than Pathan. Then I was given some rather crude and ill-fitting Western-style clothes, including some unfashionably flared and very tight fawn trousers with sharp creases down the front. I tried to explain to Zulmai that the trousers were way too small but there were no others so I had to make do. I had a leather belt with a brass buckle, a cream-coloured, lightly checked brush cotton shirt and a brown sports jacket. On my feet I wore some curious grey suede Russian shoes that tied at the side. We spent quite some time on my transformation from fake Mujahid to fake Russian. Zulmai – chain-smoking as always – knew, as I did, that if anyone suspected me of being an imposter, there would be hell to pay – and not just for me.

Weakened by illness, thin as a rake, wearing unfamiliar and uncomfortably tight-fitting clothes after weeks in the mountains, I may have looked vaguely Russian with my blue eyes and fair complexion but I was certainly not up to acting like one. However there was no time for prevarication or backing out now.

The rendezvous with the driver was set for 10 a.m. on what was Day 33 of my trip. After saying my farewells to my hosts, with everyone using the phrase '*inshallah*', or God willing, before almost every other thought – 'God willing you will return safely', 'God willing you will not be stopped', 'God willing you will return to Niazuldin' – I left the house with Zulmai leading and crossed the garden towards the door in the high outside wall where the jeep was parked. I walked straight ahead, as instructed, trying to avoid the puzzled looks of the children and feeling distinctly out of place in my strange 'Western' gear. I bade Zulmai farewell and stepped through the door as he closed it behind me.

Squinting in the sunlight, I greeted the driver, who was in Afghan army uniform. I had no idea what his name was. Then I thrust my camera into his hand, gesturing for him to take a picture of me. Whatever else I did I wanted to make sure I had this moment recorded for posterity. The image that he took that day shows me standing on a bright summer's

morning in front of the jeep, looking ghostly white and
with far too much hair for a regular army officer. Behind me
stands the dark green vehicle with its brown canvas roof and,
behind that, the tall mud and stone walls of the house where
I was staying.

Then I climbed inside and sat in the back. The driver took
his seat in front of me and after muttering a short prayer – no
doubt beseeching Allah to do his utmost to protect us – he
turned the key in the ignition and the engine sprang to life.
With my camera at the ready, we set off, the jeep bumping
violently on the rutted tracks – my head crashing against
the framework for the awning – until we reached the tarmac
roads by the Palace. Then my half-hour tour of central Kabul
at war – a tour that had taken Niazuldin so long to prepare
– began.

It was a journey conducted at breakneck speed because the
driver was beside himself with nerves and keen to complete
his mission as soon as possible. It was a shock for me to be
suddenly moving in a vehicle through Kabul after weeks of
inertia or travelling only on foot. At that stage Western journalists were banned from Afghanistan and none had reached
the centre of the city either in daylight or darkness, so I was
curious to see how the capital was faring. Leaning forward
to peer out of the windows, I saw an urban sprawl that
looked remarkably normal, with little damage in the central
districts. There were very few Soviet soldiers on the streets
and little evidence of their presence. There were Communist
Party posters here and there and the odd picture of Babrak
Karmal, but not the intensive Sovietisation I had expected.

Kabul is made up of a series of sprawling sub-centres.
Among those that we visited that morning were Darul Aman,
Kote Sangi, Deh Mazang and Chihil Sutoon. Each was linked
by main roads where military checkpoints were set. It was at
these that we were most vulnerable and my heart was in my
mouth as we stopped at the first one. I sat back, shielded by

the canvas awning from the sunlight and from the inquisitive eyes of the soldiers on the road, as the driver showed his papers, said a couple of words and then waited a few seconds before we were waved on.

'We're certainly doing this properly,' I muttered to myself, swallowing hard.

But after a while, I became almost blasé about the checkpoints because we seemed to breeze through. I was never spoken to directly, thank God – the disguise seemed to be working. The driver shouted out the names of all the buildings we passed as I snapped some of the worst tourist photos in Kabul's history. I saw the university and a big shopping centre at Shar-e Naw, where there were Afghan soldiers and many more jeeps like mine. After weeks in the mountains it was surprising to see so many people in Western dress, including women going about their shopping or stopping at tea houses, oblivious to the war on the outskirts. I remembered Niazuldin's jest about visiting the InterContinental for tea and thought 'Not today, Niaz, my old friend'; this was quite enough as it was.

It was an almost unimaginably risky tour. I was just a moment's indiscretion, or bad luck, away from the inside of a cell in Pul-e-Charkhi and a charge of spying by Moscow that, initially at least, would have been accompanied by a sentence of death. In practice, captured Western journalists were normally held for a few months or years before being released. But no one had been captured in Kabul and certainly not posing as a Russian officer. As James had warned me, the consequences would have been serious.

It could have been, and probably should have been, one of those daring-do episodes from war with a swashbuckling quality, especially a secret war of resistance. But in reality it was hard graft and I was struggling both physically and mentally with the pressures it had brought. Although Niazuldin had kept his word and shown that his network had infiltrated the Afghan army to the extent that they could pull off a jeep trip through Kabul, the notion that he could do whatever he liked in the city was stretching things a little. We completed the journey in about forty minutes but under the most onerous of conditions and things could have instantly unravelled at any of the checkpoints.

In the final minutes I was relieved to see some familiar landmarks – buildings, junctions, the odd road sign that I had seen on the way out, meaning we were nearly there. Eventually the driver brought the jeep to a stop and cut the engine. He was gabbling away, relief pouring from every sinew – he had completed his task and I had completed mine. We had not been rumbled, the jeep had not broken down, I had not been spoken to and we had got round undetected. It took me a few seconds to realise that we had parked outside a new safe house and it would not be Zulmai who greeted me. Sweating profusely, I climbed out of the vehicle and embraced and thanked the driver. The owner of the house, a stocky moustachioed individual in an ill-fitting suit, was waiting at his garden door to welcome me with a big smile on his face.

'*Salaam alaikum*, Mr Edward,' he said as I shook his hand. 'Come in, come in ...'

Inside, I sat down in another curtained reception room and gulped some cold water, served by a young boy, and collected my thoughts. We had got away with it but only now could I appreciate the risks that Niazuldin and I had taken. No one could accuse him of half-measures – we had been in and out of the heart of the occupation. It had been a classic resistance operation that blurred all the hard and fast lines that divided a nation at war. I couldn't wait to get out of my ill-fitting Western gear and soon I was swapping clothes with one of my Afghan companions. We waited until dusk before walking back to the ecstatic welcome of Zulmai and my hosts at the place where we had started earlier that morning.

I hugged everyone in turn and we laughed at the sheer imper-
tinence of what we had done.

Now all I had to do was get back to the camp and see if
I could sell a story to a newspaper about it. The plan was
that I was to return that night – my fifth in the city – but,
in the event, I was to remain for a further nine days because
just at that moment the Soviet army launched another attack
on the camps and cut the road between Kabul and Musei.
Those nine days were not in Niazuldin's masterplan and
would shorten the odds on me being detected dramatically. I
was shuffled between different safe houses, still unable to eat
much because of the dysentery, and waking from sleep with
every slight noise.

Much of the time I was back at Zulmai's and spent many
hours talking with him, often about his dreams of leaving
Kabul with his wife and children and starting a new life in
America. But he had no money and we both knew those
dreams were almost impossible to turn into reality. He was
racked by fear and smoked obsessively, always with an ear for
any strange noises that could herald a search party. I think he
accepted it might be just a matter of time before the regime
caught up with him but he was too proud, and loyal to his
comrades, to flee.

During those long nine days, I had two more sessions
hidden under floorboards. On the first occasion, soldiers
came right into the room where I was hiding and stood above
me, their feet on the rug on top of the trapdoor to the secret
compartment. I held my breath as the footsteps creaked over
my head listening to the strange voices above me, my heart
thumping so hard I was sure it must be audible. The second
time, I spent hours hiding in a hole dug under the floor of a
stable, much like the one in Zulmai's outhouse. On top of me
there was a rug piled high with mulberries that was pulled
across the entrance. Would this be the time that my luck ran
out? The hours dragged past interminably and when my host

pulled back the entrance covering, I emerged not knowing if the next face I was to see would be Russian or Afghan. As I clambered out my legs were so stiff I could barely stand.

During long daylight hours waiting for the signal to leave Kabul, I whiled away the time, sometimes listening to the English-language service of Kabul Radio and the news broadcasts of the Jomhuri-ye Demokrati-ye Afghanistan – the Democratic Republic of Afghanistan. We were told the country was living through 'difficult times'. But there was plenty of good news too – upcoming elections in Kabul, irrigation projects completed, industrial plants constructed 'with the help of Soviet advisers' and feudal debts overcome. It was classic, indescribably tedious nonsense, delivered in the deadpan style that typified Soviet-era newscasting. In the afternoons, in between bouts of funereal music, the station seemed to announce the names of those killed on the government side in a doleful and endless lament.

On three or four occasions I got the impression I was heading back to the hills, when in fact I was just being moved from one house to another. As in the camp, a lot of purposefully misleading information was fed to Zulmai's friends, as part of elaborate attempts to prevent our movements being detected.

I had seen a complex web of agents and 'doubles' throughout the two long weeks that I laid low in the city, any one of whom could have betrayed me for money, or as a result of a conflict of loyalty, but all of whom remained steadfast in the cause of the resistance. They included members of the Afghan army, men who supposedly worked for the KHAD or as paid informers for the Soviets, and small boys who had already learned to pose as budding Communists at school but who, at home, worked as lookouts and messengers for the Mujahidin. The little boys showed extraordinary self-possession for their age – sweet little chaps with smiles on their faces and ready at a moment's notice to run out with a vital nugget of information from one safe house to another. I had no doubt that the regime would have tortured them for that information just as it did their teenage brothers and parents.

My return journey, when it finally materialised, was made in three stages. On the evening of my departure, I said goodbye to Zulmai, thanked him for keeping me safe and promised to come and see him after the war was over. 'So long, Mr Edward,' he said as we stood at the garden door ready to leave. 'Have a safe journey and I will see you in Peshawar or in England!' He was polite to the end but I could see how mightily relieved this brave man was to see me go.

Accompanied by Asil and three of the original eight men that I came in with, we set off into the night. I was happy to be moving again but feeling weak and lethargic after two weeks of confinement and sickness. We walked for two hours, re-tracing our steps, out through the last houses on the edge of the city, over the sound detectors, through the searchlights and across the open ground between the guard posts with the ubiquitous helicopters above us, dropping flares. This time I was dealing with familiar challenges and I could gauge our progress, knowing when the danger was at its most acute and when we could relax. I knew I could trust Asil and did exactly as I was told.

We made it to a house outside the city where I spent two days waiting for the next step to Musei: two days listening to a family next door mourning the loss of a son who had died fighting for the resistance in Kabul. The women screamed incessantly at the top of their voices, the effort tearing at their throats. I wrote in my notebook: 'The wailing is the most chilling and disturbing sound I have ever heard – if the Mujahidin in the camps seem stoical about death, the impact at home remains dramatic.'

On our way again, we crossed the open desert towards Musei and hit the main road just as a Soviet or Afghan army vehicle was approaching in the distance, its searchlights scanning the ground on either side of the tarmac. To avoid it, we ran and yomped our way across the plain, taking about half the time we had needed on our journey in. When we stopped, safely out of range, my lungs were burning.

After spending a night at Ajab Gul's house in Musei, we set off on a baking hot Friday morning for the camp, excitement building with every step. We had made it, our mission had been successfully completed and I was looking forward to seeing the man who masterminded it.

When we arrived, the sentries welcomed us as returning heroes and everyone came rushing out to greet us. With an overwhelming look of relief on his face Niazuldin strode towards me and gave me a bear hug, lifting me off my feet. It was at that moment that I realised he had been terrified we wouldn't make it. If I'd been captured it would have ruined his reputation as a commander. I like to think he was also relieved on a personal level; I was certainly delighted to see him. We hugged each other again and laughed and joked in our broken English and Pashto – me thanking him; him bragging that he always knew that he could do this and that I was wrong to have doubted him.

He was in his most expansive mood. In his moment of triumph he seemed to be saying something along the lines that even if the Russians stayed forever in Afghanistan, he and his countrymen would fight them forever. He kept repeating the word 'jeep' as if to say 'you didn't believe I could organise that for you, did you?' and then he reeled off the names of the places I had seen. I got the gist of it, helped by the aggressive gestures that Niazuldin used to emphasise his points. But he sensed that I was struggling.

'RedWhite, good?' he asked.

I shook my head. I was exhausted – strung out after days living on my nerves, either hidden from view or curled up in secret spaces, smoking too much and suffering the deleterious effects of dysentery that had caused considerable weight loss. After all the build-up, the drive through Kabul felt unreal. Now that it had been completed I wanted to get going – in my mind I was now on my way home – I wanted to get out of Afghanistan, breathe deeply again and regain my sense of balance.

11

AFTERMATH

If all the delays in Kabul had been frustrating and nerve-racking, they were nothing to what awaited me afterwards. The plan had been to head for Pakistan as soon as possible but, once again, the Soviet army got in our way as it launched one of its biggest offensives of the war in the area between the camp and the border. As a result, I was stuck in Afghanistan for sixteen more days.

I had access to a radio and could follow the news and the reporting on the offensive on the BBC, Voice of America and Radio Australia. The BBC said that it was the largest Soviet and Afghan army operation against guerrillas in Paktia province since the war had begun. It estimated that up to 10,000 Soviet and Afghan troops were involved and that they had reached within a mile of the border with Pakistan. Heavy casualties were reported on both sides with hospitals in Kabul and Pakistan filling up with the wounded. Western diplomats in Kabul were quoted as saying that up to fifty helicopters a day were leaving for the combat zone.

I listened as the offensive ground on, watching as Nia-zuldin and others left and turned up again. As the days went by I became ever more fixated on getting back to Peshawar. I was desperate to hold an intelligible conversation again and to get away from the threat of further bombing, which was preying on my mind. I was still weakened and dehydrated from dysentery and generally strung out. Every day we saw helicopters and heard planes overflying us. We knew the Soviet army was not far away. There was a possibility we could come under attack again and that knowledge was starting to eat away at me.

The wait drove me to new heights of boredom and exasperation. I played word games in my notebook trying to make as many words as I could out of 'Interminable', 'Obstacle', and 'Thorough', among others. I spent hours and hours trying to force my addled brain to remember specific people and places, even the stops on the London Tube (I got every station right on the District Line between Baron's Court and Tower Bridge), the properties on the Monopoly board, the positions on a cricket field and the sea areas in the Shipping Forecast. I drew pictures of the yachts I hoped to own one day – the men in the camp couldn't make head or tail of those, having spent their entire lives in a landlocked country. And at one point, I spent several days trying to remember the name of the horse in the final scenes of *The Sting* when Robert Redford pulls off his big fraud. When I got it – and it took some getting – I wrote it triumphantly in heavy type at the top of a page: 'Wrecking Crew'. I dreamt of Kathy in America and of the food I wanted to eat when I got back; bacon seemed to be top of my wishlist. But the hours went by ever more slowly.

A week after I had hoped to be back in Pakistan, I wrote of the frustration that was gnawing away at me: 'Terribly weak and exhausted. Niaz told me I would have to wait in the camp for five more days – something about the Russians around Teri Mingal – I don't believe it. Sadar has told me it is a four-day holiday starting today and that no one does anything during this period. Terminally depressed at the thought of more time here. Fazil-Jan and all his men have gone to Musei and most of Niazuldin's men are on an operation. The camp is almost deserted – just Sheir Mohammad, Bokum and a few others.'

There were lighter moments. One morning I climbed to a vantage point high above the camp. I turned on the radio and heard David Bowie and Mick Jagger singing their new Number One version of 'Dancing in the Street' on the BBC. I must have looked a sight, jiving in my *shalwar kameez* halfway up a hillside with a tiny radio in my hand. I followed the cricket too. On Day 52, England were 170–1 in the sixth Test and then 462 all out. The Aussies were 52–2 at the close. That sort of thing was comforting to hear but at the same time made me feel more lonely than ever.

On another morning I spent an hour watching a little rat or a vole moving among the rocks. That day there was a heated row in the camp after one young boy accidentally shot another in the leg while cleaning his Kalashnikov. Fortunately it was only a surface wound that they were able to clean and dress but the chap responsible was given a big talking to by one of the older men who then seemed to argue about whose fault it was. I wrote a little analysis of the war to help pass the time. It was a distinctly bleak assessment that did not foresee the increase in both the volume and quality of weapons supplied to the Afghans by the CIA in the later years of the war.

Unless the Mujahidin acquire the military capability to consistently deal the Russians decisive reverses in the field, and unless they find among themselves the political will to unite, then Afghanistan will be forgotten by the West. It has already slipped back into the periphery of world events, the conscience of the West satisfied each year by the meaningless rhetoric of the UN. Afghanistan was worth one Olympics sacrificed by some, but little more than that, it seems. The war, however, will drag on for as long as the Russians remain here – for years and years (indefinitely).

On Day 59 – Friday, 6 September – things started to improve, with reports reaching us that finally the offensive was coming to an end. 'Brooklyn (in New York) has a new ferryboat, and I miss Kathy. Today our Pakistan visas run out – I wonder if James (about whose progress I had heard nothing) is fixing his or not,' I wrote in my notebook. Then I continued:

> Last night a man arrived in Musei from Pakistan. <u>Apparently</u> [I underlined the word] the Russians have f***** off and the fighting is over. The Muj might have destroyed seven choppers and one jet and are now clearing the mines on the trails. I remain sceptical with experience. I'll believe it when I see it, although this time there does appear to be some consensus about this in the camp. We were the subject of intense attention from reconnaissance aircraft this morning.

The next day, to the accompaniment of loud artillery fire, my return journey began just after lunch. The rounds seemed to be coming over our heads from somewhere behind us as we headed east and I broke out in a cold sweat. There were about twenty of us, not including Niazuldin who bade me farewell at the camp and promised to come and see me in Peshawar before I left for England.

We walked for six hours through the hills to a deserted village where we slept in the mosque for a few hours. We set off again at 2 a.m. and then walked for eighteen hours straight. We didn't hang about as we made our way through the passes that had been the focus of the offensive. There were fires still burning on the hillsides and we came across one abandoned artillery gun, but there were no mines along the way and little evidence of what was said to have been the fiercest battle of the war, except that nearly all the *chaikhanas* we had stopped at on the way in had been destroyed.

We slept for a few hours, then walked for another eighteen-hour stretch before we managed to find a tea house that was still in business. I was wrung out and physically exhausted in a way that I had never experienced before. I could barely put one foot in front of the other – I wrote in my notebook that I felt 'jet-lagged' – and conversation of any sort was beyond me. When I was offered tea and a smoke, the most intense feeling of joy swept over me. We were only a few miles from safety and I started giggling and then laughing and couldn't stop. The relief of getting close to Pakistan and the pent-up emotion of weeks living on my nerves was finally being released. The men around me must have wondered what on earth I was laughing about. I was drunk with happiness and I loved every step that took me closer to the border.

For the last mile, as we climbed up to Teri Mingal, I hitched a ride on a tractor that took me through the border post and down into the village. I had made it. Physically, at least, I was out of Afghanistan. I had gone in with James and Lawrence, I had toured Kabul in an army jeep and then endured the endless delays afterwards. After so many days of dreaming about getting to Teri Mingal I felt light-headed with relief. At last I could start to regain some control of my movements, I could get out of range of heavy weapons, and I could contemplate conversation with people in my own language.

I surveyed the scene in the village. It was sixty-three days since I was last there but it felt like a lifetime. Now I understood what I was looking at. I had tasted the war in all its raw power and intensity and I felt only admiration for the young Mujahidin all around me so eagerly preparing and packing their horse-borne loads for the remainder of the summer fighting season before the winter cold set in.

The place had been bombed during the latest offensive and twisted and smouldering piles of rubble were all that remained of some of the tea shops and stores on the hillside high street. I found one that was still in business and after an hour sitting drinking Coke, then tea, and feasting on freshly cooked chicken tikka, I climbed aboard a pick-up with several of the men and we began our journey back through the North West Frontier Province to Peshawar. But for reasons that were never properly explained we spent our first night in the town of Parachinar just a few miles down the road from Teri Mingal. On edge and desperate to get as far away from the border as possible, this was the last straw for me. I was yearning for Peshawar and the American Club but my loud protestations in a language that my hosts could not understand were futile and I had to endure one more night in *shalwar kameez*.

The following day we completed the journey back down through the hills and into the oppressive heat of the plains and the men dropped me off at the Afghanaid house in Peshawar. Recognising me immediately, the gatekeepers hugged me warmly in welcome and I strode into the quiet of the garden, feeling dazed to be back. I was hoping to find James waiting for me on the veranda but was told by the staff there that he had long since returned to England. It turned out that he and Lawrence – who was already back home in Mexico City – had taken four weeks to circumnavigate Kabul. They had had one or two very close shaves as they came near to Soviet and Afghan positions during a complex journey in which they were handed on from one commander to another.

That night I managed to call James from the Afghanaid house.

'Hey, James, it's Ed ...'

'GORMAN! Wow! You've been gone a hell of a long time. I was starting to get worried. How are you?'

'Well, I'm out. I'm a bit thinner than I was, but I'm back in Peshawar.'

'My God, that's a hell of a long trip ... how many days were you ...?'

'I dunno, over sixty? It was amazing.' I felt sick using such an anodyne term to summarise what I had been through. 'I went into the city but it took so long to plan, I almost went crazy waiting and we had quite a lot of shit in that camp.'

'Yeah, but did you do the jeep trip?'

'Yes, we got it done. I was dressed as a Russian. Niazuldin delivered – but I think … in fact I know I bit off more than I could chew. I'm seriously thin – I had dysentery.'

'Oh blimey …' There was a pause.

'How did *you* get on? Did you make it right round?' I asked.

'Yes, it was a tough trip. We nearly got trapped on a couple of occasions and we met some seriously useless people who were supposed to be commanders, but we made it in the end.'

'Good, I was wondering …'

'We had a pretty tricky time crossing the Shomali plain near Bagram airbase.'

'How long ago did you get back?'

'About three weeks. I hung around in Peshawar for a few days but I couldn't see the point of staying. Lawrence headed off back to Mexico via New York.'

'Have you managed to get anything published?' I asked.

'Yes, the *Daily Telegraph* have taken two pieces, just as they promised.'

'Oh, cool … OK,' I said feeling intense envy at his success just as the line got cut off in the normal Pakistani way.

I remember getting a shock the first time I looked at myself in a bathroom mirror. My cheeks were sunken and there were shadows under my eyes, while the bones of my skull seemed unnaturally prominent. I promised myself that I would try to eat, to build myself up again, but my appetite had shrunk. I felt out of sorts in a way that I couldn't quite put my finger on. A couple of days after I got back, my temperature shot up and I worried that I had caught some kind of infection, or that it was a side effect of the dysentery but there were no other obvious symptoms.

The delights of the American Club were beyond me for the first few days while I tried to recover and reacquaint myself with my own world. I called Kathy, who was in California, and we told each other how much we had missed each other and how much we loved each other but I got a vague sense she was going through the motions on that score. I tried to explain to her what had happened to me but the conversation was hard going and I felt a yawning emptiness as I struggled for the right words to describe what had gone on in Kabul and in the mountains before and afterwards.

'I can't wait to see you,' Kathy said, and I promised her I would be on the first flight from London once I had the money for my fare.

—◆◆◆—

Five days after I got back to Peshawar, Niazuldin showed up at Afghanaid. He had come to see me but he was also intent on exploiting the fruits of his triumph by publicising the adventure as widely as possible.

He laughed at the sight of me, stick-thin in my jeans and T-shirt, clean-shaven and pale. '*Salaam alaikum*, RedWhite,' he said, playfully punching me.

We sat in the garden under the shade of a tree talking, using one of the Afghanaid staff as an interpreter. Niazuldin was sticking to his 'I told you so' version of events.

'My Mujahidin have shown the world that we can operate right under the noses of the infidels,' he claimed proudly.

'Yes,' I agreed, 'but you have to admit it was a close-run thing.'

He wouldn't have any of it. 'Of course I knew what I was doing all along,' he claimed.

I told him that I would never forget the look of relief on his face when he saw me re-enter the camp but he laughed it off, insisting he'd never had any doubt I would get back safely.

It was great to see him in a safe environment, away from all the stress and pressures of the camp. When it was time to say goodbye I promised Niazuldin I would do my best to 'tell the world' what we had done and that I would return to Peshawar and see him again.

I stood at the gate and watched Niazuldin's jeep slowly cross the Khyber Railway tracks and head off towards the hills.

Soon after that I tried to start writing but the task of committing my story to paper in the abbreviated form demanded by newspapers, neatly encapsulated in an exact number of words, with a catchy message they could use in the headline, seemed beyond me. It was intensely frustrating and dispiriting. I wanted to tell my *whole* story, the whole truth I had witnessed, but the editors I offered it to were thinking in news terms. If I couldn't get stories published, I would be letting down Niazuldin and all the men who had taken such risks for me. I sweated over my stories but my head wasn't clear enough and the words wouldn't come.

In the end I spent about ten days in Peshawar, during which I updated my visa in Islamabad and had lunch with one or two American and British diplomats. They were almost certainly intelligence officers and were keen to hear first-hand what conditions were like in Kabul and the state of the war close to the capital. Their questions seemed to me to be always fishing for bad news for Moscow and good news for the West, but I was pretty frank about the parlous state of Mujahidin weaponry and its ineffectiveness in the face of air attack and artillery onslaught.

I was out of Afghanistan and safe but I was still facing the consequences of an experience that had drained me mentally and physically. It wasn't that I had witnessed appalling carnage – people being blown up in front of me – or horrors of that sort; it was more to do with a loss of control over my safety and destiny while undergoing stressful and frightening experiences. It seemed to me that it would have been easier to operate in a war zone as part of a regiment in the army, supported as I would have been by the camaraderie and friendships within the ranks. If someone was killed or injured, others would have been there to pull together and help take the strain. We would have been able to draw strength from our training and discipline. By contrast I was alone for long periods, unable to communicate my fears and wishes, and reliant for my safety on people who were good-natured but came from a culture largely alien to me.

The experience I had in and around Kabul with Niazuldin's men was overwhelming in its scale and scope. Much as I wanted to talk about what had happened, I found that it was almost impossible to explain to anyone – even expats in Peshawar who knew the score – what I had been through.

12

MY LOST YEAR

In mid-September I caught a flight back to London, landing at Heathrow and catching the Tube into town. After weeks in the dry lands of Logar province I was stunned by the intensity of the green foliage alongside the track.

At last, from the comforts of a friend's flat, I managed to find the wherewithal to write a series of articles that went on to be published. There were pieces in the *Wall St Journal* ('Fighting for Afghanistan's Soul'), *The Sunday Times* ('Inside Kabul'), *The Washington Times* ('A Secret Visit to Kabul, in Company of the Mujahideen') and the *Glasgow Herald* ran a four-part series, but none of them got across what I wanted to say. I couldn't begin to even touch on the scale of what I had been through and never felt I had done myself – or Niazuldin – justice. An interview for the BBC World Service's Eastern Topical Unit, which I did at Bush House in London and which went out on its Pashto and Persian radio services, was probably the most fulfilling thing I did, because I knew many of my Afghan friends would hear it.

The piece that appeared in *The Sunday Times* particularly galled me. It was all of 600 words by the time the sub-editors had finished cutting it under the direction of the foreign editor, Stephen Milligan. And when I saw it I felt utterly disillusioned with my chosen vocation. 'If that's what happens when you have done what I have,' I thought to myself, 'then I don't want to carry on.' I was angry and struggling to come to terms with my decision to go into Kabul, which had turned out to be beyond what I could cope with and beyond what I needed for the purposes of my work.

I crashed back into civilian life, broke and haunted by what had happened and looking for ways to ease my fears and anxieties. I was jumpy – sudden loud noises, doors slamming, people creeping up on me all put me on edge. A loud bang in a London restaurant even prompted me to dive under a table. I was irritable. I started to suffer from nightmares; I felt nervous without any obvious cause and I began to suffer bouts of a debilitating physical sensation of heating in my head that made it hard to think clearly. I found that, without warning, my mind would wrench me back to Kabul and the mountains and the horrible sensation of vulnerability when being shelled without cover. I craved an enclosed, protective space.

The sound of helicopters overhead in the London sky took me right back to the death of Abdullah-Jan and the times we walked under their thumping rotors at night, waiting for the growl of their Gatling guns. And the sound of a high-altitude aeroplane reminded me of the distant humming of the Soviet reconnaissance flights, the Black Tulip and of days waiting in the camp.

I was still feeling feverish and had no idea what was wrong with me so I went for tests at the School of Tropical Medicine. The results showed parasites in my blood confirming I had some form of malaria. 'This must be why I feel so wiped out all the time,' I told myself. The rather headmasterly doctor there was unimpressed by my state of mind and body and gave me a sharp rebuke. After asking me a bit about what I had been doing, he said it was time for me to learn to live more sensibly.

'You need to start making some helpful decisions about your own life,' he said in a rather detached manner.

'Yes, I know,' I replied, feeling on the edge of breaking down in front of him.

'There are plenty of people who do your sort of thing but they learn to live with it and you must too.' And then in a phrase I have never forgotten he added: 'It's time for you to start boxing clever.'

He was right, of course, and I left the building determined to try and do exactly that – whatever that was.

After two weeks in London I headed off on a one-way ticket to New York, desperate to see Kathy, even though her slightly cooler than normal responses to me on the phone from Peshawar and London had set the alarm bells ringing. It was five months since I'd last seen her and I knew instinctively that there was a distance between us that had not been there before. On our first night together she took me out to dinner at the Boerum Hill Café in Brooklyn, not far from her home – an expensive gesture for an out-of-work actress. I made the mistake of bringing up her longed-for but as yet stuttering career on the stage, a very sensitive subject. 'Had she thought about doing something else?' I asked. It was the explosive beginning of the end of our trans-Atlantic love affair.

Our lives were now on unimaginably divergent courses and already we felt like strangers in each other's company. Kathy had waited for me so patiently – 'I wonder how things have been for you,' she had written in long, unanswered letters from New York or California when I was inside for all those weeks. 'You must send me letters telling me about everything. I want to know about everything, OK?' But I was someone else when I got back to her and in no state to save the relationship. Less than a week after I arrived in New York we had parted, though she was good enough to allow me to stay on in the house until I had found somewhere else to go.

The pain of our break-up came at the beginning of a year in the States that was part bender, part therapy. I had no interest in continuing with journalism and I was trying to avoid thinking about what had happened to me, about Afghanistan, about newspapers, even the news itself. Looking for ways to escape the psychological and physical after-effects, that included acute pain in my eyes and gums that left me feeling exhausted from the moment I woke up, I took refuge in alcohol – drinking myself into a stupor – and drugs, regularly using cannabis and other substances when I could get my hands on them. I reached high points – or climactic low points – when my fevered imagination and my memories overwhelmed me. One day in New York State I was walking across a wide-open intersection between two highways, after stepping out of a diner, when I suddenly felt a creeping fear of the open space. I stood shivering with terror as people all around me went about their business as normal.

There was a black hole into which my mind would tumble when Afghanistan forced itself into my thoughts – a central vortex I could never discuss or explain and did my best to avoid. It was as if a film was playing in my head and it was always the same – the men bringing Abdullah down from the mountain, his head lolling on the back of the man who carried him, his eyes suddenly seeming alive but then lifeless again as they lifted him and laid him down. I could see it as if it had happened just minutes before.

Then there was the little cameo of the cigarettes, how they were handed to me and how I smoked them all without thinking. The burial stayed with me too. The men lined up in the darkness saying goodbye despite the threat of renewed shellfire. I remember thinking that while we were burying one of them, another might be killed right in front of us. It could have happened at any time.

After a white Christmas in Manhattan, when a school friend working in Wall St and I did our best to keep Pablo Escobar in business, I lost myself for several months painting houses for an American couple who were going through the early stages of a painful separation. First I painted her place in Long Island from top to bottom, then I hopped onto a flight and painted his in Chicago. Neil was a highly decorated Vietnam veteran and he and I spent many a long hour comparing notes on our experiences, with the benefit of copious amounts of alcohol and other stimulants.

In fact, the subject of Vietnam became a major preoccupation during my time in the States. I read new accounts of the war and grilled Neil for as much detail as I dared on his time in Special Forces. While I was in Chicago I attended the first formal welcome-home parade for Vietnam Vets ever staged in the city in June 1986. I loved every minute of it and seemed to identify with men who came from all over the country to take part.

I wrote my own account of that historic march when 200,000 Vets took part:

What struck me straight away was the up-beat atmosphere. So much has been written and said about Vietnam and the men who fought there. About the sense of national shame and embarrassment at having lost the war and then collectively not acknowledging the debt owed to those who lost their lives and limbs in Indo-China. But these men had come to finally put all those ghosts to rest. They had come as heroes, not as the downtrodden and defeated. This was the real victory of Chicago.

Listening to them you could clearly sense that they saw the day as a test for America – not for them. They were going to have a ball and celebrate the victory that most of them felt had been snatched from them by the politicians and the media, and America could either acknowledge that or be damned.

There was a great feeling of excitement and anticipation.

How many would turn up? And more importantly, how many Chicagoans would forego their busy Friday to come out and welcome them – or even shout abuse. And how would the Vets themselves react? What was it going to feel like marching down State Street with the ticker tape falling behind the Marine Band?

There were going to be lumps in the throats and tears welling in the eyes of many – spectators and old soldiers alike – and down at the pier, as the sun came up, many sat alone preparing themselves for this last but most welcome Vietnam battle.

While I could write with fluency and verve about Vietnam Vets on the streets of Chicago I simply could not string a sentence together about my own experiences in Afghanistan and whenever I tried, my mind just seemed to shut down.

'It is now almost nine months since Abdullah-Jan died. But his memory and the events surrounding his death haunt me today with terrifying clarity,' I wrote one day in black felt-tip on a page of lined foolscap. I went on: 'Occasionally an experience witnessed at first hand can be so powerful ...' But I crossed that sentence out. Then I added: 'Abdullah was a quiet, softly spoken, intelligent man. Very thin with a firmly chiselled face – features more reminiscent of a European than an Afghan.'

Then I started again. 'Although I spoke only a few words of Pashto upon arrival at the guerrilla camp hidden away in the mountains south-east of Kabul, I quickly attached myself to Abdullah.' I crossed that out. 'He was the second-in-command at the rebel camp. No macho guerrilla-type, Abdullah was a mullah, roughly equivalent to a priest in Christian society.' And that. 'When the bombing finally ended at dusk, the men ...'

And that was as far as I got.

On another occasion I wrote a long, throat-clearing

introduction to what I imagine was supposed to be a full account of what happened but it petered out after two pages of a 'preface'. In the course of that piece I dwelt on the disadvantages of the language barrier.

> The fact that I spent almost all my time inside Afghanistan without an interpreter was, and is now, a severe drawback. I know I missed so much about my Afghan companions simply because I could not understand what they were saying most of the time. Many of the conversations were restricted by my very limited grasp of Pashto and indeed my interpretation of causes and effects is clearly wanting in many cases simply because I wasn't able to ask what was going on there and then.
>
> But being without an interpreter was also at the heart of the experience. For in the comparatively short period of two months I had become completely immersed in the lives of the men and their country with no means of escape or familiar psychological landmarks against which to pace myself. The intensity of the struggle was with me undiluted and I had no choice but to get stuck in.

At some point during that year of recuperation and anger – and it must have been when my frustration and torment was raging – I did manage to get an account of my state of mind and my turbulent emotions about Afghanistan down on paper. It was called 'A Note of Warning' and it seems to reveal a mind wrestling with delayed shock and feelings of fear and guilt.

> I can hardly bear to think about Afghanistan now. It catches me out. Waiting to surprise me around the next corner. Climbing the stairs, closing the front door – something – a smell, the colour of the light. My mind races to get through it. At top speed. A beginning, middle and end.

The sickening warmth at the bottom of my spine, a shake of the head and it is gone.

The picture is often the same. The awareness of fear. The terrifying moment of unbearable violence on a cloudless, moonlit night. That moon which now shines over me, that would kill us all with its deathly glow. The twilight in which we knelt beside the body. The men whimpering, quietly tugging gently at the sleeve, intoning '*Ghoda, Ghoda*'. And the contortions of his still face in the dim light of the oil lamps. Preparing for burial. The body moving this way and that – a smile. Then a grimace revealing teeth unrelated. A hand passes gently across the face to return it to a recognisable normal. Then the shroud and the face is covered for the last time.

The problem with this – and I know it may sound absurd – the problem is that for much of the time I enjoyed myself. Weighing up the balance, surviving something real, feeling real emotion like some laboratory animal for the first time, entering into the spirit of the thing with the doctor. There were moments of terror. Moments when death, wounding or capture seemed unbearably close. But what I have come to realise a year later may surprise you. That the real terror only set in when I was well away. Back in the comfort and relative safety of Brooklyn. At some point – I like to think of it as the middle of a frightful night – I woke up. And for the first time, in dramatic juxtaposition to the comforts of modern American life, I realised fully what I had done. That was when the fear grew in me and set in for good. I still can't explain it. I suppose you'd call it a delayed reaction. The mind doing its best to conceal and hide from itself, finally surrendering to the incoming tide.

◆◆◆◆

As the months passed by in the States, I began to feel better. There were even days when I had no symptoms at all. I was nomadic, picking up friendships, places to stay and jobs, then moving on before too long. I hardly ever watched the news and if an item on Afghanistan came on when I was in front of a TV I turned away. Most of all I rested and gave myself a chance to recover.

One way or another the time off healed me to the point where I decided to head back to London in the autumn of 1986. By the end of the year I had got myself together sufficiently to try my luck on the jobs market. At first I worked hard to land a reporting role in Fleet Street but was rejected by all the papers I tried, among them the *Independent*, the *Daily Mail*, the *Daily Telegraph* (whose editor Max Hastings wrote a charming reply concluding 'thank you for troubling to get in touch'), and my old friends at the *Glasgow Herald*.

In the meantime I was invited for an interview by the secret intelligence service, MI6, who had heard about what I had been up to in Afghanistan – possibly via the diplomats I had met in Pakistan a year earlier – and imagined I might be of use to them.

I was shown into a grandiose second-floor office in a smart terrace on the Mall with large sash windows overlooking St James's Park. A man who introduced himself as 'Mr Halliday' was facing the window when I walked in. Just as in the movies he turned and approached me, offering his hand by way of a greeting. It was a fascinating interview during which I signed the Official Secrets Act and was shown various examples of recent MI6 operations. There was one that caught my eye that I assumed had to be made up. It described how MI6 had helped set up a fake arms-buying operation in Europe so that agents could intervene in the sale of Exocet missiles to the Argentine airforce during the build-up to the Falklands War. This enabled the service to doctor some of the missiles, ensuring that they did not detonate when they hit British warships – something that did happen on a number of occasions during the war. I didn't believe it at the time, thinking it had been concocted to impress would-be young spies, but many years later John Nott, the defence secretary during the Falklands War, decided he could reveal the details in his own memoirs and the story appeared on the front page of *The Sunday Times*.

I would have made a terrible spy, or MI6 officer; like all journalists I enjoy telling people what I have found out, not concealing it from them. Luckily my performance in the Civil Service exam, when my 'words-only' mind was faced with hundreds of puzzles involving numbers and shapes, was woeful.

I was house-sitting for a family friend in a farmhouse in rural Herefordshire when 'Mr Halliday' broke the news.

'Is that Mr Gorman?'

'You are speaking to him,' I replied immediately.

'I'm afraid the news is not good, I'm afraid,' he said, repeating himself.

There was no need for him to, as he put it, 'break the rules' by explaining why I had failed, but he did anyway and he sounded genuinely disappointed. 'Unfortunately, your performance in the cognitive tests was really not very good across the board.'

'Oh,' I said. 'Oh dear. That's rather irritating.'

'More than anything it's rather surprising,' he went on. 'I mean broadly, you are close to what we are looking for, which is a great pity.'

We chatted politely for a few minutes with Mr Halliday mulling over what 'a remarkably odd result' it had been. In that way, my career in the intelligence service evaporated before it had even started.

Next on my list was the City of London. While I had been risking my neck in the wilds of Afghanistan, several of my university friends had been earning big money in the City.

Perhaps, I mused, I should forget about journalism and join this gold rush. I wrote a series of letters to various banks that explained my unusual journey to their door.

'You will no doubt be curious as to why it has taken me three years since leaving Cambridge to elect for merchant banking,' I wrote to one recruitment executive. 'It would have been inconceivable for me to walk straight out of university into a potentially life-long career. Journalism – both on business magazines and in the field in Afghanistan – gave me the opportunity to find out a bit more about myself and the world outside that protective environment. And certainly I have now exhausted my curiosity in that respect. In particular I have elected not to continue the rather life-threatening business of war reporting. Risk-taking is one thing, but when the penalty for misjudgement may be death, one can hardly claim it is a career with a future.'

Surprisingly, I got two interviews, one of which produced a job offer as a Eurobond trader at Credit Suisse First Boston on a salary of £22,000, plus bonus – not a bad start even in late 1986.

I duly turned up in a suit, getting to the office on Bishopsgate, not far from the new Lloyd's Building, at 7 a.m. each morning in time for the daily briefing about what had been happening in the markets in Japan overnight. And I began the fiddly business of trying to understand the various monetary instruments that I might one day buy and sell. On my first morning Justin, the head of sales, sized me up and down.

'What do you know about this business?'

I told him I knew virtually nothing apart from the contents of an introductory booklet on Eurobonds that I had been given.

'Do you know about yield-to-maturity?'

I said I didn't and he winced.

'You realise you are going to have to do at least two hours reading every night after work for the next month?'

'Of course,' I replied sounding as enthusiastic as I could but with a sinking feeling.

My putative switch to banking was never going to be less than painful but I quickly realised I was only doing it to prove a negative. I wasn't interested in money. I wanted to be a foreign correspondent.

I completed four days at Credit Suisse, staring at little green numbers on the screen in front of me and nodding to Justin. On the fifth day I told the secretary on my desk that I was popping down to the research department on the floor below and walked out of the building. I went to the cinema and watched *Down by Law*, in which Tom Waits fittingly plays a disc jockey escaping from a jail in New Orleans across the alligator-infested swamp of the Louisiana Bayou. I got back to my flat and wrote a grovelling apology to the managing director who hired me. He tried to persuade me to think again but I knew what I wanted to do and within a few weeks I was working on Robert Maxwell's new London evening paper, the *London Daily News*. I worked there every day of its short life – from February to July 1987 – covering all the news that was fit to print in London under the excellent editorship of Magnus Linklater – until Maxwell pulled the plug without warning.

With time on my hands and a little money saved up, I was dreaming about going abroad again and I hunted for a freelance commission. It came from the up-market glossy travel magazine *Departures*. I offered the editor, Lucretia Stewart, a first-person feature from inside Afghanistan. I explained to her my background and experience in the country and she jumped at it. She wanted 3,000 words at £200-a-thousand and offered a £1,000 advance against expenses. I was launched. To boot, *The Times* was also interested in taking the odd freelance article.

I could not say that I had recovered from my adventures in Kabul but I was certainly determined not to let Afghanistan beat me. I felt that I had done the groundwork two years earlier and, having reaffirmed my ambition to work as a professional journalist, I wanted to capitalise. Despite the troubles I had been through and was continuing to contend with, Afghanistan was my speciality and the place where I would try to make my name. But it would be dishonest not to admit that I also felt I *had* to return in some sense. I did not want people to think that I had buckled or could not face the war again. I knew, even if most of my friends had no clue, that true bravery is not going somewhere dangerous for the first time; it is returning freely once you know what risks await you.

13

THE UNFORGIVING SUN

In September 1987, almost exactly two years after leaving Kabul, I was back in Afghanistan, in the company of a young freelance photographer from Northern Ireland named Colin Boyle – a hard-smoking recent graduate from the Royal College of Art in London.

Armed with letters of introduction from *Departures* magazine and from an assistant foreign editor at *The Times*, Colin and I made our way to the offices of the resistance groups and linked up with a thirty-year-old mullah named Bilal, who was the chief provincial commander for one of the larger Mujahidin resistance groups.

Bilal offered to take us into Kunar province, not far from where James – who by this time was well into his new diplomatic career in the Foreign Office – and I had travelled during our first trip in 1985. On this occasion I had no plans to stay in Afghanistan for more than a couple of weeks and Colin and I vowed to work as a team.

'We're fuckin' well going to stay together, right, Ed?' he affirmed. For some reason everyone knew Colin as the 'Vicar' but he swore an awful lot for a man of the cloth.

We drove up to the frontier and crossed into a rugged land-scape where the Soviet hold was at best tenuous and where Moscow's ground troops rarely ventured from their secure garrison towns. As before, we crossed the border on foot. It was the second day of the trip and a moment I recorded in my diary:

> At once, the stinging reality of war is upon us. As we take our first steps down the trail towards the mountain pass that will take us into Kunar, young Afghans – red-faced, sweating profusely and gasping for breath – are running towards us, shouting to clear the way. Behind them, carried on wooden beds, are three young fighters whose legs have been shattered by the Soviet mines that litter the valley.
>
> Commander Bilal tells us, as we settle down in a snug mud and timber house for our first night, that we can go back if we want. There will be fighting, he says. There are government troops in the valley and already today forty Mujahidin have been wounded by the mines and ten have been 'martyred'. It's a chilling thought but we have come to report and he has come to fight. We have no hesitation in continuing.
>
> Our anxieties about mines and the mind-numbing business of concentrating on every footstep quickly subside as the gruelling, steep mountain paths take their toll. Walking for hours in the burning sun, stopping only for the men to pray and the occasional gulp of ice-cool melt water, we make our way through country of stunning natural beauty in the border area.
>
> In the foothills of the mighty Hindu Kush range in late September the neat terraced fields fed by intricate irrigation canals are ripe with sweetcorn, beans, wheat, walnuts, mulberries, mint, tomatoes, heather and marijuana. After burning summer days, the evening air under spectacular cloudless skies is pungent with the sweet smell of woodsmoke as we – the honoured guests – are treated to specially killed lamb, chicken and goat.

Back in the heat and dust of the Kunar valley, there was no sign of the war nearing an end. It still felt like a stalemate, although a greater volume of better weapons, including some anti-aircraft missiles, was starting to tip the balance in favour of the Mujahidin. In the combat zone along the Kunar River, I again came face-to-face with the dismal effects of the Soviet scorched earth policy. After the bucolic paradise of the hill country, we now moved through broken villages and deserted and overgrown fields, and again encountered the stubborn resistance of the hardy few.

We soon found that Bilal, our new commander, had nothing on Niazuldin in the charisma stakes. A small, wiry individual who scampered up and down the hills like a mountain goat, he was a proper fighter but I did not connect with him the way I had with Niazuldin. Perhaps I had grown older and wiser. There was not the same devotion to him among his men as I had seen in Niazuldin's group, something that immediately registered as a negative in my mind. This was more gritty and less fun.

Surprisingly, I wasn't feeling any of the sort of paralysis or the over-heating symptoms that had plagued and haunted me in the States. Somehow I had moved on enough to make this return trip possible. I invested heavily in my newfound working partnership with Colin and enjoyed the *craic* with him as he – and I – swore and smoked our way through our adventure together. We also benefited from the services of Abdul, a stocky individual in his fifties with a white skull cap, who proved an excellent translator. Compared to Kabul two years earlier I had everything in place to cope with most of what might lay ahead. I was with the Vicar, it was a short trip in countryside that was vaguely familiar, we were not trying to infiltrate the capital and we could communicate with our hosts. More than anything I knew what I needed for a good story – there was no requirement for anything extravagant.

For several days we toured Bilal's bases, moving gradually up the valley towards the old fort at Barikot with an armed escort of around fifteen men. We took the toughest of routes to avoid detection by Soviet gunners and to arouse as little curiosity among the locals as possible. The hundreds of men under Bilal's loose command were scattered throughout the valley in old farmhouses or classic guerrilla-style fortified compounds dug into the hillside, which the best set designers in Hollywood would have difficulty matching. There they spent their days discussing the war, the philosophy of the Mujahid, praying to Allah for his help in the fight, eating their simple meals of meat and rice, talking enthusiastically of great victories – some real, some imagined – and planning their next attack on the local Soviet base at Asmar.

Inevitably, travelling in an area little visited by Europeans before the war, Colin and I were the source of unending fascination to many of the villagers, who were startled to see their first Europeans bristling with strange 'machines'. Everything from our quite ordinary toothbrushes to our Walkmans received detailed attention.

On our second day inside Afghanistan Colin and I went to watch an 'operation'. Anxious to demonstrate that, unlike many of his counterparts, he did more than just talk about fighting, Commander Bilal took us up a tortuous and heavily mortared hillside to a vantage point above the town of Asmar. There we crouched in the bushes, observing like two badly behaved visiting generals, as he coordinated a chaotic rocket strike on the town. Bilal would scream into his short-wave radio giving the order to fire. Then the Chinese BM12s, launched from a neighbouring base, would fly through the valley in pairs emitting a low whistling sound before veering away from the target and exploding in the distance. 'Fuckin' typical,' was Colin's succinct summary.

After firing eighteen rockets, wild-eyed and happy with his work, Bilal shepherded us back down the mountain. We stopped briefly as a lone Soviet jet overflew us, releasing five bombs that glistened in the sun before landing with a resounding crash among the hollyoaks in the valley below. The munitions left a thick blanket of smoke and a rich stench of high explosive. High altitude and inaccurate bombing, which often set fires among the hollies and pines, became a daily feature of the trip.

Continuing on up the valley, we began what we expected would be an eight-hour walk to reach the only bridge across the Kunar River under Mujahidin control. But to our surprise we were able to cross lower down in a French-made Zodiac inflatable. The young Afghan boatman, making a precarious living negotiating the raging torrents of the icy river, worked frantically with his one paddle to prevent us being swept away downstream. The men meanwhile, looking more nervous than at any other time on the entire trip, prayed continually throughout our five-minute voyage.

We had come to report what Bilal assured us was the site of a great victory for the guerrillas. A Soviet convoy moving down the valley from Barikot to Asmar had been ambushed. There were at least thirty tanks destroyed, he said, and 400 Soviet soldiers had been killed in the ensuing five-day battle. Having succumbed to a certain scepticism on such matters, we were surprised to find that he was as good as his word. There, littering the road, were at least forty Soviet vehicles, rusted and shattered, lying in demented positions, caved in on each other or blown upside-down. Although none actually qualified under the strict definition of a tank, there were several APCs and howitzer field guns in among the jeeps and supply trucks.

All around us lay the evidence of a fierce and protracted battle. There were tank shells and cartridges of every shape and size, bits of vehicle blown across a wide area and thousands of Soviet army ration tins. All along the road at regular intervals, neat line trenches or square fox holes had been dug with impromptu stone-walled battlements piled alongside where Soviet soldiers had sought refuge after leaving their vehicles. We never managed to get a completely unambiguous version of events, but evidently the soldiers had dug in and fought it out with the Mujahidin firing down on them from the rocks. We were told that scores of helicopters had come in wave after wave, blasting the hillsides with rocket and cannon fire, though the Muj claimed – absurdly – that only one of their number had been killed by the time the last of the Soviet troops had been plucked to safety.

We clambered among the debris, the armour plating burning hot in the midday sun, searching for trophies for our mantelpieces. I picked off a couple of instruction plates from the cabs of Soviet APCs. For the first time we were getting a glimpse of the other side of this war. I imagined what would have been going through the mind of a young Russian conscript cursing his slow progress, as he rattled ponderously down that road at the wheel of a hopelessly vulnerable supply truck. Looking out at the surrounding hills, fearful of ambush at every turn, his senses straining for the first hint of impending disaster. Then the deafening crash of an RPG round, his fear turning instantly to shock, sending adrenaline coursing through his body as the chaos of battle enveloped him. He would have scrambled to get out of the truck to find cover among the rocks and then come face-to-face with the reality of a violent death at the hands of vicious bandits in a wild and remote landscape.

The Muj told us they looted the Soviet corpses and then threw them in the river. We had no way of knowing how many there would have been. As we wandered haphazardly back down the road to our rendezvous point with the commander, it seemed almost as if we were reviewing the evidence of a war long-since finished, the gruesome details lost in the haze of history. But the sudden eruption of rocket and mortar fire somewhere not too far off down the valley was enough to remind us that the killing was still going on and the agony of Afghanistan was not over.

'I could really handle a steak sandwich with cheese on top in the Main Street Diner in Richmond, Virginia,' muttered Colin in his Ulster brogue, between puffs on yet another cigarette. 'And a whisky and Coke to wash it down with ...'

The long summer days of Afghanistan were upon us and the simple charm of Afghan cuisine was beginning to rub a little thin as we both succumbed to the inevitable internal disorders. Then, in the way these things always happened in Afghanistan, we found ourselves stranded for five days in a tiny village, halfway up an alpine-style valley. The commander was suddenly 'elsewhere'. We couldn't go this way and we couldn't go that. We had no choice but to sit it out and wait for him, doing our best to conceal our frustration.

We made detailed studies of ants, shared appalling Pakistani cigarettes – they may well have been the aforementioned Red & White – discussed at length our favourite foods, played quiz games with the assorted Afghans passing through and gave pompous and long-winded dissertations on the major political questions of the day. We drank endless cups of green tea. Dragged unwillingly into the twentieth century, the Afghans were preoccupied – even obsessed – with politics and their war. They kept Abdul busy. What did I think of Iran's ambitions in Afghanistan? Why won't President Reagan give us more arms? Who did I think was responsible for the bombings in Peshawar?

When the commander finally returned, he was in high spirits. After supper he summoned Abdul, then drew himself up to his full, but not very impressive, height and addressed me.

'What I want more than anything,' he said, 'is a good English wife.'

'There are not many of those to be had unfortunately,' muttered Colin, smirking.

'I'll see what I can do,' I said, trying to be polite.

'You are to take me to London and find a beautiful woman who will obey me,' he went on.

This prompted more irreverent asides from Colin.

'I will think about it,' I said, 'but even if I could find you a wife, it is very unlikely that she will obey you.'

'Of course she will,' replied Bilal affronted at the idea that an Englishwoman might ignore the wishes of a proven Mujahidin commander. 'I will give you, in return, as much land as you want, a horse and six wives.'

The exchange reminded me of a melancholy occasion during my year off between school and university when I sat with a desperately poor Palestinian man on the beach at Gaza, listening to him offering me the hand in marriage of any of his three daughters.

The following day we began the last and most testing part of our journey, during which our relationship with Bilal deteriorated dramatically. We had been 'inside' for almost two weeks and felt it was time to leave. Having travelled in the area two years previously, I knew that a safe but tough pass over the mountains to the staging point on the border was just a day's walk away. But Bilal was adamant. It was impossible for us to go that way, he said. Every conceivable excuse was made: there weren't enough men available to take us, he had to stay, and, most ludicrously of all, he claimed that were we to take that route, he would most likely be shot by Mujahidin from another party. In view of the fact that he had spent the previous ten days introducing us to fellow commanders and telling us how united they were and that all their old divisions had been patched up, this latest claim struck us as far-fetched. But we had no choice. We had to go where he went and he was heading north to Barikot where the Mujahidin – still surrounding the Soviet garrison – were preparing for a major onslaught in the coming days.

Wearily we began plodding our way along the old Kunar road where several days earlier we had seen the wreckage of battle. The valley felt hotter and drier than before, and we rapidly began to suffer from heat exhaustion as the unforgiving sun bore down on us. We covered perhaps a twenty-mile stretch of road that, even in its heyday, would qualify elsewhere as no more than a passable farm track and now bore the scars of repeated ambushes and bombing. In some places huge boulders and avalanches of rocks blown off the hillsides forced us to take long detours. We encountered more Soviet wreckage, an APC sunk in the river, its gun turret just showing on the surface, and numerous other 'tanks' lying rusted and smashed in the bushes.

By mid-afternoon, ten hours into the walk, our patience was running out. There seemed no respite from the burning heat of the afternoon sun and at every break in the journey we scrambled down to the river for another stomachful of silty, grey water. We had got ourselves into that dreaded merry-go-round where, having drunk too much early on, no amount of water could now satisfy our thirst. At four o'clock we stopped for lunch. It consisted of a few lumps of dry bread that we nibbled at disconsolately, watching ants at our feet scurrying away with the crumbs. Again we tried to persuade Bilal that we should turn back. We had passed several pulley-system bridges across the river that would take us on our preferred route. All we needed was a couple of good men to guide us and we could say goodbye to him there and then. But still he would have none of it.

Our anxieties about the journey reached new heights as our increasingly lacklustre progress brought us gradually nearer to Barikot and the insistent chatter and thump of battle. Far from being the safe way, it became starkly obvious that Bilal was taking us into the thick of it. At five o'clock we spotted explosions to our left and almost casually inquired of him whether we too would soon be the object of attack.

There was no chance, he assured us. After all, as he had repeatedly said, this was the safest of routes.

Imagine our surprise when, thirty yards in front us, an artillery shell exploded with fearsome power. Then another, and another. As the barrage picked up momentum, with shells landing to the left and right, we ended up lying flat out along the open road cursing.

'I could fuckin' kill that bastard,' screamed Colin as we lay there waiting for the next rounds to come in.

As the shelling got ever closer we decided we had to move. Desperately tired, our rucksacks like lead weights on our backs, we started to run across the cornfields, stumbling and panting like old men, crashing on our faces as each round whizzed over our heads. Bilal ordered us to go one by one, taking our chances to cross the main target area and then gather among the trees to our left. He set off first, nimbly negotiating the rocky slope as we crouched, discussing who should go next. There were eight of us altogether and, with the help of Abdul, we decided that two men should go first and then we would follow. After they set off, Colin duly followed as another round came in. Then Abdul went and I followed him. I was running as fast as my tired legs would carry me, diving to the ground as the shells screamed in, the adrenaline pumping and my heart racing.

But Colin and I had both reached the stage where being hit was the least of our worries. The sheer exhaustion of running and the now desperate need for water had come to dominate our dulled senses entirely. When we reached the rendezvous point among the trees we discovered that Bilal had vanished. Pinned down, the group was now split, with five of us together in the trees and the remainder still out in the open but unable to move because of the intensity of the barrage. Immediately the men with us began to argue about whether we should stay where we were or carry on to our left. This time it was not a case of the 'living martyrs' but just plain incompetence. It became starkly clear that the commander had never given them instruction on how to deal with these situations.

So there we were, huddled against the rocks, waiting for the Soviet gunner to lose interest and with the commander nowhere to be seen. This was all too much for Abdul who began preparing for death, frantically reciting verses from the Koran. At one point he shouted across to Colin who was smoking while crouched behind a boulder.

'Mr Colin! Put out your cigarette. They will see your cigarette.'

Colin was having none of that. 'They'll see your fuckin' hat before they see my fag,' he thundered in a reference to Abdul's white skull cap.

I found myself thinking about our adversary. Who was this man casually sending shells our way? I tried to imagine what was going through his mind. Perhaps he would break for tea in a few minutes or maybe just bang off another twenty for the hell of it. Maybe there would be a guy on the nightshift, known to his comrades for his prodigious use of ammunition, who would take over and try out a couple of new angles. The men with us called and whistled for their commander but there was no sign of him as the rounds crashed about us. We decided we had no choice but to sit it out.

At dusk, with the explosions registering a new target somewhere ahead of us, we tentatively ventured out from cover and continued in the direction of the camp. Far worse than anything we had experienced so far, what Bilal had billed as a 'ten-minute walk' became a gruelling hour-long test of willpower as we stumbled like drunks under the weight of our packs up a dry riverbed to the camp. It was a true taste of Afghanistan. Our stomachs were empty, our mouths so dry that our tongues seemed to have grown into great lumps of glue sticking to the roofs of our mouths.

Finally we spotted the dim glow of an oil lamp ahead

and the sickly sweet smell of roasted goat meat filled our nostrils. We met the advance party – two men with torches, talking and laughing. We threw our packs down in a gesture of defiance and sat on the ground trying to summon enough strength and willpower to cover the last ten minutes to the camp. Somehow we did it, stopping at the first sound of water to drench ourselves in it against the advice of the men, who told us it was dirty. We couldn't care in the least, even though it turned out that they were right and we would pay the price in the usual way the following day.

We had made it. The camp turned out to be yet another Hollywood classic cut out of the rocks with perhaps fifty men, the commander among them, sitting around a fire drinking tea and chatting away like guests at a cocktail party. Colin and I just sat there, apart from the group, shivering in the cool air. We had decided not even to raise the issue of what had happened in the cornfield with Bilal. We knew he didn't have a leg to stand on. He had taken us into the line of fire and then abandoned us. All we cared about now was getting out of the country as soon as possible.

Two hours later we were on the road to recovery with the aid of delicious goat's cheese baked on the fire and the usual succession of cups of green tea – we were unable to face the round of naan bread and what we were repeatedly assured was sheep, not goat meat.

The men were preparing for battle. Some, the bravest, were going to creep up on the post that had been firing at us all afternoon and attack from close quarters while others launched their 'deadly devices' from the hills. It was an eerie place, reminiscent of the tough camps around Kabul that I had visited two years before, where young men came to fight and to die. There was an indefinable look about them – a kind of haunted preoccupation that washed over them. They were there to fight for God and they were resigned to it. I looked around at the faces smiling at me across the fire and wondered what fate lay in store for each one in the next twenty-four hours.

After supper we politely declined the kind offer of one of Bilal's commanders in the area to 'stay with us for a few days to watch the battle'. It was to be a good fight, we were assured, and, besides, it would give us the chance to rest. Bilal, looking just a little shifty, quickly consented to our request to leave. We would have four men and we would depart at two o'clock in the morning, retracing our steps in the darkness, returning back to the river and crossing to Pakistan by the route for which we had long argued. It was with a bittersweet sense of victory that we settled down for three hours of fitful sleep in that camp.

At 2 a.m. the alarm on my watch woke me and I found my torch. I had slept nose-to-nose with the severed head of a goat. Its dumb eyes had been staring at me all night. Was this some sort of grisly revenge for refusing the rest of him, I wondered?

After downing cups of sweet tea under the stars and exchanging the most cursory of goodbyes with Bilal, we set off, stumbling our way back down the riverbed, sending rocks crashing around our feet. We made good progress, crossing the now peaceful fire-zone within two hours, listening to the percussive popping noise of the flares sent up from the post.

What a wonderful feeling it was to be heading in the right direction at last. We found new strength in our weary legs as we marched back down the river. We made a precarious crossing one-by-one – this time in a basket suspended above the water that was controlled by a pulley system anchored in the rocks on the banks. By midday we were halfway up the long pass nearing the border and well on our way to our first, ice-cold Coca-Cola, followed by a beer and a burger in the American Club in Peshawar.

Before I set out on that trip to Kunar, I had been to the Harakat offices in Peshawar and left a message for Niazuldin, letting him know I was in town and that it would be great to see him. When I got back, I was handed a note to say that he was on his way. A few days later, there he was, the 'Lion of Kabul', climbing out of a jeep at the Afghanaid house, large as life, laughing and joking and almost crushing the life out of me with one of his bear hugs.

Looking a little older, a little heavier, his long jet-black locks a little shorter, he was still Mr Charisma himself – everything that I remembered and had missed in Bilal.

'*Salaam alaikum*, RedWhite,' he intoned in his deep, sonorous voice.

He came with two of his men and we greeted each other like the old friends we were. I was delighted to see the man I thought of as 'my commander' and we spent two hours talking through what had happened over the last two years.

I was saddened to hear that twelve people in the group had been killed since I left – 'martyred', as Niazuldin put it. They included Asil, who looked after me on the way in and out of Kabul, and Zulmai, who had been ambushed on the streets outside his home one night about six months after I left. The news about Zulmai winded me. Had he been shot as a direct result of harbouring me, I wondered? Or was it the almost inevitable result of the double life he was leading? I knew that the latter explanation was almost certainly the right one – the realistic one – but the alternative thought planted itself indelibly in my subconscious.

It was clear that for Niazuldin, Zulmai's death was a hammer blow. 'He was my friend,' he said of his cousin, smiling at the thought of him. 'It's always difficult when you lose someone from your family with whom you have lived, fought and shared life together.'

Listening to him and mulling over what he was saying I

began to feel that familiar heating sensation in my head, and my eyes and gums began to ache. Once again I felt as though I was succumbing to some sort of fever, the way I had after my last trip during those lost months in America. Perhaps it was a recurrence of the malaria. But I hid my discomfort. I didn't tell Niazuldin about the waking nightmares I had been having about Abdullah's death or that seeing Niazuldin himself was making me feel ill. I felt I needed to put on a good show for him.

Niazuldin talked about the war. He said he was still fighting and the Soviets, afraid of the new Stinger anti-aircraft missiles supplied to the resistance by the CIA, were no longer using helicopters to such devastating effect. He was losing more men to mines, with thirteen wounded in addition to the twelve he had lost. The route I had taken into Kabul, he told me, was now impossible with much of the open ground in front of the guard posts heavily mined. Two years ago they had been able to infiltrate the city twice a week. Now they were lucky to get in twice a month.

Niazuldin went on at length about his need for more weapons but he was also looking forward to an eventual victory. He talked of his dream of seeing Afghanistan ruled by 'a good Muslim' who would allow him to return to his house in Kabul, with his wife and three young sons, and relax in his garden. And, he said, he wanted to come to Britain – could I sort out a flight and we could spend some time in London seeing the sights?

After two hours it was time for him to go. I had enjoyed being with him, even if the experience left me exhausted. I had no explaining to do in his company. Niazuldin knew what I had been through. We hugged each other and shook hands and he climbed into his nice new jeep. As his driver prepared to leave, he called the interpreter over. There was something else he wanted to tell me.

'We are the same old tigers as we always were,' he grinned.

'We will always make ourselves kill the unbeliever. Don't think that the Mujahidin will ever give up.'

And with that, he was gone.

14

CHOWNI

After my visit to Kunar with Colin, I continued to build my relationship with *The Times,* which had published a short news story on that trip. I based myself in Peshawar and made a precarious living reporting for the paper on what turned out to be the final years of the Soviet war and occasionally made forays back into Afghanistan.

I went into Paktia province a couple of times, once in the depths of winter in the snow, and I re-visited Teri Mingal, just after yet another bombing raid. I had no plans to go further than the village – I knew what was beyond it, after all. On that visit I met two Palestinian fighters who had come to help the cause, one from the West Bank, the other from Gaza. 'I will stay here,' said twenty-two-year-old Ali, wrapped up in his Palestinian scarf against the cold, 'until the victory of Islam or I am martyred.'

But much of the time I lived off the steady stream of information about distant battles and political manoeuvring among the resistance groups that I picked up in Peshawar. Alongside the news I looked for feature material and managed to interest the paper in a story examining the psychological impact that the war was having on generations of Afghans, an idea prompted – perhaps – by my own experiences.

I visited Dr Mohammad Azam Dadfar at the Psychiatry Centre for Afghans, based in University Road. A former lecturer in psychiatry at Kabul University and a victim of torture himself, Dr Dadfar had set up his clinic to try to help the tens of thousands of his countrymen struggling with combat neurosis, survival guilt or the mental scars associated with debilitating injury. But he was overwhelmed by the sheer number of patients who presented.

Among the cases we discussed was that of a seven-year-old girl called Saira from Kunduz in northern Afghanistan. She had been brought to see him nine months earlier just after her family had completed a disastrous journey on foot to exile in Pakistan. On the way they were caught in an air raid at the Hajigak Pass in central Afghanistan. Saira's grandfather, mother and one-year-old sister were killed in the attack and the little girl had not spoken since. 'She displays doubtful emotional reactions towards friendly contact,' the doctor had written in her case notes. 'She avoids looking other people in the eye and shows anxiety. She has chosen mutism.'

'When we started, we just wanted to establish a rehabilitation centre for victims of torture,' explained Dr Dadfar, 'but I found it was difficult to restrict it because we found a rush of patients with other psychological disorders. Everybody manifests some minor psychological problem and we have thousands of cases that we can't treat. I feel guilty sometimes because, even when we can help, often what we offer is not effective – we only have time to give tranquillisers and this is not a cure.'

It never occurred to me that perhaps I should consider signing up for treatment with someone like Dr Dadfar. I had had my difficulties but I seemed to be coping and this was just another aspect of the war and the suffering of the Afghan people that I wanted to cover in the pages of *The Times*.

A few weeks after that interview, I went with the television news cameraman Peter Jouvenal into Paktia province to visit a Soviet base that had just been abandoned. It was May

1988, just nine months before the final deadline for the Soviet withdrawal from Afghanistan under the timetable that had been agreed at the UN in Geneva following six years of negotiations. An eccentric Englishman from Henley-on-Thames, Jouvenal was regarded as the doyen of the Peshawar-based Afghan media corps. He had been going inside with the Mujahidin for years and had captured some of the best combat footage of the war.

Peter had started life in the army, where he had been trained to use a TV camera. One of his great stories was of the time he was lifted on a crane over the walls of the H-Blocks of the Maze prison in Northern Ireland during protests by the IRA, the better to film what was going on inside for the benefit of army commanders. He turned his expertise into a stellar career as a combat cameraman. Like me, he loved Afghanistan, and it was there that he did most of his best work.

Peter and I got on like a house on fire and when we travelled together to the Soviet base at Chowni he had already completed more than fifty trips with various Mujahidin groups. His fiftieth expedition consisted of him driving all the way to the border, stepping across it for a few minutes, and then returning like a batsman who had scored a century to the 'pavilion' at Peshawar to celebrate in the American Club.

Peter is profoundly dyslexic and he and I were constantly joshing each other over his spelling. When we heard about the pullout from the base at Chowni, we scrambled to get there using all his contacts and we hoped to be the first in. But as we picked our way through the minefield guarding its approaches we saw our colleague Rory Peck, who was working for NBC News, coming the other way with his TV camera on his shoulder.

We got to the base forty-eight hours after Soviet and Afghan troops had abandoned it and there was an unmistakable sense of victory in the air. The guerrillas were swarming all over the huge fortified area, jumping around in gas masks and Soviet helmets, collecting ammunition and cigarettes, sitting at the wheels of jeeps and armoured cars and, like children, making engine noises, or lounging on deck chairs and beds that only two days before had been slept on by their enemy.

Perhaps the single most striking thing about Chowni was the sheer size of the base and the adjoining area of country guarded by its satellite or forward posts. The Kabul government had said it was withdrawing from minor exposed positions but Chowni, about twenty miles from the frontier, ranked by any standards as a key garrison. It took two and a half hours to walk the length of the valley occupied by the fortifications. The Mujahidin estimated that 4,000 Afghan and some 100 Soviet troops were based there and that seemed, if anything, on the low side.

It was a measure of the newfound strength and confidence of the resistance in Paktia that we were able to take a jeep from the border almost all the way to the edge of the base. From there we followed in single file through minefields that the guerrillas were in the process of clearing by hand and which, they said, had claimed three lives in the past two days. The forward positions were spread out at regular intervals on the hilltops along a main river valley that led down to the central area. On our way down we passed, with increasing regularity, abandoned artillery positions marked by huge piles of gleaming shell casings, houses converted into small barracks or command bunkers, and garage facilities cut out of the hillsides.

The base itself was spread out on a plateau about a mile long with the command position at one end, next to it a large helicopter landing area, then a series of barracks and officers' accommodations, numerous ammunition dumps, the camp hospital, a large mechanics shop and, finally, the cookhouse. All the buildings had either suffered serious structural damage or were peppered with shrapnel. The entire area was pockmarked with ground-to-ground rocket impacts fired by the Mujahidin from the hills. The decision to evacuate Chowni must have been taken at very short notice because all the ammunition dumps were left stacked high and intact and there were probably thirty vehicles, including two tanks and several field pieces, left abandoned. In the mechanics' shop, armoured cars had been left jacked-up waiting for new wheels, and at the bakery the shelves were crammed with loaves.

You could tell where the Soviet officers had lived because the accommodation was smarter. I found bottles of Stolichnaya vodka, abandoned pet dogs, one of which had been shot, discarded packets of Russian cigarettes and walls covered in pictures of Russian women. In one house there was even a sauna made out of wood from ammunition boxes. There were also piles of books, mostly political works, including an English-language pamphlet on socialism, advertising on its cover articles entitled 'A world without war: how to achieve this' and 'Can an army replace a revolutionary vanguard?' Chowni had been left in disarray and even an attempt by the regime to bomb it the day before our arrival had largely failed. Kabul's loss had been a big gain for the Mujahidin, who were benefiting from the tons of ammunition left behind and the advantage of being able to launch operations inland.

'We are very happy because this place was important for the Russians,' explained a Mujahidin commander to me. 'We want to make it a very big Mujahidin camp and we will go from here to the fronts in Logar, Gardez and Kabul.' And in his moment of victory, he added with a grin: 'Perhaps we will even go from here to Tadjikistan and Uzbekistan.'

In my despatch from Chowni, I wrote of a macabre find:

The last soldier to die defending this huge combined Afghan and Soviet army base, set on a dusty plateau below

the wooded hills of Paktia, was a young Afghan tank commander. He now lies in a shallow grave about twenty-five
yards from where his T55 tank broke down in the early
hours of Sunday morning. The Mujahidin guerrillas here
claim that they shot him as he ran down the road, trying
to catch up with the rest of the convoy as it moved on its
way to the main base at Gardez, thirty miles to the south.

He would have been one of the first to benefit from the
Soviet decision to pull out of Afghanistan and the Kabul
regime's new strategy of withdrawing from exposed bases
in border areas, like this one, to concentrate on holding
the big cities. But now he is dead and the Mujahidin – in
their high spirits – have taken to digging him up, calling
him names, and hitting him over the head with a spade. It
seems likely that this young man, dressed in the uniform
of a lieutenant, died heroically. A brief inspection of his
tank shows that it is now useless. A journalist colleague,
well-versed in such matters, believes that he disconnected
the hydraulic system supporting the barrel and then fired
a single shell, sending the barrel crashing back into the
turret – a process that disabled the tank's main weapon
and would have taken just enough time to cost him his life.

The blatant disrespect for his body may seem barbaric,
but for the Mujahidin it was an expression of victory at
Chowni, and perhaps a way of avenging the thousands
who have died over the years attacking the base.

It was Peter's technical knowledge of weaponry that helped
me to trace what had happened to that unfortunate Afghan
soldier whose body was being abused by the jubilant guerrillas. A picture of Jouvenal and I with five of our companions on that trip shows us smiling at the camera, dressed in
shalwar kameez, and with all but one of us wearing either
Soviet tank headgear or Soviet army helmets. In addition to
my notebook, I am carrying a blue hardback book with a

bust of Lenin embossed in gold on the front that I found in one of the barrack rooms at the base. It is a collection of Lenin's works in Arabic that has two bullet holes in it. A round had travelled through the front cover and then every page before exiting through the back cover.

Compared with my experience of the summer of 1985, this was almost the perfect trip. We were in and out in a day, we got a great story and I was working alongside the best in the business. No time for reflection on this one.

Yet when I got back to Peshawar I immediately got sick again. My mystery fever had returned and I was debilitated by an illness that I continued to believe to be malaria. Two weeks after the visit to Chowni I noted in my dairy: 'Whatever it was there was no possibility of work. But it dragged on and coincided with too much drinking, dope-smoking and cigarettes.'

Later, in the States, on a brief holiday from Peshawar with a new girlfriend, I reached a crisis one day and she took me to the casualty department of a hospital in Texas. I felt scared, I couldn't think clearly and my head felt like it was on fire. Having first seen my credit card to ensure that I could pay for his expertise, the young duty doctor decided I was suffering from 'Acute Nervous Exhaustion'. He told me to rest (which was what I was trying to do anyway).

◆◆◆◆◆

Throughout the summer of 1988 I continued beavering away for *The Times* in Peshawar and Islamabad until, in the autumn, I was offered a contract working in the newsroom in London. My determination to find a way into a full-time journalism job had paid off. I flew back to London but was there for just one month before the editor, Charlie Wilson, offered me what, at that stage in my career, was the posting of a lifetime – the chance to fill in for Michael Hamlyn, the paper's distinguished, mustachoied and white-suited Delhi correspondent, who was returning to London. I had South Asia to myself for six months, based in Hamlyn's elegant villa in south Delhi complete with a staff of twelve – among them cooks, *chowkidars* (guards), bearers (domestic staff), *dhobi wallers* (washing women) and a driver – and I had the time of my life.

I travelled widely around India. I covered wars in Sri Lanka – the Tamil Tiger rebellion in the north and the Communist insurgency in the south by the Marxist terror group, Janatha Vimukthi Peramuna. I travelled secretly into Burma from Thailand to visit the Karen rebels, an experience marked by all my old demons coming back, including aching gums and eyes and the usual fever. I covered a cyclone in Bangladesh, bouts of communal violence in Pakistan and an attempted coup in the Maldives that required me to stay in a five-star hotel for a week on an atoll that I had mostly to myself.

Being 'our man in Delhi', Afghanistan was also within my remit and I visited Peshawar several times to catch up on the latest news from the war. As 1988 came to a close the final pullout of the Soviet army from Afghanistan was drawing near and just before Christmas I got a call from *The Times* in London. It was Dennis Taylor, one of the last gentlemen foreign desk staffers in Fleet Street.

'Hello, Edward,' he intoned, as usual never in a rush, despite spending his entire professional life working to deadlines. 'After all your efforts with the resistance in Afghanistan, we wondered whether you would be interested in an opportunity to go and see the other side of the war and spend a few weeks with the Russians in Kabul?'

'What did you say?' I replied in disbelief.

'We and the BBC have been offered visas for a correspondent to travel to Kabul as a guest of the Soviet army and we naturally thought of you,' he replied.

'Well, yes, of course I would love to go but ...'

My first instinct was that I should probably decline this extraordinary offer. Surely the Russians must know about my escapades with the Mujahidin from all the articles I'd published? They could clap me in jail and throw away the key. 'No, that's nonsense,' I heard a voice in my head say. 'The Russians would never allow an official correspondent of a world-famous newspaper into Kabul and then put him in jail.' On the other hand, my ride around Kabul in 1985 must have really pissed them off ... I tried to put the thought out of my head. Perhaps this was another manifestation of *glasnost* – the Soviet army was finally going to allow reporting from both sides of this brutal war, even if there were only a few weeks left ...

'Dennis ... do you think it is wise to go there after all the work I have done with the Mujahidin? It just occurred to me that ...'

Taylor dismissed the notion that I might be placing myself in special danger. He reassured me. 'Things are changing fast,' he said. 'Gorbachev wants to get out and the Russians need some good publicity.'

I trusted his judgement and put my fears to the back of my mind as Taylor explained that I was to pick up my visa in Delhi. The plan was for me to remain in Kabul all the way up to the final withdrawal deadline on 15 February 1989, more than seven weeks away.

After the call my mind was racing. This was going to be a real challenge. How was I going to react when I was introduced to men who had inflicted such misery on so many Afghans? I felt nervous but I was fascinated at the prospect of meeting the Russians who up until now I had inevitably viewed as the enemy. I got my visa, and jumped on the first plane out of Delhi with a bag of my own clothes. On this trip there wasn't going to be any need for Chitrali hats or *shalwar kameez*.

Ghostly white, with too much hair and uncomfortable in my ill-fitting clothes, I am ready for my tour of Kabul on 13 August 1985.

Jeep trip: some of the worst photos of downtown Kabul ever taken – but then again, I was no ordinary tourist.

Downtown Kabul.

The aftermath: back in the camp on 23 August – exhausted, weakened by dysentery and wracked by fear.

At the Afghanaid house in University Town, Peshawar, after more than sixty days 'inside'. Niazuldin is alongside me.

An image taken in downtown Peshawar that appeared in a *Mail on Sunday* magazine article about young British freelancers chancing their arm in the Great Game of the 1980s. (John Gunston/*You Magazine*)

The last time I saw Niazuldin; he came to visit me in Peshawar in 1987 after my trip into Kunar with Colin Boyle. (Jana Schneider)

Dressed up in Soviet army headgear at the base in Chowni in May 1988, just after it had been relinquished by the Soviet army. I am standing in the middle holding notebooks. The figure on the right is the legendary British cameraman Peter Jouvenal.

Looking haunted … in the year before diagnosis.

Visiting Soviet troops on the outskirts of Kabul in the
run-up to the final Soviet withdrawal in February 1989. I am
in the bottom left of the picture. (Jana Schneider)

Interviewing President Najibullah at the palace in Kabul. 'Sure, I'm confident,' he told me – but he would end up being castrated and hung.

Russian reporter Misha Kozhukov. 'All the truth about this war will never be written,' he told me. (*The Times*)

Downtown Kabul ravaged by civil war during my final visit in April 1994.
It looked more like Dresden after Allied bombing than the Afghan capital.

Off work and non-functional. I spent much of my
time with my noble black retriever Blue.

Sailing on *Nutcracker* was always a form of solace. (Daniel Green)

Jeanna: I fell in love with her from the moment I first saw her.

15

SPECIAL CORRESPONDENT

When you found yourself somewhere that all your competitors in other papers would like to be and you had the story to yourself, *The Times* had a charming tradition of billing you as 'Our Special Correspondent'. It only happened to me once and that was when I got to Kabul at Christmas in 1988, ahead of the deadline for the Soviet army withdrawal. The deal was that the Russian-led force would complete its pullout by 15 February, marking the conclusion of a disastrous ten-year occupation that had cost between one and two million Afghan lives, with millions more injured or condemned to the misery of exile in Pakistan and Iran.

Deadlines drawn up by diplomats act as perfect news targets and, as this one drew closer, the speculation about what might happen grew ever more intense. Would the 'puppet' regime of President Najibullah – the feared former head of the KHAD, the KGB-trained Afghan secret police – survive for more than a few days? Was Kabul about to descend into a bloody reckoning as the Mujahidin came down from the mountains to purge their countrymen in the Afghan army who had fought alongside the enemy? Was this going to be a bloodbath and a humiliation for Moscow, as the West fervently hoped? Would Najibullah himself end up like Mussolini swinging from a lamppost? There were comparisons being made with the undignified final exit of the

Americans from South Vietnam as the last few diplomats and soldiers were lifted off in helicopters from their compound in Saigon, kicking away their former allies who were trying desperately to escape with them.

I flew in on Christmas Eve. As we approached Kabul the plane began an unnerving corkscrew descent right on top of the airport, turning such tight angles as it spiralled towards the ground that you felt the wings would be ripped off. The reason for this bizarre and frightening approach was to avoid a long, slow and low trajectory over the snow-capped outlying hills, which would leave the plane vulnerable to Mujahidin fighters armed with anti-aircraft missiles. Although I couldn't see it, our jet was also firing bright chaff or flares in a probably futile attempt to draw incoming missiles away from its fuselage.

Safely on the ground I made my way, once again, into a city at war, past long lines of visa-hunting Afghans queuing outside the Indian embassy, and checked into the Hotel Inter-Continental, the very place where Niazuldin had so often joked I should stop for tea during my earlier whirlwind tour of the city. My room commanded panoramic views across the brown low-rise capital and to the majestic mountains beyond, where I had spent so much time with the Mujahidin. The only other Western journalist in the place was Lyse Doucet of the BBC, the brave and highly respected Canadian-born radio reporter who was just beginning to make a name for herself. Only *The Times* and the BBC had been offered visas at that stage so Lyse and I had the place to ourselves.

I stood at the window of my room looking out over Kabul, trying to spot landmarks that I had seen four years earlier during my impudent jeep tour. Had I travelled down that road? Was that one of the roundabouts we circled at breakneck speed? Where was Zulmai's house? Which were the suburbs we had walked through on our way in and out? The wire sound detectors, the searchlights ... Then I was risking imprisonment, execution as a spy and an imposter by being in Kabul; this time I was an invited guest of the enemies of my friends.

Beyond the densely packed centre of the city with its busy markets and suburbs crawling up the sides of the hills, I looked again to the mountains on the skyline. Up there in the snow I imagined the Muj sitting around their camp fires cleaning their weapons, praying, chatting and eagerly awaiting the end of a ten-year struggle for national liberation. I thought of Niazuldin, of Abdullah-Jan and Fazil-Jan, and of how impenetrable Kabul had seemed from those mountains. Now I was right in the heart of it.

Being in Kabul in those days was a special privilege. Everything you did, everyone you spoke to, every story about the war took on added poignancy and urgency. These were the dying days of a failed superpower adventure and the city offered unlimited scope to cover the mood of subdued panic, the sense that things would never be the same again and that something awful lay around the corner. There was a buzz about it that gave a heightened sense of reality to everyone's lives. And a jobbing news reporter could hardly ask for a better canvas on which to paint. Everyone from street traders to Russian generals, to nervous diplomats eyeing their escape route, was in the same boat and had something to say.

As I set about my reporting task as a guest of the Soviet occupiers, I decided not to broadcast my past. I wasn't sure if any of my Afghan government minders, or the Soviet or Afghan army officers I met, knew what I had got up to in my previous life and I was frankly too nervous of the possible consequences to tell them.

But there was one exception with whom I did share my secret and that was a Russian journalist I came across in those final weeks and with whom I knew, within seconds of meeting him, that I had something in common. Mikhail Kozhukhov had been covering the war from the other side for many of the years that I had been working from Pesha-war. He had been with the equivalent of the Americans while I had been with the equivalent of the Viet Cong and, if I thought I had paid a high price for my adventures, I could quite clearly see that Misha had paid an even higher one.

It's an old cliché to talk about the thousand-mile stare. With Misha, it was not so much a stare as a sense of horror in his bloodshot eyes. He spoke only vaguely about what he had seen but I had no doubt that he knew things and had experienced things that had changed him forever. He seemed old for his thirty-two years and smoked one cigarette after another as he recalled three and a half years on the Afghan beat for the organ of the Communist Youth League, *Komsomolskaya Pravda,* which had a circulation of 18 million.

We were introduced one evening by an official Russian interpreter. Misha was sporting a thick moustache. An unlit cigarette hung from his pursed lips and on his head was a paratrooper's beret flattened to one side, a symbol perhaps of the blurred line he pursued between reporting and soldier-ing. Despite the language barrier, we hit it off immediately, drawn together like brothers who had seen two sides of the same war through opposing prisms. I had written unselfcon-sciously of the Mujahidin as freedom fighters, whereas he had been required – or did see them – as bandits and terror-ists. I had seen the Soviet presence as the result of a hostile invasion whereas he had viewed it through the perspective of Communism's drive to spread its doctrine. Like him, Soviet army soldiers I came across would say they were not occu-pying or subjecting anyone in Afghanistan to their presence, but fulfilling what they termed their 'international duty'. They were responding to an invitation to enter the country by the Communist regime in Kabul.

I got the impression Misha had seen far more action than I had, travelling and working with an army that never got a grip on how to fight a counter-insurgency war, trying to make its occupation work in the dying years of its mission. He had gone regularly on operations with Soviet special forces or Spetsnaz. I remember thinking that, compared with him, I had seen and done almost nothing of consequence. He had been wounded twice, had spent months in military hospitals with typhoid and amoebic dysentery – something I had also experienced – and he had been recognised with the Order of the Red Star for his eyewitness reports of combat.

'All the truth about this war will never be written or told,' he told me in English over a beer at a Soviet army base.

'Well, you can tell me, Misha,' I said flippantly.

'There are some things I know that I will not even tell my son, let alone a foreign journalist,' he growled. 'I consider war is so bad that those people who are lucky enough not to have seen it must not know the details.'

Even then Misha seemed to understand the price he had paid for his work in Afghanistan, far more clearly than I did about myself. He quoted the Russian writer Andrei Platonov: 'Battle is life at high speed – war itself is like this,' he said. 'It has made me older.'

I told him of my adventures with the Mujahidin – not that he accepted that term – and he was fascinated to hear about the war from the other side. But he accused me and my Western colleagues of 'not being absolutely sincere and honest' in our reporting.

'Come on, Misha,' I goaded him, 'you don't really believe all that crap about coming here to do your international duty?'

'Maybe I was not objective too,' he admitted. 'We were on different sides of the same war.' He said that soldiers had often pleaded with him to 'write the truth' in his reports. 'They mean that we didn't describe their feelings and events correctly,' he said, 'that we tried to make things sound better than they were.'

I had seen pictures of appalling carnage inflicted by

Soviet soldiers and helicopter gunships on Afghan villagers in retaliatory attacks for harbouring guerrillas. I'd been
shown images of piles of dismembered bodies stacked up in
the backs of trailers being towed behind tractors for burial.
I had also heard stories of Russian soldiers captured by
the rebels being skinned alive and left to die in the roaring
midday sun. And when I had been with the Mujahidin in the
mountains south of Kabul, I had fretted about an operation
against us by the kind of men Misha had spent time with:
highly trained and ruthless special forces soldiers dropped
by helicopter some miles from their target who crept up on
rebel camps at night and, silently at first, killed everyone in
them. It was simply fascinating for me to hear about those
men from someone who had worked with them.

'When I got in a helicopter with the paratroopers or a
Spetsnaz team and I had no idea what would happen in the
next five or ten minutes, I was always surprised by the faces
of the soldiers,' Misha told me. 'They were absolutely calm.
They would always prefer to say they "worked" in Nangarhar or Paktia, rather than they took part in combat.'

We talked and drank long into the night, chewing over
experiences that both set us apart and brought us together,
and exploring our competing versions of the truth. Misha
went on to become a popular television personality in
Moscow after the war, presenting his own travel show, and
was briefly a spokesman for Vladimir Putin, when he was
prime minister. He also wrote an account of his experiences
in Afghanistan entitled: 'Alien Stars Over Kabul'. My report
in the paper on Misha appeared under the headline: 'Soviet
reporter changed by hell of Afghan war.'

I got out and about in the city on those crisp, cold winter
days. I interviewed the Russian general in charge of the withdrawal and went to see families burying their dead after the
nightly incoming rocket attacks from the hills. In the little
hillside suburb of Bibi Mahro, I attended the funerals of

fourteen-year-old Rahimullah and eighteen-year-old Farza-
nah, both killed by rockets fired at the city by the Mujahidin.
Rahimullah had been sitting with friends in the graveyard
where he was now being interred when the missile came
scything through the air. A piece of shrapnel tore through
his neck, inflicting wounds from which he died in hospital a
few hours later.

Among the relatives standing in the rain that day was
Nasir Afzaly, whose smart grey suit and white mackintosh
marked him out as someone who had thrown in his lot with
the regime. His anger and disgust at the men whom I had got
to know in the mountains was visceral.

'Those people who are against our government did this.
I am sure they will achieve nothing – they will get nothing,'
he fumed. 'They have no target, they just want to continue
the killing. They are like animals. If they had any feeling for
human life, they would not do this.'

I had Niazuldin, Fazil-Jan and Abdul Haq and their men
in mind when I wrote up my account of the funeral in the
next day's paper. 'One wonders what the young Mujahidin
fighters who launched the rocket from the Logar hills to the
south of the city would have thought if they could have seen
the results,' I wrote. 'Rahimullah's death highlights perhaps
their biggest dilemma in the coming months: how not to kill
hundreds, perhaps thousands of "innocent" civilians as they
step up attacks on the main regime-held cities after the Soviet
withdrawal.'

I visited Soviet soldiers in their outposts, nervously ticking
off the days to the moment when it was their turn to head
north to safety and their families. I found I enjoyed being with
the regime. I was always busy – there was a hot news agenda
in play – and it was safer, more structured and more familiar than the challenge of life with the Mujahidin. I slept in a
comfortable bed, was served hot meals and drinks, and could
phone the paper whenever I needed to. The InterContinental

had access to one of the very few international phone lines out of Kabul and I made sure I could get on it whenever I needed to by bribing the hotel phone operator with $200 in cash, the equivalent of several months-worth of his regular salary.

On a place the Soviets called 'Hill 31' on the north-west perimeter of the city, any remaining preconceptions I had about who these soldiers were evaporated when I found a group of conscripts manning a post built around an old concrete water tank. Some had been there for a year dodging incoming but largely inaccurate Mujahidin rocket fire and responding with shells from a 122mm howitzer. They couldn't wait to get home. When I got there the place was alive with country music. The bored soldiers were listening to Willie Nelson as they stood around in the perishing cold. At that stage, before the collapse of the Soviet Union, this was quite an astonishing discovery. It just wasn't in the playbook in the late 1980s to think of Soviet army conscripts passing the time in Afghanistan listening to country and western music all the way from Nashville.

My host, a thirty-six-year-old chain-smoking lieutenant colonel named Viktor Astapushenko – who enjoyed quoting old army sayings such as 'War is war, but we must have lunch on time' – was realistic about what had been achieved by the occupation.

'We will not be eager to fight any other war after this one,' he said. 'It was complicated here and we had problems, but it did not come as a shock. We are realists and we understand the situation. We are against exporting revolution and against exporting counter-revolution.' He added: 'The Afghans must decide for themselves what they want; there must be a middle way in Afghanistan.'

One of his men, Vasily Savenok, a twenty-year-old radio operator from Minsk, brought a wry smile to my lips when he talked about the Mujahidin. 'I can imagine how they look,' he said, 'because I have seen a lot of films made by

Western television crews in Afghanistan. I believe most of them are fighting for money – we are not here for the money,' he added earnestly.

President Najibullah spent those desperate days holed up in his big palace in the centre of the city, secretly trying to calculate his odds of surviving after the Soviets had gone but talking up his chances in public. He did not miss the opportunity to do so when I asked for an interview. By then, of course, he was 'wide open' to compromise and was offering the Mujahidin leadership almost any concessions he could think of in return for a quiet transition after the occupation.

The Ox, as he was known, was a large man in a big black suit with an invasive case of halitosis. There was something absolutely dreadful about him as he sat at his desk in front of one of the only other telephones in Afghanistan connected to the outside world, trying to sound civilised. But I had heard stories of his personal enjoyment in torturing his political opponents and I knew how much he was hated by so many of his ordinary fellow Afghans. Men like Niazuldin would have castrated him alive given half the chance, so it was hard to believe I was sitting opposite him in his lair – deep in the heart of the heavily guarded Presidential Palace – listening to him talk of a future that he did not deserve and of the odd 'vagabond' who might interrupt it.

I asked whether he would consider stepping down – a key precondition of resistance leaders before serious talks could take place about the future.

'As for myself, as President of the Republic,' he replied, 'I have been elected by the *Loya Jirga* [Grand Assembly] and by the will and determination of the deputies. The question of the stepping aside of this or that personality or political group is not for discussion.'

Failing that, was he prepared to hold direct talks with representatives of the Mujahidin, in the unlikely event that any of them would consent to enter the same room as him?

'We are ready to hold talks with all groups who are interested in ensuring peace in the country,' he said. 'It makes no difference whether they are moderates, representatives of the Afghan refugees, supporters of Zahir Shah [the exiled King] or extremists, so long as they are interested in peace. Victory will be with this position.'

'Do you feel confident about your own future?' I asked him at the end of our encounter.

The old Ox seemed remarkably sure-footed: 'I draw strength from the reality of my society, and from the demands of my people,' he said, before breaking into English. 'Sure,' he added with a smile. 'I'm confident.'

In fact the Ox would go on, as one Western diplomat put it later, to play a weak hand 'really rather well'. But in the end the bankruptcy of his position, plus his fatal decision many years earlier to choose dialectical materialism over Islamic fundamentalism, would catch up with him. When I heard he had been castrated and then hanged in Kabul in September 1996, I mainly remembered the halitosis.

⟡

Everyone who could was leaving the city. The fear of what might happen once the last Soviet soldiers headed up the Salang Highway was corrosive. Most ordinary Afghans had no exit strategy and the ones who had thrown in their lot with Najibullah and his cronies were close to panic. As the deadline approached, even the last remaining Western diplomats were being pulled out. I had got to know the young British envoy who had been left in charge of the British embassy, one Clovis Meath Baker. We met regularly to compare notes on what was happening, whether we thought the rump regime could stand on its own feet without Moscow's military support, and the more prosaic details about what flights were available and to where. In the end, and much to his irritation, Meath Baker was ordered out by London. In a formal letter on headed embassy notepaper, and addressing me by my surname alone, he informed me, in his capacity as chargé d'affaires, that it was time for me to get going too.

British Embassy,
Kabul
Tel: 30511

Dear Gorman,

I must advise you that you should leave Afghanistan without delay while normal flights are still available.

It is entirely your responsibility to decide whether or not to act on this advice, but I must make it clear that this is a final warning and there is no question of any subsequent evacuation by the British Government. If the Embassy is obliged to close there will be no British Consular protection once the Embassy staff have left the country. If you should decide to stay, please inform the Embassy immediately.

W.J.C. Meath Baker
Chargé d'Affaires
Kabul 19th January, 1989

I ignored Clovis's advice to leave and phoned the embassy as instructed. I have kept that letter and framed it as a reminder of those days waiting to see what would happen in the cockpit of the Great Game in the closing years of the twentieth century.

Like soldiers in any army coming to the end of a war, Soviet troops had grown excessively nervous and superstitious about the final days of a conflict that had cost them some 14,500 dead and more than 50,000 injured. The war had delivered a blow to Soviet pride from which the-then superpower was never to recover. I had arrived in the city prepared to dislike the occupiers. I had spent good portions of the previous four years reporting on the destruction and misery they had wrought on Afghans from all walks of life and part of me felt it was a betrayal of those people to now look at the endgame of that struggle through the eyes of their persecutors.

But as I got to know them, especially the serious-minded young Russian men who were detailed to act as my translators, I couldn't help but warm to them. In most respects they were far closer culturally to the British than were the Afghans. We could laugh at the same jokes, we could drink together, talk about women together, eat familiar food together, all of which were areas of dissonance with my Afghan hosts. It still felt uncomfortable, though, and it felt like I was looking at the world back-to-front as I peered out from a Soviet guard post trying to figure out what the Mujahidin were going to do next, imagining them praying, eating their meagre rations, preparing for battle and fearing the consequences.

The Russian who made the biggest impression on me was one of the last I met before *The Times* pulled me out of Kabul two weeks before the 15 February deadline – Colonel Aleksander Golovanov who was in charge of the main air base in Kabul. (For reasons that were connected to a dispute between the paper and the Soviet authorities over the appointment of a new correspondent in Moscow, I was unexpectedly sent to Moscow and then to Tajikistan. I was tasked with covering the aftermath of an earthquake and landslip that had buried two Tajik villages in their entirety with the loss of all the inhabitants. This was seen as a way for *The Times* to show a bit of heart when it came to the Soviets. At the time I was irritated to have to leave Kabul but the diversion would pay dividends.)

Apart from the general commanding the capital, Colonel Golovanov was the most senior Russian officer I interviewed in Kabul. Having been attacked by them in the mountains years earlier, and having grown to hate the sight and sound of them, I was especially curious to see the Mi-24 Hind helicopter gunships up close, and I was curious to meet the man who ordered those gunships out on their killing missions.

I badgered my Russian contacts until one day I found myself being driven past the sentries and along the muddy track towards the helicopters and the giant Ilyushin transport aircraft on the apron of the military headquarters at Kabul airfield. Colonel Golovanov of the 103 Guards, Airborne Division, was organising the final elements of a hugely complex logistics operation as the Soviet army and its air assets packed up and headed for home.

The colonel could not have been more charming. Getting up from beneath a portrait of Lenin in his jerry-built office – which was surrounded by sandbags to protect him against the threat of incoming rockets – he warmly shook my hand. He spoke about what he considered to be the success of the mission, the reasons for the withdrawal – according to him they were political not military – and his respect for the fighting qualities of the Mujahidin. But the part of the interview that struck a nerve was what he said about his wife and his superstitions about leaving. Here was a leader of men in battle who had no qualms about admitting that he was nervous about the odds of being killed in the dying days of the Soviet occupation.

He was not at all bashful about his love for his wife, Antonina, a teacher who was waiting anxiously for his safe return at their home in Kaliningrad. It was a proper love story. When I asked him about her, Colonel Golovanov pulled out a bundle of more than seventy letters his wife had sent him and laid them on the desk.

'In all these letters there are words that show how worried

she is: it is usual for any woman to be like this. Of course I miss my wife,' he said through an army-supplied translator.

I asked him if he had any regrets about the mission he had overseen, one that had inflicted countless deaths and widespread destruction on a peasant society that would take generations to recover.

The colonel's response would have stuck in the craw of many an ordinary Afghan who had seen first-hand the work of Moscow's gunships. 'We came here at the request of the Afghan government,' he said. 'We never wanted to change the Afghan way of life; we just wanted to help the people to build a new life. I believe that everyone will remember us because everything we have done was from the heart; whatever happens they will remember.'

Then we talked about leaving Afghanistan and turning the lights off. Colonel Golovanov did not tell me that he planned to be on one of the last helicopters to leave. I assumed he would go in a transport aircraft. He explained that none of his fellow soldiers and airmen would ever talk of the 'last time' they were home in the Soviet Union, lest they were tempting fate.

'We are always ready to go home,' he said. 'We don't have any special celebrations planned, but everyone knows the withdrawal will end soon; the time has come. When we receive our orders we will board our aircraft and leave for home.'

I had a good story. I filed it with the paper and thought little more about the charming colonel at the airbase. When it was my turn to leave I packed my bags and headed down to the market in the centre of town to change my dollars into the local Afghani currency. The hotel would only accept cash and inflation was raging out of control, Weimar Republic-style. I returned to the hotel with carrier bags full of well-thumbed Afghani notes. By the time I had piled them up in front of the cashier I could no longer see him behind a wall of money. I was getting late for my Aeroflot flight to Moscow and when he said, 'First I have to count it,' I headed for the door.

After a weekend suffering severe food poisoning in a Moscow hotel, I travelled down to Tajikistan and duly reported the horrors of the earthquake and subsequent landslide that had swallowed the village of Shorora. It was then that I realised I had the perfect opportunity to see the formal end of the Soviet war that had occupied so much of my time and had made an indelible impact on my life. I got on the phone to London and received approval from the desk to make my way to Termez, a depressing, end-of-railway-line dump of a place in neighbouring Uzbekistan. It was there that the last convoys of Soviet troops were making their way across the Oxus River Bridge.

Waiting for them on the Soviet side I spoke to thickset mothers, who understandably cared little for Afghanistan's future but had come to welcome their sons with tears and hugs and loaves of bread with the word 'peace' baked into them. It was a moment in history and my report of the stage-managed final convoy that crossed into the Soviet Union on 6 February was published on the front page. That final admission of defeat by Moscow and those images of tanks crossing the bridge have come to be seen as among the first cracks in the Soviet edifice that would lead to the beginning of the collapse of the entire empire later that year, something that was far from clear at the time.

I was running out of energy then, the weeks of incessant reporting in Kabul having taken their toll, and I never properly wrote up the saddest part of my visit to Termez: what I found out about Colonel Golovanov. Milling around with other journalists there I started to hear rumours that the last man killed on the way up the mountainous Salang Highway was a brigade commander from Kabul who, it was said, had been determined to lead his men from the front.

The final exit by the last of Moscow's forces had been preceded by heavy Soviet air strikes on villages close to the highway, which the US State Department said had caused hundreds of casualties among Afghan civilians. Had Golovanov been involved in those attacks on civilians? I found it hard to imagine the gentle and caring man I had met opening fire on defenceless peasants.

But it had been a difficult extraction for the Soviets with the last armoured column forced to halt while snow and ice were cleared from the road and two soldiers had been killed in an avalanche. Gradually it became clear that it was indeed Colonel Golovanov who had gone missing. His helicopter was described as having 'disappeared', either shot down by a Mujahidin missile or perhaps Golovanov had lost his bearings in the snow and crashed.

Whatever happened, the colonel never got to see his beloved Antonina again and I have always wondered how she coped with the news that her husband had gone and, not only that, that he had probably been the last man to die in the Soviet Afghan war.

It was left to Mikhail Kozhukhov to write the final paragraph in *Komsomolskaya Pravda* of that disastrous adventure started by an ailing Leonid Brezhnev ten years earlier. The Soviet commander-in-chief, Lieutenant-General Boris Gromov, was the last Kremlin soldier to leave and he gave Kozhukhov his final scoop of the war. He wrote: 'On 15 February at 10 a.m. local time, Lieutenant-General Boris Gromov will be the last to cross the bridge. He will pass without looking back. Then he will stop and "deliver a speech", but just to himself. It will last one minute and seven seconds. It will not be written down or listened to.'

16

LIVING WITH THE GHOSTS
OF AFGHANISTAN

After my days in Kabul with the Russians and my visit to Termez, I imagined that my Afghan adventures were over – and for a few years they were. I came back to London, now on the staff of *The Times,* and within a few months was offered the post of Irish Affairs Correspondent. I had carved out a reputation for covering trouble spots so where better to send me than the biggest trouble spot on Britain's doorstep?

I was summoned by the editor, Charlie Wilson, to his office upstairs in the old wine warehouse where *The Times* was based at Wapping. It was a typically brief encounter. With a reputation as a Glasgow hard man, Charlie scared the wits out of me and, like most on the paper, I did whatever he told me to. The conversation went something like this. 'Would you like to become our correspondent in Ulster, laddie?' That may look like a question when written down, but it came across more as an order. I replied in the only way possible – 'yes'. And that, give or take a few details on practicalities, was about it.

That was a Friday in June 1989, and on the following Tuesday I was standing behind a police cordon in the centre of Belfast watching army technical officers deal with a 400lb IRA bomb. It was lunchtime and I was fighting the strange sensations that had dogged me since my time in the mountains in 1985. My eyes were stinging, my gums and teeth were aching and I felt stoned, finding it difficult to follow simple conversation. In those days, whatever it was that was eating away at me was back in full spate. I was waking up feeling more exhausted than when I went to bed and I was taking painkillers every day to deal with the sensation of heating and headaches. It was hardly the best way to start a four-and-a-half-year posting to Northern Ireland when the Troubles remained a wearying source of bad news.

During that time I covered every conceivable variation in Republican and Loyalist violence, assassinations, bombings, SAS hits on the IRA and the controversy over collusion between Loyalists and the RUC and army. Then there were the meandering details of attempts by successive Secretaries of State – Peter Brooke and Sir Patrick Mayhew – to broker some sort of settlement, early attempts at a popular peace movement, miscarriages of justice and the last hurrahs of Charles Haughey, the legendary and corrupt Fianna Fail leader in Dublin. Over the years I developed a sort of sixth sense for the pattern of violence and could more or less tell when it was time for each side to make a move. I discovered too how clever the Republican PR operation was in Belfast and, to this day, have yet to see anyone deliver a controversial message more effectively than Gerry Adams's team in the Falls Road.

I enjoyed much of the job and the chance to be part of a regular press corps but it was unrelentingly hard work and the demands from the office in London were heavy. Matters were made more difficult by having to compete against David McKitterick, the Belfast correspondent of the *Independent*, then in its heyday, who was in a class of his own. McKitterick knew the story inside out and wrote about it with an authority that no one could match. It was soul-destroying being called night after night by the news desk in London to be told, 'David McKitterick has got this or that, can you match?' Of course I couldn't and I admitted defeat from about week three. McKitterick himself was extremely nice about it and always helpful to newcomers like me.

I made the most of my brief to cover the whole island of Ireland. I bought a guide to the best Irish golf courses and picked story ideas near as many of the choicest ones as I could find. I climbed Croagh Patrick, the holy mountain in Co. Mayo, visited pony fairs in Connemara and reported from villages that had yet to get electricity. Even in the north I found occasional alternatives to the daily diet of misery with the odd ploughing competition. But those stories were very much the exception that proved the rule during the Troubles – the job was almost entirely about communal hatred and the battle between two competing ideas of nationality, something I found difficult to understand, having been brought up in the certainty of peaceful rural Warwickshire.

After six months living off Belfast's Malone Road in a flat rented by my predecessor, I bought my first house, a little cottage in the rolling hills of Co. Down. It was on its own at Killinchy, close to Strangford Lough, where I sailed a dinghy whenever I could get away from the demands of the office. I loved living out in the country and gained some peace of mind in my rural and sometimes lonely isolation. The landscape was beautiful and the people round about were friendly enough, but I never felt at home in Co. Down or anywhere else in Ulster. It seemed to me to be a land dripping in blood, the place names alone enough to conjure images of dreadful bombings and murders, and I found the Protestant and Loyalist culture entirely alien. I always had more in common with those who considered themselves Irish than I did with Unionists.

The years I spent in Ireland were dominated by the work – I regularly travelled abroad as one of the paper's foreign 'firemen' in addition to my duties in Ulster – but they were also years when I was carrying the physical and psychological baggage left over from Afghanistan and it influenced much of what I did. The everyday battles I was fighting became almost routine for me and I often wondered whether there was anything abnormal about me at all. Maybe all journalists responded to frontline news roles with night terrors, sweating, then waking up feeling shattered with a soaking pillow and mattress. Not only were there the daily painkillers I took in a futile attempt to clear my head, but I drank quite heavily and threw myself into activities and distractions that seemed a refuge from anything that I might associate with work. Sailing was bliss and I bought my first dog – a noble black retriever I named Blue after the farmer's dog in Ufton in my childhood – who accompanied me almost everywhere I went. And I got stuck in on the land around the house, planting roses and trees, building rough stone walls and buying more land from the local farmer, taming it and planting hedges.

Looking back, it seems to me that I was battling to try to find some peace of mind, to clear the storm that had exploded in my subconscious in Afghanistan during the summer of 1985. I was trying, on my own, to build a home, plant a garden, buy furniture, curtains, pictures, and look after a dog and then another one, a Field Spaniel called The Lord Chief Justice. The isolation I chose was deliberate: I wanted total peace, no noise and nothing unexpected. What I got was all of that but also a solitary existence that left me with little distraction from my demons.

There are hundreds of episodes and hundreds of ways of describing what was haunting me. One pattern that came and went was a manic slideshow for which I always had a front-row seat. The old circular cassette with the pictures loaded would flick through its menu of shudder-inducing imagery and I could do nothing to stop it except try to speed it up to get to the end and hope it would stop there and not go back to the beginning.

I would see images of Abdullah-Jan, his body in death, the burial, a moonlit night, then Abdullah again, his body twitching, then me out there as if seen from afar, then the terror of shellfire, the images accelerating as I tried to escape. I would shake my head to finish it. Helicopters were all bad and I could hear the sound, and sense the feel and the fear of explosions as if I was still on that hillside, waiting for a gunship to pick me out instead of Abdullah. I had a visceral mental picture in my mind of an explosion happening in front of, inside me, all around me, that I could conjure at any moment – an intrusive destructive and destabilising force that I could not stop invading my subconscious and conscious mind.

It is a difficult balance to describe because the real me that was being choked by these demons is a gregarious and happy individual and (perhaps) few of the people I knew in those days will recognise the inner torment I describe here. There were long periods when I was able to handle the pressures with ease but there were also plenty of indicators that something was wrong.

In the early days of Ulster, I visited my eldest sister Jane and her family at their charmingly chaotic home near Hay-on-Wye in Herefordshire. I had driven down from Scotland, after taking the ferry from Larne to Stranraer, and had been planning to return in a couple of days via one or two golfing stops in the Borders. Then the phone rang in Jane's kitchen. Was Ed there by any chance? It was the foreign desk asking whether I was free to return to Afghanistan. They wanted me to go the next day. I cannot recall the news event that prompted the call but the assignment involved heading back into Kabul, probably via Pakistan.

Almost as soon as I put the phone down, the heating began, pulsing through my body. I started to feel I was losing focus, losing the ability to think clearly, my mind in flight mode as I contemplated what lay ahead. Irrelevant or unimportant details preoccupied me and prevented me from thinking fluently and keeping up. I assumed I was experiencing another of my recurring bouts of malaria and was infuriated that *that* disease had returned just at the wrong time. How was I going to explain it to my editors? They would think I was hopeless.

Motivated by the drive to succeed that had accompanied me from childhood, I decided to complete this new task whatever the consequences. I packed and headed down to London but by the time I made it to Heathrow I was in no state to fly. I called the office and explained that I had a fever – which was true – and that I believed I was experiencing a bout of malaria. It was just a cruel coincidence, I added, because there was nothing I would rather do than go back to Afghanistan. In my conscious mind I genuinely believed that to be true. We agreed that I would not fly and instead I checked into the Post House Hotel at Heathrow. Maybe I would be feeling better the following day. But the next day I felt worse and I never got on the plane. Someone else went to Kabul and I headed back to my day job in Co. Down.

That episode was the beginning of a pattern. Confronted with extreme challenges, stressful environments, a return to a war zone, my mind would go into meltdown. There were good reasons why no one else spotted what was going on. For a start I never talked about Afghanistan because I was engaged almost full-time in trying to avoid thinking about it. I rarely admitted to having episodes of collapse because I was terrified that I might lose my standing at the paper. And when necessary, I had a reasonable explanation with the malaria narrative – although I now suspected something else was going on, something connected with stress.

By my second year in Ulster I was travelling abroad quite regularly. I accompanied the Defence Secretary Tom King on a pre-first Gulf War trip to the region in August 1990. Then during the build-up to the war and after the fighting started, I spent more than a month based in the Jordanian capital

Amman, where I endured King Hussein's interminable press conferences and made regular trips to the Iraqi border to interview refugees coming out of Baghdad and elsewhere.

Later that year I went to Iran with Lynda Chalker, the Overseas Development Minister. I caused a minor diplomatic embarrassment on that trip by abandoning her official helicopter at the Iran–Iraq border and jumping across the fence, the better to report on the misery of Kurdish refugees who had escaped their homes on the plains, fearing that Saddam Hussein was about to attack them. The reckless instinct that had got me into trouble in Afghanistan seven years earlier was back in play. In the few moments that I had to make a decision whether to get back on the Iranian air force Chinook or not, I forgot my passport and everything else that I needed. But I managed to get away with it and then spent several weeks reporting on the Western intervention in northern Iraq to protect the Kurds. I enjoyed myself in Kurdistan, taking US army helicopter rides in and out of Iraq, persuading a terrified Kurdish taxi driver to take me into the abandoned Kurdish city of Dahuk, and reporting on American and British troops deployed on Operation Provide Comfort, which imposed a safe zone on the ground and in the air over northern Iraq.

It had been going well; I was getting tons of copy in the paper until one morning somewhere in eastern Turkey I woke up and knew immediately that the assignment was over. I was no longer fit for reporting. It was as if my mind had hit a brick wall. Where before I had been thinking with reasonable clarity, now I felt complete paralysis. I found it difficult to assemble sentences and I was slipping behind an invisible veil, preoccupied by something that drew me in and would not let go. I was distracted from everything around me and I knew I would have to go home.

I assumed that it was yet another recurrence of malaria and felt panicky because once again I would have to tell the office that I was sick. I was always careful to avoid the 's' word – stress – but concentrated on the malaria theory. The foreign desk told me to get home as soon as possible, which was not that easy. Fortunately, the Royal Air Force stepped in to turn a long and complicated journey into a long, simple but noisy affair. They offered me a ride in a Hercules transport aircraft heading to RAF Brize Norton in Oxfordshire. I jumped aboard with some off-duty Chinook pilots and headed back to Blighty.

I am not sure why I caved in at that time. Weeks earlier I had witnessed appalling suffering in the mountains, where families were stranded in the snow and the elderly and very young were dying of exposure. But I had 'survived' that and had gone on to report on refugee camps and on the progress of the international operation to reassure the Kurds. I had pushed myself hard but I had never been under direct threat, yet still my mind – or perhaps my body – had reached its limit.

I managed to overcome a similar episode when confronted with the prospect of reporting on the Balkan war for the first time. This was another of my 'holiday' destinations while I was based in Belfast. The paper was running a rotation system for this – the nastiest of wars – and my name was next on the list. I flew to Zagreb in September 1992 on a 'fireman' job that started in rural Croatia and ended up in Sarajevo at the height of the siege. It goes without saying that this was hardly a sensible way for me to be earning a living.

On this occasion the very thought of working in a war zone induced the now familiar impairment of my faculties. In the bar of the hotel where I was staying I had met up by chance with the American author and humourist P.J. O'Rourke, who was working for *Rolling Stone* magazine and looking for material for his next book. We hit it off immediately and agreed to travel together along with the veteran BBC radio reporter Bob Simpson. We hired a car and the following day headed off to the outpost town of Slavonski Brod, on the Croatia–Serbia border, which was being shelled by the Serbs.

Even before we got there I was tumbling into trouble. PJ was great fun to travel with. There was endless banter and jokes, and the irregulars at the checkpoints loved his business card. *The Times* was one thing, *Rolling Stone* magazine was quite another. 'Wow, that's cool, *Rolling Stone* is here to cover our war,' they would say in their broken English, their strong features breaking into smiles. But I was trying to work out whether I could complete this task before it had even begun.

On our first day we stopped at a roadside bar on our way to the besieged Muslim enclave of Bihac. We weren't even in the danger zone and I was feeling stoned and struggling to keep up. PJ appeared to be loving every minute of it. In his subsequent despatch for *Rolling Stone*, he began his account of that day – entitled 'Gang Bang Bang' – with a classic PJ gag that typified his cleverly irreverent approach even to a deadly case of inter-communal hatred.

> I drove to Bihac with London *Times* reporter Ed Gorman, BBC reporter Bob Simpson and Croatian translator, Sonja, who pretended to be Serbian when we were stopped by Serbian soldiers. It was easy for Sonja to pretend to be Serbian because Serbs and Croats are so much alike that the only way they can tell each other apart is by religion. And most of them aren't religious. So the difference between Serbs and Croats is that Serbs don't go to Eastern Orthodox services and the Croats don't attend mass. And the difference between Serbs and Muslims is that five times a day the Muslims don't pray to Mecca.

While PJ was laughing all the way to another chapter in another successful book, I was scared. I was suffering from my usual fever, my mind looking for avenues of escape as I crashed head-on into exactly the wrong assignment for my underlying condition. Standing by the side of the road, I thought 'I am going to have to tell PJ that I can't do this'. But I couldn't face the humiliation of that – I hardly knew him after all – and I resolved to soldier on.

I guess being with PJ was the best thing for me in the circumstances. He was everything that I did not have in Afghanistan in '85. Here was someone who helped me deal with my feelings of fear and apprehension, mainly through endless discussion with Bob about his main passion in life – high-performance road cars. Our assignment, reporting what he enjoyed referring to as a battle between the 'unspellables and the unpronounceables', was strictly of secondary importance to car-talk

Sadly, PJ did not come with me to Sarajevo. I wish he had. By then the besieged Bosnian capital was a valley-sized torture chamber for its Muslim inhabitants, who were being starved, shot at and shelled from the hills by their former Serb neighbours. It was the last place on earth I needed to be. The journey in, along the airport road, guarded by Serb snipers, was terrifying. I drove what was arguably the most dangerous road in the world at that time with the *New York Times* correspondent John Burns, in an entirely unprotected Lada jeep full of cans of fuel that he was bringing in for his contacts in the city. One high-velocity bullet and we would have gone up in a fireball.

Life inside the former Olympic city could not have been designed better to aggravate a mind fevered by memories of war. In Sarajevo, every time you stepped out of the hotel you were in danger of being shot or hit by shells. The Holiday Inn was burned and blackened in its upper floors where it had caught fire after being hit, and the place stank. On the streets, stacked shipping containers were piled high at intersections to offer protection from snipers, and in the hospitals the dead and wounded arrived at every hour of the day. People were living with little food, fresh water or medical supplies.

In comparison with my experiences in Afghanistan, where I was alone for much of the time with guerrillas with whom I had little in common, life was made easier by the fact that Sarajevo was a whole city in the grip of terror. This was a modern European society under siege and as a visitor you quickly became part of it. Everyone was in it together. People drank and smoked to ease their fears and life speeded up; all sorts of unlikely relationships blossomed because the whole population was living with the knowledge that tomorrow could be their last.

I managed to struggle through it for a week, going through the motions of trying to convey what I was seeing, but I was expending as much energy on keeping my own head together as I was on reporting on the conditions for the brave people I met there. My imagination and reality were blurred at times. I remember sleeping in the hotel – or trying to – and hearing gunfire in the suburbs in the early hours. I took it to be the Bosnian defenders taking on the Serbs in their efforts to break out. In the morning no one else seemed to have heard what I had. Was I imagining things as my fevered brain tried to cope with a daily diet of fear and misery?

I visited a tower block where a mother had lost a child to shellfire on an upper floor and got a sense of how ludicrously dangerous the place was and how angry the people were. I found it hard to believe that just a couple of hours' flying time from most European capitals this sort of slaughter was being allowed to continue.

On the way out of Sarajevo that time – I returned eighteen months later when the siege had eased somewhat – I got a souvenir in the form of a nasty headwound. I had to leave the city in a rush after my then-girlfriend, Salwa, was taken ill. I needed to get back to Belfast so I made my way out of Sarajevo with a group of British and American journalists

– among them Allan Little of the BBC and Christiane Aman-
pour of CNN. We were standing outside the police station in
the Serb-controlled village of Ilidza, waiting for our papers
to be stamped, when an APC that had been guarding the
airport road came trundling towards us. The soldier at the
wheel of the APC, who I have no doubt had nothing but contempt for Western journalists conveying to the wider world
the war crimes being committed in Sarajevo, was looking
straight at us as he approached. His tracked vehicle was
accelerating and kicking up clouds of dust.

As it reached us, without any warning the driver tipped
the APC into a spin, making a hard right-angle turn to the
left. The last thing I remember was the tracks kicking up
stones as we dived out of the way to avoid being hit by the
back end of it. I was at the front of the group and either
moved too slowly or perhaps had no chance to escape as the
vehicle smashed into a signpost next to me. It came down on
my head, as Allan put it, 'like a club'. Its leading edge sliced
into the left side of my forehead and the impact knocked me
over, unconscious.

'It was a really nasty moment – it looked like he was going
to kill one of us,' recalled Allan. 'You were clean out and
when you woke up you looked stunned. There was blood
streaming down your face, which was completely white. Your
pupils were dilated and you looked as if you weren't there.'

Christiane, who was already a household name around
the world, immediately took charge, and an ambulance was
called. Its siren blaring, it took me a few miles down the road
to a Serb military field hospital where soldiers with far worse
injuries than mine were being treated. The surgeon got to
work without waiting for the anaesthetic to dull the pain,
shaving my head and then doing what doctors in London
later said was a top-class filleting job on the wound. I was
sewn up, given a white expandable net bandage to put over
my head and sent on my way. Christiane accompanied me

to Zagreb and sat up with me for much of the night in the Esplanade Hotel, worried that I might lose consciousness again.

The next morning she organised for me to be taken to the airport and I flew to Frankfurt with a towel wrapped round my neck to keep my head straight. I got some odd looks on the plane and then wandered around the airport looking, and feeling, like a zombie, before catching a connection to London. On arrival I took a taxi to the Royal London Hospital where tests showed there was no serious damage to my brain or skull.

Much later I discovered through a friend that my eccentric former history teacher at Marlborough, one Omer 'John' Zametica, who went on to become the spindoctor for the Bosnian Serb President and now war criminal, Radovan Karadzic, had heard about my injury. Zametica, who ranted and raved in those days from the headquarters of the Bosnian Serb government at Pale, had reportedly described what happened to me at Ilidza as an 'RTA' – a road traffic accident. Even I could see the funny side of that.

—••••—

I had met Salwa in January 1991 during my posting to Amman in the first Gulf War. She was an attractive young Palestinian journalist who had been sent to the Jordanian capital from her home in Beirut to work for one of the leading American news magazines. In her late twenties, with long wavy hair and strong features, Salwa was an accomplished operator who exuded confidence in a part of the world she understood. She spoke fluent English and was a survivor in her own right. When she was still young, her mother had walked out on her father, leaving her, the eldest of nine children, to run the house. A refugee family that had originally fled Palestine in 1948, they had been living close to the frontline of the civil war in Beirut. This was a woman who knew far more than I did about living in a war zone.

We got on well from the start, and over a month in Amman during that winter our relationship blossomed. We spent hours together in the hotel and sneaked off for quiet dinners in the old city. Salwa was fun to be with and I admired her determination, confidence and competence. Compared with me – a boy from a well-off, middle-class family – she had been dealt a tough hand yet she had broken out and was building a career despite the fact she'd had little training or education.

After the war we stayed in touch and began to speak regularly – me in Belfast, Salwa back home in Beirut. Then over two years we swapped visits to each other's 'capital' of sectarian conflict. She had to conceal from her father that she was seeing me, because in the Muslim world relationships like ours started after marriage not before. So we made up cover stories for her visits to Northern Ireland where I showed her the sights of the Troubles. In Beirut we stayed together at an apartment belonging to a colleague of Salwa's and she introduced me to her circle of friends. Many of them were journalists, among them *The Times'* own correspondent in the city, Juan Carlos Gumucio from Bolivia, who had an apartment overlooking the seafront. A passionate reporter and bon viveur, Juan Carlos – who committed suicide in 2002 – became a champion of our friendship.

Eventually, we decided to get married and her father gave us his blessing. In early 1993 Salwa's family put on a hell of a party in Beirut for us attended by several of my friends and two of my sisters – Kate and Fiona – who flew out for the week. But even before the big day I was having my doubts. This was a huge challenge, crossing distant cultures, and Salwa and I had already begun to argue over the minor details of life. Her view of what was appropriate, or right or wrong, clashed head-on with mine in many respects.

When Salwa came to live with me in Co. Down, in the rural isolation of the cottage where I had existed alone for four years, the impossibility of what we were attempting hit us. We started to row almost immediately and I had little capacity to cope. Faced with a new source of torment, I yearned for the peace that had taken me to Killinchy in the first place and I knew within three months that I had made a terrible mistake.

Painful and humiliating as it was for both of us, we separated after just six months of marriage and then divorced, with Salwa moving to London just ahead of me, as I brought my years in Belfast to a close. Our relationship, which had begun in the unlikely setting of Amman on the eve of war and had then developed during brief snatches of time together, was never less than ambitious. But it was mainly my problems that brought about its decisive and untimely ending.

The truth was that the demons I carried from Afghanistan affected all aspects of my life, including my ability to forge relationships with women. I guess the simple explanation for this is that if you have a storm raging in your mind and you are expending inordinate energy in dealing with it, there is not much space – or mental energy – left for reaching out to others, let alone for tenderness, compassion or love. I had lost my easygoing nature and had become brittle, irritable and difficult to live with. Even at the best of times, I could be distracted, distant and hard to reach. None of this helped in a marriage, which should have been built on trust and affection. It was doomed from the start.

17

THE LAST TIME

After four and a half years in Northern Ireland on the treadmill of the Troubles and with a disastrous attempt at marriage still smouldering behind me, I came back to London in the summer of 1993 to try and make a new start. My posting in Ulster was over and I was being redeployed to the office. I was still battling the ever-present deleterious affects of 1985 but I was able to function as a news journalist, even if I hated the idea of 'home news'.

Most of the time in Northern Ireland I had lived a lonely life in a remote cottage that I shared with my two dogs. Back in London and required to go to the office at Wapping every day, I had no choice but to hand my dogs on. The Lord Chief stayed in Ulster with the owners of my local pub, Kitty and Morris Crawford at the Dufferin Arms in Killyleagh, where he became something of a fixture in the bar. My black retriever, Blue, went to live with my sister Kate near Colchester.

Having made a little money from my first step on the property ladder in rural Co. Down, I was now able to borrow enough for a three-bedroomed Victorian terrace in Balham in south London. It was at the end of my first week there that one of my new neighbours invited me round for dinner. There were five guests that night and one of them stopped me in my tracks. Sitting opposite me was a divorced mother of three, whose beauty, grace and stillness captivated me from the moment I set eyes on her.

As the evening went on I became more and more convinced that I had to see her again, if only I could find a way. Jeanna lived up the hill in much smarter Clapham and had come to the dinner party on her bicycle. I lived four doors up the road and therein lay my problem. I could hardly offer her a lift home. When it was time to leave, I squeezed her hand more in hope than expectation as I kissed her goodbye, thinking nothing would ever come of it.

But Jeanna was curious about me. Although she was going out with someone at the time and would continue to do so for another two years, there was something that spurred her normally reticent self to track me down. She has since reflected that very early on she felt that I needed some help and that, at the very least, she could be of assistance. Even though she barely knew me, she regarded me as a friend in need. A few days after our first meeting, she called me at *The Times* and a few days after that we met for a drink. For months thereafter we met regularly for dinner, as our friendship grew stronger. For the first time in my life I was building a relationship that had proper foundations, even if her heart lay somewhere else. I found Jeanna's calmness – she was known as Slow-Mo by her friends because she never did anything in a rush – and strength of mind irresistible. She was everything I wasn't. Never impulsive, hers was a measured approach to life and she found the sorts of decisions I had been making about mine utterly unfathomable. I dreamt that one day she would be mine.

At the paper I duly got stuck in, writing about whatever forced itself on to *The Times*' home news agenda – the rise of the British National Party, the troubled birth of the Child Support Agency, a deadly coach crash on the M2, the continuing row with Libya over the Lockerbie bombing or the election of a new professor of poetry at Oxford. But it was never my thing and I yearned for the life of a foreign news reporter.

In March 1994, seven months after my return from
Belfast, I was let out on a two-week trip to Bosnia where the
siege of Sarajevo was coming to an end. I was on hand on
the remarkable day that the band of the Coldstream Guards
flew in and played at the football stadium in the city ahead
of a match between soldiers from the United Nations Protection Force (Unprofor) and a team from Sarajevo FC. I
wrote about the strange cocktail of euphoria and anxiety
among the brutalised people of the Bosnian capital as they
began the painful process of trying to re-build their lives. I
covered the death of Corporal Barney Warburton, a twenty-
seven-year-old Class 1 bomb disposal engineer, who died just
twenty-four hours after shaking the hand of visiting prime
minister John Major. He had been trying to diffuse an improvised bomb on the confrontation line between Croat and
Muslim forces at Vitez.

I loved this work and when my time was up I reluctantly
returned to London. Back on home news, my first story concerned the continuing battle against drug addiction of Jamie
Blandford, the heir to the Duke of Marlborough. But I was
on the hunt for another foreign assignment and a few weeks
later my big chance came.

It had been five years since I had last visited Kabul and by
April 1994 it was being dismantled block by block by a civil
war that had ravaged the city since the fall of Najibullah.
The former president had managed to hold on for two years
after the Soviet pullout but then the place had imploded into
a vicious and destructive conflict as the Communist Afghan
army, sponsored, trained and armed by Moscow, melted
away and the Mujahidin factions moved to centre stage.
They did so not in unity but as deadly enemies, taking out
on each other years of distrust and jealousy and destroying
large parts of the old city in the process, something that even
the profligately destructive Soviet army had not managed.

The new Afghan war had already claimed, according

to the Red Cross, 13,500 lives with 80,000 wounded since Najibullah's death. It had created thousands more refugees who had either moved within Afghanistan to escape the fighting or fled to Pakistan and Iran. After almost fifteen years of continuous bloodshed, the country had become a basket case among nations and no one seemed to know what to make of it or what the West's response to this latest traumatic episode should be.

But Afghanistan was still my speciality so when I suggested to the foreign desk that perhaps I should go back and have a look around, they didn't hesitate to give me the green light. I was to head in via Pakistan, spend a few weeks reporting in Kabul and then write a four-part series on the state of play for the foreign pages. I was excited about the assignment but from the moment I walked out of the office my old tormentors returned.

Sweating, heating, on fire, my eyes and gums in revolt, I started to slip behind that ghostly veil once again, so that what was going on around me seemed suddenly beyond my reach or interest. I had to fight to keep a conscious grip on what I was trying to do. I barely slept in the days before I left and indeed I have only patchy memories of that trip, because I was struggling all the way through it to keep my mind on track. It was an effort of will simply to get on the plane, something I had failed to do on at least one previous occasion when offered the chance to return to Afghanistan. But I was determined to get the job done. I had failed in the past and this time I was going to deliver, come what may.

I flew out to the Pakistan capital, Islamabad, and then for the first time went overland by road to Kabul, entering the country through the front door, as it were, at the famous Khyber Pass. Even in the state I was in, I am sure I would have had a little *Carry on Up the Khyber* chuckle at that point, as I passed through the imposing stone gateway at what was once the north-eastern edge of imperial India. This was the way that British soldiers who had fought in the Afghan wars more than a century earlier would have entered Afghanistan.

Then I made my way by car to Kabul through the magnificent hill country that I had walked during my previous visits, passing various checkpoints where bribes were paid, some manned by very young boys shouldering powerful weapons. The atmosphere was tense and unpredictable and kids with weapons in their hands did nothing for my peace of mind. As we got closer to the city the road climbed through impressive gorges, with great cliffs reaching high into the sky on both sides, and I looked for signs of the old war that I knew so well: a roadside grave of a Mujahid fighter, its flags threadbare and faded in the breeze; the turret of an old Soviet APC jutting out of the river hundreds of feet below.

In Kabul, and later in the provincial capital of Jalalabad, I stayed at the houses of the International Committee of the Red Cross (ICRC) and it was with their staff and in one of their vehicles that I travelled into the city.

My first job was to get to grips with the civil war – something I had no experience of – so I arranged to visit the frontline in the heart of the wrecked centre of the old city. I walked along streets that had once been tidy, tree-lined and busy thoroughfares edged by shops that were now pummelled to rubble. The place looked more like Dresden after the firestorm that followed the Allied bombing at the end of the Second World War than an Asian capital city. I was taken through a maze of smashed buildings and broken trees to the frontline of a conflict that struck me from the start as being pointless and self-destructive.

In the trenches of Kabul it was boys of twelve or thirteen years old – the same age as the ones I had seen at the checkpoints on the roads – who had been hoodwinked into doing the killing. It was a bloody stalemate featuring the mainly Tajik forces of President Burhanuddin Rabbani against the mainly Pathan ones of Prime Minister Gulbuddin Hekmatyar.

Our guide brought me and my interpreter to a point where I could observe a youngster wedged into the rubble of a half-destroyed house, manning a machine gun. He was smoking a joint. Crawling back to sit alongside me, one of his friends told me that they regularly fired RPG rockets at what, I could all too clearly see, was point-blank range at their enemies across what remained of the street.

'Would you like us to show you? We can fire a round now,' he offered, gesticulating in the direction of the ruined houses opposite.

'No, I would not like that to happen. Tell him I do not want him to do that,' I whispered firmly to the translator through gritted teeth. The boy just laughed at my squeamishness.

I could see that this precarious vantage point could be transformed, in the blink of an eye, into a living hellhole. In the background we could hear the chatter of gunfire else-where on the frontline and I was determined that the centre of the fighting that afternoon would remain there, not here. The place was like a vision of madness and I desperately wanted to get out and get some air.

Having persuaded the grimy boys not to show off with their RPG, I crawled back to safer territory where I took the only picture I have ever had published in *The Times*. It shows a street in what was once a prosperous district of central Kabul with not a single building intact. Most have shards of walls standing jaggedly amid huge piles of rubble and broken trees. The once busy thoroughfare has been reduced to nothing more than a clearing through a junkyard. In one corner three Afghans, all carrying Kalashnikovs, have gathered under a tree for a smoke. It is an apocalyptic image of a broken city and a wasted victory.

A couple of days later, I was sitting on the roof of the ICRC house some way from the fighting zone. It was a still, early spring afternoon. I had come up with a book and a cup of tea to enjoy the warming rays of the sun. In the background I could hear the pop and crackle of distant battle. Then, quite quietly, I heard 'whish, whish … whish …' It sounded like an invisible bird gliding past my ears. I will never know for sure, but it suddenly dawned on me that someone might have been taking a pot shot at me. Were these bullets rippling in the air, close to my head? I decided not to wait around for confirmation of my fears and leapt for the stairs.

Getting away from the war, I spent a day touring the majestic old British embassy compound standing serenely but abandoned in front of Ali-Abed Mountain, where a Mujahidin faction had dug in tanks and artillery. Under an old agreement with Pakistan, dating back to Partition, the embassy was shortly to be transferred to Islamabad, where Britain's diplomats in exile were already based.

The place felt, smelled and looked like a country pile somewhere in Surrey. It was dominated by an elegant two-winged ambassadorial residence overlooking what were once immaculately tended formal gardens, including a rectangular pond complete with a fountain and red roses guarding each side. There was a tennis court, swimming pool, hockey pitch and squash court. Dotted about elsewhere in the twenty-six acres of terraced gardens were the homes of junior diplomats who had lived in English-style Victorian country houses done up in whitewash and green trim and reached by roads fringed by hedges. Inside, the houses had the familiar damp smell of an old English or Scottish country home, festering after months of winter cold.

The main residence included spacious reception rooms looking out on extensive terracing, guarded by archways, and onto the lawns beyond. There was a large ballroom and an oak-panelled library. The grand piano that once stood in the main hallway had been removed, as had the grandfather clock and the books. But in the ballroom large portraits of George V and Queen Mary were still awaiting their turn for the movers, and the drinks cabinet – once used by my British

Embassy friend Clovis Meath Baker – was still stocked with bottles, some of which had been untouched for five years.

The compound had taken more than sixty hits from shell-fire during the civil war and a 100mm tank shell had found its way through the front veranda of the main residence, ricocheting upstairs, crashing through a chest of drawers and then hammering into the ambassador's bedroom where it destroyed a television set before coming to rest without exploding.

Randhoj Raj, a retired Gurkha captain from east Nepal who was in charge of security at this relic of Britain's once grandiose imperial past, was my nervous guide to what he called his 'little Buckingham Palace'. He was terrified that he would be reprimanded for giving a reporter from *The Times* a final peek before the handover. He admitted that his had become a lonely job since the last diplomats left, but said he would be sad to see the embassy go.

On another day I stopped by a nondescript, crumbling shed by the side of the road, not far from the old royal palace. I was pretty sure that this was a road I had been driven down during my jeep trip through Kabul almost a decade earlier. Someone with me said it was worth having a look inside. The shed looked like all the other wrecked buildings in Kabul, but in this one there were a couple of old relics of a different kind that demanded a moment's contemplation. Here, damaged by shellfire and by parts of the roof that had fallen on top of them, and covered in fine grey dust, were the custom-built cars that used to convey the Afghan king in the days before he was overthrown in 1973. Among them was a Rolls-Royce of a similar vintage to the one owned by my grandfather. These once-majestic machines would have been worth a fortune had they been looked after. But their political significance condemned them to the destruction that now swept so much of the Afghan capital. Like so much else of the nation's past, they were being left to rot.

And then the moment of truth.

From the day I arrived in Kabul, I had been asking round for news of Niazuldin. How had he coped with this post-victory internecine power struggle? Where was he living? Was he in Pakistan or had he returned to Kabul, perhaps to re-open his shop, or was he fighting in the civil war? I sent out feelers and within a few days received news that floored me.

'Niazuldin is dead,' said my translator matter-of-factly one morning as we met at the beginning of another day of reporting.

'How do you know? Are you sure?' I demanded. It seemed impossible that the Lion of Kabul, that larger-than-life figure who I had last seen four years earlier in Peshawar, would not have survived.

The translator shrugged: 'That's what I have heard.'

I found it hard to believe that Niazuldin – a man I regarded as a great survivor and someone with an almost invisible protective aura around him – could have gone. I continued with my enquiries. There must be another explanation. Was Shams still knocking around Kabul all those years after we first met in the mountains? Might he be in touch with Niazuldin?

At last I managed to make contact with someone from Niazuldin's group and arranged to go with him to a house where he insisted I would find people I knew. He picked me up from the ICRC house and drove me to the area of the city where I had stayed back in 1985. This time I was not wearing *shalwar kameez*. In fact I looked more like I did when I was dressed up as a Russian officer than a fake Mujahid as I walked through the door to the garden of Zulmai's house in jeans and a long-sleeved shirt. Would I be welcomed or was this going to be awkward, formal or even hostile?

But they were ready to meet me: the men and even the women, who gathered behind a half-opened door. I shook hands with the men and hugged them. '*Salaam alaikum, Salaam alaikum … Salaam alaikum …*' We smiled at each other and laughed together.

'We are glad that you have come back,' one of the older men – perhaps one of Zulmai's brothers – said through the translator. 'It means a lot to us that you are here and that you came to find us.'

This was unexpected after all those years of sweating over what had happened and wrestling with my own guilt about Zulmai's death. It hit me right between the eyes and I was tearful with gratitude for their generosity of spirit.

We talked about Zulmai and his vain hopes for a new life.

'He was a very brave man,' I said, 'and I was so sad to hear that he had died.'

His little children were grown up by then. I had been afraid that they might blame me and see me as part of the reason for his death but instead their warmth almost over-whelmed me. If anything, it seemed, my presence reaffirmed his life and his 'glorious death' as they saw it. We talked a bit more, recalling those dreadful days in the heart of the Soviet occupation and that extraordinary escapade in the jeep that had become part of the folklore of the family.

Then the conversation turned to Niazuldin. They all said his name but in the respectful tones that Afghans reserved for those who had been 'martyred'.

'We too have heard that he is dead,' uttered the translator after listening to the family discussion. So it was true. My great friend with whom I had teamed up as a twenty-four-year-old novice war reporter and then carried out that crazy stunt in Kabul, that huge presence and force of life – the man whom I had trusted with my life – had gone.

'We don't know what happened to him exactly,' he added, 'but he is thought to have had a disagreement with a rival commander who threw him down a well and he died down there.'

Even though I had heard the rumours, this information – and the abrupt way it was conveyed – shook me to the core. I had always imagined Niazuldin would survive whatever the war threw at him even though he'd had a few close escapes by the time I met him. But his cloak of invincibility was just a figment of my imagination, conjured up to help me deal with the risks I had taken under his guidance.

I was lost in thought reflecting on those long days in the summer of '85 when someone asked if I would like to see one of the places where I had hidden, nine years earlier. We went to the shed. The lumps of earth that used to fill the entrance to the secret compartment were gone. In their place, there was just a gaping hole in the floor. I walked over and peered inside the cramped space where I had spent many hours hiding from Soviet and Afghan soldiers and members of the secret police. It looked impossibly small. How did I get in there?

We were all laughing but I was just going through the motions. My subconscious was taking me right back to the camp, to Abdullah again, his burial and those days under fire. It felt raw and immediate. I hadn't expected this – neither the welcome nor the sudden confrontation with the reality of what happened all those years earlier. It was time to go. We all shook hands and I hugged the men again. I thanked them and said my goodbyes. May God be with you. We walked slowly out of Zulmai's garden and got back in the car for the journey to the ICRC house on the other side of town.

The following day, on my way back to the Khyber Pass and Pakistan, I stopped at the village of Khushgumbad, just outside Jalalabad in Nangarhar province. I was with some foreign aid workers who wanted to show me the problems of poppy-growing. I walked in a daze slowly up a track in the heat of the midday sun to where an old man greeted us in his fields. The West had never stopped lecturing the Afghans on what they should or should not be growing in their fields, thousands of miles from the streets of London, Paris or

Milan, and the resentment among the villagers was all too obvious to see.

'Why are you manufacturing weapons and sending them here where they will kill people?' he ranted. 'The problem is that we have less land and we have to live and feed our families. There is nothing to compare with the poppy yield. The people who buy it from us take it abroad – that is their business.' It was a defiant performance and it was my last interview in Afghanistan.

That evening I was at the ICRC compound in Jalalabad, ready to cross the border the next day. Outside the streets were crowded with thousands of internal refugees, many of them armed, many of them sleeping rough after fleeing from Kabul. All about us were tales of human misery. The compound had a satellite television connection and we gathered in front of the TV to watch – in stunned silence – reports of Ayrton Senna's death at Imola. The juxtaposition was startling. A legendary multi-millionaire Brazilian racing driver dying at a Grand Prix circuit in Italy while taking part in the richest sport on earth. Outside was the milling throng of Afghans, to whom he meant nothing, battling for survival at the bottom end of the world poverty rankings, battered by fifteen years of war (and with at least another twenty-two to go).

◆◆◆◆◆

Three days later I was back at my desk in the old wine warehouse at Wapping and, somehow and definitively, I knew that my mind had shut down. Totally. Not like before. Not like at Heathrow, three years earlier, or in Iraq. This time the mechanism had stopped completely and I knew immediately that I could not conceal this. In the past, however seriously I had been affected by experiences on the road, I always knew that given some time off I would recover. Not this time. It was crystal clear to me that a different order of paralysis had taken hold.

I had flown back from my trip to Afghanistan a couple of days before. I had ground out the pieces I was asked for on the civil war and Afghanistan's dismal future prospects, and I was supposed to be starting the working week, once again as a home news reporter. But I had only one thought in my head: I had to leave the office, whatever the consequences.

Using the internal mail system on our computers, I sent a brief message to my boss, the home news editor James McManus, while my friends and colleagues around me set about their inquiries for the day. My mind was elsewhere – in fact anywhere other than there.

'I need to see you for a brief chat, please,' I typed and pressed 'send' without hesitating.

McManus, who was busy constructing another day's news list, replied instantly. 'Can't now. I'm busy.'

'Sorry, James, but I really do need to see you.'

'Look, if you want a pay rise, this is the wrong time to ask,' he replied.

Normally I would have laughed at that and waited my turn. But there was nothing normal about this. I sent him a third message: 'James, I'm deadly serious. I *have* to see you now. *Something is seriously wrong.*'

McManus understood this time and called me to meet him in the main conference room.

We sat down and I had absolute clarity about what I needed to say. I knew, as if someone had spelt it out for me in the capital letters of a newspaper headline, that my mind had closed down and I could no longer function in the office.

I did my best to explain: 'I have a serious problem. Something has gone "snap" in my head and I need to get out of here.'

'Hang on a minute, Ed. You can't have just lost your marbles ...'

'I know it sounds weird and it *is* weird – I don't know – something's definitely not right and I know that I cannot stay here.'

McManus paused to take in what he was hearing. 'OK, OK … right.'

'I guess I should just go home and hopefully things will improve,' I said.

By then he knew this was real – I suppose he could see it written all over my face – and there was nothing he could do to stop me.

'Is there anything I can do to help?' he asked. He went on to make suggestions about who I might see and so on; his attitude was nothing but understanding and helpful.

A few minutes later I walked out of the building, unaware that my career as a foreign correspondent was over, although I sensed deep down that things would never be quite the same again.

18

NON-FUNCTIONAL

In the early summer of 1994 I found myself at home in south London, having ejected myself from the office and with my life in a mess. I was a thirty-four-year-old divorcee with no girlfriend, no job and a scrambled brain. Like James McManus, Peter Roberts, the managing editor of *The Times,* was supportive from the outset and showed nothing but concern for my welfare. During the entire period I was off work that was never to change, something for which I remain extremely grateful.

Initially I saw a GP who thought I had depression and prescribed Prozac. In those early days I slept a lot and wandered around town drinking too much accompanied by my black retriever, Blue, who came back to live with me and keep me company. I kept well away from the paper and my colleagues – in fact I felt allergic to the whole idea of going anywhere near Wapping – and tried to concentrate on the inexact business of getting better. But after a few weeks I could tell that nothing was changing and I sought another doctor.

A friend recommended Martin Scurr, who worked in private practice in Notting Hill. Martin had a spectacular waiting room in an elegant whitewashed Victorian town house. It featured a full-scale snooker table and a collection of beautiful antique miniature yachts. The yachts were an interesting detail because my longstanding passion for sailing was playing a big part in my imagination as I looked for an alternative focus – an escape even – for my tortured mind. Later that summer, I decided to sell my house and buy my first proper yacht, a 35-foot wooden classic named *Nutcracker* that I spotted in a canal basin in Maldon in Essex. The boat required lots of work and, while completely incapable of expending any energy on my professional career, I had unending enthusiasm for *Nutcracker* and the work I was doing on her – a contrast that would eventually provide an important clue to what was wrong with me.

Martin is a wonderful doctor and was nothing but attentive to my needs, but he was convinced, for want of any other explanation, that I was suffering from depression. He asked me a lot about my family history, about the early death of my mother, the traumatic break-up with my father and the impact it had on both me and my sisters. He could find plenty of antecedents in my background for his diagnosis. His notes of his first assessment in July, when he reached the conclusion that I had a 'depressive illness', provide some interesting clues to my underlying condition.

> [Ed is] lethargic, lacks energy, and is unable to write with any fluency. As soon as he is required to do anything he feels stoned and loses mental agility. He exhibits a complete loss of enthusiasm for his job. He feels negative about it. He is amazed to be in this state. He is usually good at making a go of things. He constantly feels overheated, a sense of heat in his face. Sweating ... paroxysmal [tending to uncontrollable outbursts].

I told him that I'd had two episodes of fever in Pakistan and Afghanistan and then recurring problems with feverish symptoms. Martin noted, in a conclusion that even I had reached by then, that malaria was a red herring. 'He now thinks these bouts were "stress",' Martin wrote.

I explained that I had experienced these symptoms on arriving in Ireland, when assigned by the paper to Bosnia on my trip with P.J. O'Rourke, and before my final visit to Kabul.

'It commenced,' Martin wrote of the Bosnia example, 'THE MINUTE he walked out of the editor's office – a panic attack – all throughout preparing [to go to Bosnia] for four days. It went on as he arrived in Vitez, having come from Split.'

Then Martin started a new page in his black fountain pen and wrote: 'Following Afghanistan,' a word that he underlined, 'he plunged into a deep hole from which he has not emerged.' There is an arrow from the word Afghanistan to a comment lower down that gives an indication of how tricky this was to understand back then. It reads: '[Afghanistan] by which he was incredibly invigorated … he felt he had rediscovered his journalistic enthusiasms.'

No wonder Martin was struggling. To put it simply, I was exhibiting confused symptoms and signs of a love-hate relationship with Afghanistan, which had given me the most exciting, important but also terrifying moments of my life.

Martin doubled the Prozac and I went off to try and recover. I think I played a little golf and got out of town for some fresh air. I saw Jeanna every now and again but my chances to have dinner or go out for a drink with her were few and far between while she remained involved with someone else. I saw Martin again in August when he prescribed, in addition to Prozac, Lithium, quite a heavy-duty drug.

By the time I saw him in early September, the picture was still mixed. I was feeling better in the days immediately preceding the appointment but I had been 'bad' or 'worse' for much of the time since I had last seen him.

'He has been drinking a lot. He still hasn't opened a newspaper or listened to a news bulletin. He feels he must get back to work soon.' Martin noted that I was sleeping for long periods but that I was still feeling exhausted. He dwelt a lot on my family history, and wrote that he was certain 'it is' – he underlined 'is' with a scribble five lines deep – 'a case of depression'.

A month later I appeared to be getting worse. Martin's notes are dominated by my own preoccupation with his diagnosis. I did not believe it.

> [Ed's] got a sort of 'thing' about the diagnosis, i.e. being 'mentally ill'. He was previously obsessed with the diagnosis being ORGANIC. He feels it's a failure, that he may never work again, etc. He doesn't seem to be feeling better – if anything he's lost motivation. Manically busy in the past, now not bothering about ANYTHING. Previously fastidious about points of detail ...

A few weeks later I hit rock bottom after a night out on the town with Bill Frost, a colleague from the paper. Tall, wiry, with a shock of fuzzy greying hair and with a cigarette or a pint always in his hand, Bill was a partner in crime if ever there was one. Highly intelligent with an evil sense of humour, he and I got on well and enjoyed comparing notes on our foreign adventures. Bill had enjoyed a distinguished career as a BBC radio journalist before joining *The Times*. He had experienced far greater horrors than I, particularly in Bosnia, where he saw the bodies of people who had been crucified impaled on the walls of their houses. I know how much that had disturbed him because I had to force it out of him. Bill died in 2000, aged fifty, as a result of addiction to alcohol and cocaine.

That night, we got together for a session in south London, which involved copious amounts of both those poisons. It had a devastating effect on my mind, already addled with Prozac and Lithium. Bill was trying to come to terms with the recent death of his mother and spent some time trying to persuade me to reconcile with my father, whom I had not seen for several years and who had no idea I was ill. When I got back to my own house, I flipped. Martin's notes say: 'When he got home: an explosion, he "went nuts" – a sort of emotional storm – it terrified him. He trashed the house. Became distraught. He felt very strong and could tear the banister off the stairs.'

Another note at this point records that I was threatening suicide. It also records that I stopped taking all the medicine I had been prescribed by Martin from that night on. As Martin put it: 'He wonders … is it the drugs?? Is he ill??' Also on that page Martin wrote his new diagnosis that he ringed in black pen: 'Rapid cycling bipolar.' It wasn't just depression but a more serious form of the condition that he now believed I was suffering from, in which my mood would swing from one extreme to another.

It would be fair to say that at this point, I was in serious trouble. But one thing remained crystal clear to me. Despite the drugs, both prescribed and recreational, I knew deep down that my underlying condition was unchanged from the moment I had walked out of *The Times* office four months earlier. I had no idea what the problem was but I knew I had either not been correctly diagnosed or that the medicine had not worked as expected.

It was not long after this that I completed the purchase of *Nutcracker*. Then I started working on her with an enthusiasm and intensity that amazed my family and the doctors. I spent my days working and sleeping aboard her in a small, unheated and poorly lit boatyard in the seaside village of Maylandsea in Essex, where I had her laid up in a shed. Just as I had done when learning the trumpet as a teenager, I focused all my energy into making the best possible job of the re-fit and repairs to that boat. It was going to be perfect.

When I saw Martin in mid-November he wrote 'BETTER'

at the top of the sheet. 'He now has energy. Stripping the boat, working at a tremendous rate. He has worked there for nine days non-stop. His sister and brother-in-law think he's getting better.' Martin noted that I was no longer drinking as much as before. I had started dreaming again, 'as if a blockage has gone'. There were still moments of doubt but the sharpness of my mind had started to return. At the bottom of the page, again ringed in black pen, Martin wrote: 'He now thinks that the GENESIS of this might be his first trip to Afghanistan.'

The plan was for me to return to work in early December 1994. I had gone back on the Prozac for a while and was also taking carbamazepine, a drug I have since discovered is used, among other things, for the treatment of bipolar disorder. But at the same time, partly because he was still a little unsure about my progress, Martin referred me to David Curson, a consultant psychiatrist at the Royal Masonic Hospital in west London who had previously worked in the army.

I saw David at the end of October. At first he backed up Martin's view, confirming that I was suffering from rapid cycling bipolar disorder. I went away, took the pills and continued working on *Nutcracker* until what, by any estimation, has to be one of the most important days of my life finally arrived.

It was on 12 December 1994 – 3,347 days since I had reached Teri Mingal at the end of my long visit to Kabul and Logar province in 1985 – that I made my way to Ravenscourt Park in west London to see Dr Curson for a second consultation. By that time I was beginning to feel sceptical about my treatment and frightened that no one would ever work out what was wrong with me. After eight months off, a return to work seemed a distant prospect to me that morning and I had no idea there was about to be a breakthrough. Although I can still remember Dr Curson's embarrassed reaction when he suddenly realised what was wrong with me

– he put his hands up as if in surrender when it hit him – I rely on his account, as told in writing to Martin Scurr, of that appointment.

When I started the reassessment Ed immediately described how he was worried that he looks better than he feels and is still disinclined to consider returning to his work as a journalist for *The Times* because of continuing attentional deficit, fear of failure and making mistakes, impaired short-term memory and his lack of self-confidence. On asking him directly about what had happened since his first visit to me, he described how he had increased his dose of Tegretol [carbamazepine] to 400mg twice daily and the daytime drowsiness and some ataxia [incoordination] are well-known side-effects. Furthermore, he said he had not taken the Prozac even though you suggested that he should do so. There have been no manic episodes and the 'bouts of overheating' had completely gone until sitting in the waiting room immediately before seeing me!

On reviewing the complex list of symptoms that he first described to me, I was somewhat taken aback when he said he had been 'working like a maniac' in a boatyard refurbishing and re-painting a 35-foot yacht and had been at it for anything up to twelve hours per day. I pointed out that this level of activity was hardly compatible with the profound fatigue amounting to leaden paralysis which he described when he first saw me. In a similar vein, Ed described how he had become 'totally obsessed with yachts and sailing' and the other week in the boatyard had found a sailing book and had read it from cover to cover in no time at all. Again, this was quite remarkable considering that he still struggles to read newspapers. In other words, his complaints of physical fatigue and attentional deficit seemed to be highly selective and it was at this point that I asked him directly whether he wanted to return to his job and he told me firmly that he did not. Although he still loves journalism, he cannot face returning to *The Times* and he said he would rather do a boat-building course.

As you will see, all of this was not really hanging together and it was at this point that Ed told me that a woman friend of his [Jo Morris, a former girlfriend whom I saw regularly when I was ill and who went on to work at *The Times* herself], had raised the possibility that he might have post-traumatic stress disorder. This came out of the blue and although Ed had told me a little about his work in Afghanistan in 1985, he had not at that first assessment described the horrifying experience he had gone through and what had followed in the years afterwards.

Not only had he been attacked by the Russians and at least one guerrilla he knew had been killed close by him, he felt completely isolated and helpless with no translator and had then gone on a covert mission into Kabul where he had hidden for ten days in a house and was convinced he would never get out of Kabul alive. When he did manage to escape from what was a prolonged and very frightening experience, he left Afghanistan and it was at that time that he developed the 'bouts of overheating' which were originally diagnosed as malaria. I had diagnosed these as a manifestation of autonomic overarousal and this is, of course, a feature of PTSD described in the DSMIV [Diagnostic and Statistical Manual of Mental Disorders, published by the American Psychiatric Association] under criterion B5 as 'physiological reactivity on exposure to internal or external cues that symbolise or resemble an aspect of the traumatic event'. Ed went on to describe that in the year after he left Afghanistan [following the 1985 trip] he was in the United States where he drank very heavily and did not engage in journalism but painted houses instead. Now, as he pointed out, he was just painting boats.

When the Gulf War started and he was offered an assignment, he really got into quite a state and could not face it and then matters really came to a head in the spring of this year when he returned to Afghanistan and visited the house where he had hidden and it was following that that he broke down and became non-functional. In the limited time available, I ran through all the criteria for PTSD listed in the DSMIV and Ed confirmed that he had experienced all of them at some point and continues to experience quite a lot of them even now. Several of these criteria make more sense now. Good examples include his markedly diminished interest or participation in significant activities, his feelings of detachment and estrangement from others, he has restricted range of affect, a sense of foreshortened future, irritability and outbursts of anger such as the one he had soon after seeing me, difficulty in concentrating and continuing hypervigilance and exaggerated startle response.

It was around this time that Ed began to cry, expressing ideas of failure and embarrassment about what may have happened to him. I suspect, therefore, that he either had not made the connection between those events of nine years ago or, more likely, he had made a connection but had been too embarrassed to describe them to you, me or anybody else. In the circumstances, it is vitally important that he receives appropriate treatment for post-traumatic stress disorder and the sooner the treatment starts the better.

As I sat in front of him at the end of that consultation Dr Curson picked up the phone to the leading authority on the treatment of PTSD in the UK, Professor Gordon Turnbull, a consultant psychiatrist who had developed a two-week residential treatment course at an old hospital in Ticehurst, East Sussex. Dr Turnbull was well known for having treated some of the returning Beirut hostages a few years earlier. Dr Curson explained briefly my journey to that moment and asked Dr Turnbull if he would see me.

A week later I was sitting in Dr Turnbull's large office in rural Sussex in tears again after having scored almost a full-house in the official PTSD diagnostic test. This is a series of questions that you answer, giving you a cumulative score. They range from questions about 're-experiencing symptoms' (nightmares, panic attacks, flashbacks) to 'avoidance symptoms' (avoiding anything that reminds you of a traumatic event, plus suffering depression, loneliness, suicidal thoughts or resorting to substance abuse) and finally 'arousal symptoms' (questions about anger, hypervigilance, night sweats, being easily startled and so on).

In a phrase that has remained with me ever since, Dr Turnbull, a calm, reassuring and moustachioed Scot from Edinburgh with a shock of greying hair, told me in his gentle lilt, after I had finished ticking almost every box in the test, that I had a 'rip-roaring' case of PTSD. Then he signed me in for his next two-week debriefing treatment course, starting in the middle of January 1995.

19

TICEHURST

In America I had been diagnosed with 'Acute Nervous Exhaustion'. In London at the Hospital for Tropical Diseases I had been told to slow down and 'box clever'. For many years I had convinced myself I had malaria. Then in the months that I had been off work I had been diagnosed with depression and then bipolar disorder. Now, for the first time, I had a clear diagnosis that made sense, even if I knew little about post-traumatic stress disorder and had never considered that it might be the key to my condition.

PTSD was, at that time in the UK, not a particularly well-known condition and most doctors, including Martin Scurr, were not familiar with it. In the United States, where PTSD was first described by practitioners treating veterans of the Vietnam War, it was far better established and I guess that, had I been treated there, I might have received a diagnosis quicker.

One of the best descriptions of what was wrong with me the day I walked out of *The Times* office – and indeed the symptoms that had been bugging me for years – is the definition of PTSD in the *Diagnostic and Statistical Manual of Mental Disorders*. Reading this beautifully concise summary of my own illness – some doctors tell you PTSD is not an illness, more a natural reaction to extremely stressful events – it feels as if the people who wrote it had read my mind.

I only came across it while researching this book and yet, even decades after the events that sparked my own PTSD, I still found it utterly compelling and re-affirming to read, as it charted so calmly and clinically the stormy waters I had sailed since 1985.

> Criterion A1: 'The essential feature of Post-traumatic Stress Disorder is the development of characteristic symptoms following exposure to an extreme traumatic stressor involving direct personal experience of an event that involves actual or threatened death or serious injury, or other threat to one's physical integrity; or witnessing an event that involves death, injury, or a threat to the physical integrity of another person; or learning about unexpected or violent death, serious harm, or threat of death or injury experienced by a family member or other close associate.'

I just have to think of the kindly features of Abdullah-Jan and the day he was killed, the failing light at dusk as they brought him off the mountain, Fazil-Jan weeping over his lifeless but moving body, and on and on goes the tape in my mind. Or the discovery that Asil, Zulmai and now Niazuldin had all been killed.

I had quite a lot of experience of the threat of injury and a 'threat to my physical integrity'. On that score I tend to drift, strangely, not to the days of bombing preceding my trip into Kabul or the shellfire with Bilal or even Sarajevo, but to the journey on foot out of Kabul province in '85 when I was heading back to Teri Mingal. For some hours at the start of those frantic few days of route marching, we were subject to intermittent shellfire. These were incredibly loud explosions around us and they got to me in a way that more immediate threats did not seem to. I was at my lowest ebb. My resistance to fear had collapsed. I was nakedly scared and intensely determined to get out of harm's way. The gunfire induced physical shivers in my body as I walked and I remember dwelling – especially in that *chaikhana* where I could not stop laughing – as I have done many times since, on the massive imbalance between the destructive power of modern weaponry and the utter vulnerability of the human body.

> Criterion B, C and D: 'The characteristic symptoms resulting from the exposure to the extreme trauma include persistent re-experiencing of the traumatic event, persistent avoidance of stimuli associated with the trauma and numbing of general responsiveness, and persistent symptoms of increased arousal.'

This reads like a handbook to my demons – I spent years trying not to think about what had happened in the mountains but as my 'Note of Warning' written in 1986 during my year in America makes clear, I fought a losing battle. Those experiences haunted me in my sleep in nightmares and night terrors. During the day, the sound of a helicopter, a smell, a loud bang or the quality of the light could set in train thoughts that brought it all back. And then there was the debilitating overheating in my body and mind, which attacked me whenever I faced new challenges in dangerous places – Iraq, Sarajevo, even going to Jordan in the build-up to the first Gulf War, and arriving in Belfast.

On each occasion I was impaired, sometimes to the point of not even being able to get on an aeroplane, by symptoms of 'increased arousal' – my mind and body on alert, in fear of sudden, unexpected violent events. When you are thinking like that, there is no room for trivial matters such as normal conversation, the consideration of an interview, the construction of an article, or a loving response to a gesture from someone close to you. What you crave is escape, by way of a drink, a cigarette, painkillers or something more powerful.

The manual describes the sorts of settings in which PTSD could develop and 'military combat' is the first one on the list. It also describes how intrusive recollections of the event that caused the condition, sometimes sparked by a dream, can create 'dissociative states' that can last for a few seconds or days at a time. Dissociative states is a brilliant term to sum up the alienation from normality that a PTSD relapse provokes. Your body and mind feel under attack. You are with people physically but in your head, you are not there. You are back where you do not want to be, in the centre of the black hole, waiting with every fibre of your being to react to the next onslaught.

Through the sweat and heat, it always feels as if a glass wall has come down or that a film of me is being played out on the surface in front of the real me. I have slipped behind that other narrative and am living in a parallel world fighting for air, fighting to get back to the reality of the restaurant I am sitting in. Naturally, impairment of this kind can play havoc with interpersonal relationships.

The manual is interesting on the causes of these episodes. Criterion B4 and B5 state: 'Intense psychological distress or physiological reactivity often occurs when the person is exposed to triggering events that resemble or symbolise an aspect of the traumatic event.' It gives examples of cold or snowy weather or uniformed guards for survivors of concentration camps in cold climates, or entering a lift for a woman who was raped in one.

For me this fits with what happened in the late spring of 1994, immediately before the onset of full-blown PTSD. I had been to Afghanistan several times since the summer of 1985 and to Kabul in the winter of 1988–89 with the Russians, without suffering too badly. The difference in 1994 was that I sought out the people and places I had visited in 1985. I met Zulmai's family and saw one of the hiding holes where I had taken refuge. I was emotionally on edge before that meeting and nervous about the reception I would get, but then stunned by the warmth of the welcome I received, even as I tried to come to terms with the details of Niazuldin's death. It seems clear to me that this overwhelmed my ability to resist the PTSD symptoms that had been lurking for years.

The manual deals with a unique quality of PTSD – the tendency for people with it to avoid anything associated with the traumatic event. In my case this included my job, *The Times*, Afghanistan, news in general, writing articles, watching news on television or even buying newspapers. By the time I walked out of the office I had become allergic to my own vocation and during the months that I was off, and for many years afterwards, I continued to avoid news. This is quite tricky when you are trying to make your living as a journalist.

This aspect of PTSD made it very hard for my doctors to identify what was wrong with me: I was reluctant to talk to them about what had happened in Afghanistan, the key to my symptoms, even if, deep down, I suspected it was the cause.

The manual goes on to describe other associated symptoms, all of which I was contending with to a greater or lesser extent. Diminished interest or participation in previously enjoyed activities, feeling detached or estranged from other people, having a reduced ability to feel emotion, having a sense of a foreshortened future – a feeling that I would die young; the break-up with my father and my mother's early death left me with that even before I had started my career in journalism – persistent symptoms of anxiety, which include difficulty sleeping or staying asleep, outbursts of anger and irritability and difficulty concentrating or completing tasks.

There is also a passage dealing with guilt. 'Individuals with Post-traumatic Stress Disorder may describe painful guilt feelings about surviving when others did not survive or about things they had to do to survive.' I have only to think about smoking Abdullah-Jan's cigarettes or my lingering feelings of responsibility for Zulmai's death to fit this part of the diagnostic test.

A final symptomatic detail is something called 'exaggerated startle response'. Someone who has been through terrifying events and has sought to defend themselves thereafter by adopting a hypervigilant state, is in no position to cope with the unexpected. I am a virtuoso in this area. In the months after Afghanistan I dived under a table when hearing a loud bang, but years later I still jump out of my skin when someone walks up behind me unexpectedly or, say, a mountain-biker glides past me from behind on a footpath when I am walking in the hills.

As I drove back to London after seeing Dr Turnbull I was euphoric. Finally I could think about treatment and even a cure. But as the weeks ticked by over Christmas I grew increasingly anxious about facing up to my condition and I could not see how working in the sort of group therapy setting Dr Turnbull was proposing – with three other PTSD sufferers – was going to help me. By early January I had resolved not to turn up. It was only the entreaties of my sister, Kate, and other friends that persuaded me to take this chance to start what, they argued, would be a new life.

So on a dank winter's afternoon I walked out of the boatshed at Maylandsea, my eyes on pins because of the carbamazepine, and pointed my car south down the A12 to London. I was in no fit state to drive and should have accepted offers from friends to be driven to Ticehurst. But I was embarrassed about going to what I viewed as a 'mental hospital' – which is what it had been in its heyday – and I was determined that I would admit myself to the oldest privately run psychiatric hospital in Europe with no one else on hand to witness it.

Within an hour of setting out I stopped the car in a lay-by on the A12 and thought about turning back. Almost every fibre of my being was against going into treatment, which would last two weeks. I didn't want to face the process of having to talk about what had happened to me and with strangers to boot. But there was a voice in my head reminding me that this could be a chance finally to break free, even if the prospect of what I thought of as 'surgery' to my brain, my imagination and my memory, terrified me. I fell asleep in the lay-by for a while and then, reluctantly, continued my journey south.

I was the last to arrive. When I did so, I found the other three – my fellow PTSD casualties – chatting away to each other in a waiting room upstairs in the old Victorian hospital. As I walked in and sat down, Jim, who had worked on electricity power lines and seen several of his colleagues fried alive and now could not even touch a light switch, was telling the other two that one of the people coming was a former war correspondent. They did not seem to think it could be me because, they told me later, I did not look like their idea of a journalist. My hair was quite long, I was scruffily dressed after living on the boat and my hands were covered in a black rubbarised industrial fixing compound called Sikaflex. I had got it all over myself working on *Nutcracker* earlier that day and had not had time – or, more likely, had not bothered – to scrub it off before I left. I must have looked more like an amateur plumber than a correspondent for *The Times* and they were quite surprised when I finally summoned up the courage to say 'Er, that would be me.'

The idea of the course was that each of us, under the overall supervision of Dr Turnbull and his colleague Dr Bo Mills, and the daily care of two psychiatric nurses, Tim and Sarah, would engage in detailed debriefing sessions within the group. The aim was to create a safe, non-judgemental environment, in which we could each delve into our heart of darkness and almost physically eject from our minds and bodies the rotten memories that were haunting us and debilitating us. Even before we arrived we each knew that a moment of truth was around the corner when it would be our turn to bare our soul before the group. To my mind it felt like a brutal extraction was about to happen – an operation to remove rotten flesh but without anaesthetic – and I was terrified at the prospect.

The notion that this delicate and traumatic process would take place without painkillers was the first of many misconceptions I held about the excellent treatment I received at Ticehurst. For the first couple of days we did nothing but create a sense of bonding, trust and security between us as we attended our first group sessions, repairing in between to our own rooms to fill in our diaries of each day's progress. These bonds were the anaesthetic that would help minimise the pain of what was to come. One of our first exercises involved each of us, in turn, being blindfolded and relying on another member of the group to instruct us as we walked down the corridor, through one of the doorways and then around one of the rooms where we were being treated. The idea was to encourage feelings of trust in each other.

We were given early instruction by Tim and Sarah to help us understand the process we were going to go through and the nature of the condition we had been suffering from. In addition to the trust exercise, we did something called 'Lines' where we looked at all the good and bad bits of our lives, ranking them on a scale ranging from +5 to −5 and we set down our goals and ambitions in an exercise called 'Ladders'. We were encouraged to set targets for six weeks, six months and one year in our professional lives, our leisure activities, finances, personal lives and relationships.

Tim and Sarah, who ran the group therapy debriefing sessions, told us about the 'Pint Pot Theory'. This describes how a mind subjected to an extreme traumatic event will try to fend off being overwhelmed by it as a result of subsequent triggers. The stress level will rise, as water or beer might do in a pint glass, and the mind will find ways to keep it within bounds – perhaps by use of drink or drugs or by physically removing oneself from the place or sound that is causing the symptoms. But if the trigger is too powerful, or the exposure to it too intense, the stress level will rise to the point where it is overflowing the rim of the glass and then continues to do so, leaving the rational mind incapable of stemming it. At that point you are in trouble.

This made sense to me. I realised that on many occasions in the past I had managed to keep the level inside the glass, but in the early summer of 1994, on that last trip to Afghanistan, I couldn't stop it rising too far and by the time I got back to London it was in full flow. The Pint Pot Theory felt like a neat visualisation of what had happened to me and proved an effective tool in understanding my condition and coming to terms with it.

Monday was our first day of group therapy and I dutifully wrote about my state of mind in the diary we had each been given. We had to hand them in every now and again for the nurses to read, as a way of assisting them in understanding our difficulties and what progress, or lack of it, we were making. 'I feel totally exhausted and tearful,' I wrote in blue pen at lunchtime. 'I have the impression that I am coming into the group at a more acute angle than the others – probably because my condition goes back over a longer period and has been building over successive episodes.'

By the evening of that day I must have presented to Tim and Sarah a fairly classic 'before' case. I remember thinking at the time that the diary was a total waste of time and an unnecessary diversion. Early in the evening, I was using a black pen.

Writing of any kind is difficult – it reminds me of my job and my job reminds me of all sorts of other things. I have chosen, throughout the autumn and winter, to work with my hands. Part of the problem with Afghanistan in '85 is that my rational self keeps throwing into doubt the possibility that *that* was where and when I was first traumatised. (What about the death of my mother in 1978? And the break-off of relations with my father in '83?) I thought I was doing reasonably OK in the last few weeks, but I can see now that, actually, all I have been doing is concealing the wreckage.

Then at 11.06 p.m. precisely I added one line: 'And this is going to be horrible.'

I spent much of the following day helping in the group as two others, Michael and Jackie, took their turns to have a go at starting the process of unburdening themselves. Michael had been in the air force and had lost a family member in appalling circumstances, while Jackie had been employed as a social worker in Leeds and had been kidnapped and threatened with rape. Later that day I had an opportunity to speak about my own demons and reveal the wreckage in my mind for the first time. I talked mainly about my family background, the death of my mother and my non-existent relationship with my father. The questions came thick and fast from the others and I did my best to answer them but I knew the difficult part was yet to come.

That evening I returned to the diary, a bewildered and frightened patient. 'I am helping Jim and I am helping Michael but I don't feel I'm helping Jackie enough. I feel guilty about this,' I wrote. 'Michael says he feels better for talking about [his relative]. At the moment I still feel worse.' Then later I started a new entry. 'I think I must be going down. I hope this is *only* PTSD and I'm not going mad. I still hate my job. How on earth will I be able to go back to it soon? I feel ashamed about my account today. I am so weak. I miss my dog, but not people. I love my boat but what will I think of her if I get well?'

Then I wrote about the section of the hospital that we occupied, which was separate from other areas, and the upcoming weekend break when we were allowed to go home. We each had our own room where we took our meals on trays. There was a 'group room' furnished with sofas and two armchairs where the debriefing took place and that was regarded as sacrosanct. I wrote:

> To me the unit is a bit like an aeroplane with the corridor, with a film in the evening and food on trolleys. When I fly I fight the boredom for the first few hours but then I stop and surrender and start to relax. I didn't like it here and thought I couldn't possibly stay at the weekend. Now I think I will have to tear myself away on Friday even though (or because) we still won't have reached our destination by then.

Dr Mills encouraged us to go home for the middle weekend to combat any possible dependency on the hospital environment that might develop. I left a one-line gap in my account and then added: 'I hope one day I will be sane enough and enthusiastic enough to look back at this and see how crazed (or something) I had become.'

My main moment to unburden myself came the next day when I had to go through the entire chronology of what happened in 1985 in every last detail, something I had steadfastly avoided doing up till then. The other members of the group had, by that stage, got the hang of the technique and would not allow me to skip any aspect of the story they asked for. There was no escape and I had to re-tell it all in graphic terms – the journey to the camp, the days of waiting, the attacks on the camp, the death of Abdullah-Jan, the journey into Kabul, the days hiding out in the city, then the return to the camp and, finally, the return to Pakistan.

This was a traumatic process and, like the others, I found

it impossible to complete without regularly breaking down. These were long, emotionally exhausting sessions but they were critical to making progress, and I felt the impact almost immediately. Speaking about what was haunting you was a physical process, like taking the rubbish out. There was no need for medicine. It was all about articulating and thereby letting go of the dark thoughts, fears and preoccupations that had festered for nine long years.

That night I returned to my diary at 9.35 p.m.

I have been in bed since 7 p.m. listening to the storm outside and imagining I am surfing down the waves in front of it on *Nutcracker*. I need some more time in the group to discuss: 1. My mother – just a bit about her death and my reaction. 2. My father – why I hate him. 3. Why I recall Niazuldin, Abdullah-Jan, Zulmai and Asil – all dead. (Thought prompted by Tim: 'What do they have in common?' – all dead, all friends/guardians/father figures, no chance to grieve for them, guilt about my role in their deaths.)

The group therapy technique was working its magic on me. Having feared exposing my thoughts to the others at first, I was now keen to speak further. In subsequent sessions I told the group about returning to Kabul the year before, confronting the places where I had been hidden in 1985, meeting Zulmai's family and discovering what had happened to Niazuldin. I also talked through the collapse of my marriage.

As a reasonably articulate person, used to expressing myself through my work, I responded to the challenge of the group environment more readily than some of the others. I sensed that I was making faster progress than them and even five days into the ten working days at Ticehurst, I was starting to see the light at the end of the tunnel. By early in the second week I was complaining in my diary that two of our number – Michael and Jim – had gone to the village pub for the evening. They had stepped out of the group and I felt we should try and stick together. I had certainly bought into the group ethic.

'Meanwhile, I'm feeling a bit better,' I wrote. 'It's a painful process getting better. I suppose lots of people say it, but when you've lived with a demon for so long, it can be quite hard – believe it or not – to finally say goodbye to it. I'm ready for next week.'

Then I recorded another step towards the daylight. If Jim had turned up unable to touch a light switch – he would rather eat cold baked beans than risk turning on the cooker – I had arrived unable to listen to or watch the news. I bet David Dimbleby has never imagined that just watching *Question Time* could have seemed such a challenge.

'Tonight I watched *Question Time* on TV,' I wrote. 'It's the first time in over six months that I've actually enjoyed and stuck with (for at least half the programme) anything to do with news or current affairs.'

During the final days, I was racing ahead of the other three, clearly benefiting enormously from the treatment – it felt like a self-reinforcing process, as one positive development compounded another. 'I am glad,' I noted, 'that I have got all the main "work" traumas over with. There are others, but I think I can break them down myself and "file" them.'

The only dark cloud was the dawning realisation that I would have to return to work – I referred to the 'dreaded return to the office' in my final diary entry – which was coming two weeks after the course finished. 'The whole prospect of going back to work is scaring the shit out of me. I genuinely do not want to go. I feel a lack of interest and a lack of enthusiasm. I am frightened that it will re-establish either/or my PTSD reaction, depression.'

At the end of the course we prepared to leave in an

atmosphere that reminded me of the last day of a boarding term at prep school. Dr Mills, a psychiatrist who specialises in the impact PTSD and trauma has on relationships, told me he was happy with my progress. But he warned me that there was a limit to how far I could go and that my PTSD would always leave scar tissue. He said the best way to avoid a full relapse was not to go to war zones. It may sound simple but it proved to be invaluable advice.

In the course of my research for this book I went back to see Dr Mills, now working out of his own practice in the village of Battle in East Sussex, not far from Ticehurst. Originally from Sri Lanka, he is the kind of practitioner with whom you immediately feel a bond of trust. Patient, a good listener and a wise counsellor, Dr Mills felt to me like an old friend, as we talked in his tastefully decorated rooms above the historic high street on a lovely early summer's day twenty years after my treatment.

We discussed the extraordinary progress that I made under his and Dr Turnbull's supervision. (Dr Mills had not debriefed me directly during those two weeks in January and February 1995 but it was his job to debrief Tim and Sarah each evening as a safety mechanism to ensure that they were not affected by the disturbing accounts they were hearing.)

Although I had been living with PTSD for nearly ten years at that stage, my rapid response to treatment was not unusual. 'We saw a lot of people who had had many years of PTSD recovering fairly quickly,' Dr Mills told me. Then he looked at the charts from the hospital of my case file. 'They show massive significant progress really from six weeks onwards,' he said in his heavily accented English, referring to assessments he made of me during regular follow-up visits to Ticehurst after the initial treatment. 'Some people improve after six months, some people can take up to a year but in your case at six weeks you are sorted. Your brain has sorted it out and then you maintained it at six months. It suggests that you worked really well at Ticehurst and the course suited you really well and that everything clicked in a way.'

Dr Mills also reminded me just how tough the first couple of days had been when we had to confront our demons head-on for the first time. My early scepticism about the efficacy of group therapy was, of course, misplaced.

'Group therapy is scary,' he explained, 'but what people found is that it's easier to talk it through with strangers than with somebody who is close to them. The process is not easy because avoidance of the events triggering PTSD kicks in. You don't want to go there, you don't want to deal with it. But it's also about talking about facts, thoughts, feelings and what symptoms you have now. So debriefing is a process. A lot of people can talk about it but they can't actually share their feelings. Or a lot of people can show their feelings but they can't talk about it.'

It was great to see Dr Mills again and to feel how far I had travelled. I still felt very emotional about the whole process I'd been through but, using the metaphor of the Pint Pot Theory, it was as though I had been emptied out and I now had lots of space available to deal with the stresses and strains of everyday life – just so long as I did not go to a war zone again.

20

A NEW LIFE

A fortnight after I left the hospital at Ticehurst in February 1995, I returned to London and made my re-entry to the offices of *The Times*, feeling self-conscious, nervous and out of sorts. It was nine months since the day I had walked out and I only went back out of a sense of duty. I felt I owed it to the company, to Peter Roberts and James McManus and other colleagues who had been so supportive. But my heart was never in it as I went through the motions of working, once again, on the treadmill of home news. This time I knew, even if they didn't, that there could be no escape to foreign climes on temporary assignments and certainly not to any war zones. I had no interest in doing that and knew, as Dr Mills had warned, that it would do me no good.

During my career at the paper I had always assiduously kept my cuttings. The company used to provide us, free of charge, with large black hardcover books to store them in and, over the years, I have filled twelve of them. But in those months after I returned following my treatment, I didn't keep a single piece that I wrote. I wasn't interested.

There were one or two little things nagging away at me. I had noticed that one of the news desk staff to whom I reported, who shall remain nameless, had taken to saying things like 'Here comes mad Ed' as I wandered down the office towards him. I was worried that his views reflected those of everyone else and that others were talking about me behind my back. I started to feel that perhaps my interests would be better served doing something else.

Drifting along, feeling better and stronger all the time, I determined to find an alternative to news. It came in the form of an offer out of the blue one day from David Chappell, then the deputy sports editor. I had written a light-hearted news story about the giant All Blacks rugby star Jonah Lomu, who had come to Britain during his preparation for the 1995 World Cup, and what he ate for breakfast. Having commissioned it, home news decided against publishing it and someone suggested I offer it to sport, a part of the paper that was entirely unknown to me.

I made my way down to the sports desk and got chatting to David, who had heard about my interest in sailing. It turned out he was looking for a new sailing correspondent to take the place of the incumbent who was moving on. I knew immediately that this was the perfect compromise for me. I could carry on writing but get away from news and the office and indulge my love of a sport that had always been the perfect antidote to work, helping to relieve the lingering after-effects of what had happened to me.

Peter Roberts was horrified at my determination to, as he saw it, chuck in my career and leave the main staff for the sailing correspondent job, which would be on a freelance contract. He asked me to wait three months, until January 1996, as a cooling-off period before confirming my decision and warned me there would be no way back from such a frivolous diversion. I waited three months as instructed and then went to see Roberts and told him I was keener than ever. Sailing correspondent was what I wanted to be.

When I discussed this with Dr Mills many years later, he was intrigued by my determination to head for the sea as I continued my recovery. Perhaps this was not a mere coincidence and it was the water I was after more than the boats on it. 'One of the interesting things that's coming out is that anything to do with water calms the right side of the brain down. So what you were doing was seeking out water to calm your right brain,' he said.

That was the beginning of fourteen years in sport at *The Times* – ten years of sailing, then four covering Formula One – that I thoroughly enjoyed but which I sometimes think of as being part of my long road to recovery. When I was writing about sailing I immersed myself in the sport and ignored news and current affairs for years. In those days, before *The Times* shrank to its current compact or tabloid format, there was plenty of room for minor sports and I revelled in the opportunity to travel the world reporting on my favourite pastime. I had the best job in Fleet Street, I told myself, even if it didn't pay much.

There were pit stops during round-the-world races in places like Cape Town, Fremantle or Rio de Janeiro; there were Olympic regattas in Savannah, Georgia (the Atlanta Games), Sydney and Athens; and there was the remarkable career of Ellen MacArthur, whose extraordinary feats in solo ocean-racing occupied acres of space in the paper. I covered it all, took it incredibly seriously – that 'unbridled intensity' was back in play – and forgot about my other life.

Whenever I felt nervous or stressed, I would remind myself that at that moment I was not lying in a cornfield in the Kunar valley being shelled by the Soviet army, while listening to the frantic mumbling of an Afghan warrior reading himself the last rites, or trying to infiltrate Kabul. Apart from reporting about sailing, I also spent a lot of my spare time on the water, cruising *Nutcracker* all over the British Isles – the east coast, the West Country, south-west Ireland and the west of Scotland – and as far afield as the Galician coast of Spain.

I am not sure what the close-knit world of sailing journalism thought about this intruder in their midst but Bob Fisher of the *Guardian*, Tim Jeffrey of the *Daily Telegraph* and Stuart Alexander of the *Independent* put up with me as I slowly learnt the ropes of a technical and rather obscure sport. Recalling his first impression as I turned up at my first regatta in Miami, Fisher – the top dog in the group – remembered feeling that there was something slightly odd about me that he couldn't quite place, a 'reserve' as he put it in my character. 'You look at it and think there is something wrong somewhere – I couldn't put my finger on it at the time,' he said. He was right. I was on a slow journey of recovery and by then I had barely started.

At home my long years – two of them in fact – of wooing Jeanna finally paid off when, after she ended her previous relationship, we started living together in late 1995. I had been drawn to her like a magnet from the start; deep down I knew she was exactly the companion for life that I needed. Amazingly, despite my appalling record and all the troubles I had been through, she agreed to take me on and in December 1996 we married in a simple and low-key ceremony at Wandsworth Town Hall. I became not only her husband but stepfather to Tilou, Florence and Marcus who, over the years, have grown to seem like my own.

No-nonsense but caring and compassionate, Jeanna learnt to live with me and with the scars that Dr Mills had predicted would always remain. She says that during all the time I was getting to know her before my stay at Ticehurst, I never once talked about Afghanistan or what had happened to me in 1985. If she tried to prise open that part of my life, I would change the subject. In our early years together there were times when I was present physically about the house but my mind was elsewhere and we developed our own method of dealing with relapses. She would often spot them before I owned up to what was going on and we would, quite deliberately, sit down in a quiet room and she would ask the questions that would force me to unburden myself. It was simple and effective.

Recalling those episodes, Jeanna said: 'You are physically present but you are not there – you have nothing to give. You are completely trapped within yourself. I would say that the effect of it all is that you don't deal with stress or getting overtired – it just makes you fragile.'

Jeanna is the perfect foil to me – a balanced, sensible and loving person. She struggled with my lingering sudden startle syndrome, something that might otherwise seem a minor remnant of a much bigger problem. 'It has really been a big thing because it is quite difficult to deal with,' she said. 'If I come up to you and touch you affectionately from behind and you don't realise I am there, your reaction is to get really annoyed and it hasn't got better over the years.' She noticed – how could she not? – that I was often extremely agitated when asleep as, for years, I continued dreaming about events that had once haunted me when awake and she noticed too that, more than most, travelling was a major issue. 'It is always very bad for you – it always causes you stress. I think PTSD has scarred you and does definitely affect you at times.'

━━◆◆◆◆━━

In 1996, shortly after retiring as a deputy High Court judge, my father collapsed one night. He had suffered a brain haemorrhage and died four days after being admitted to hospital. Our relationship had never improved and I had not seen him for years. I could never forgive him for the way he abandoned his children; I loved him but I couldn't come to terms with what he had done especially now that I was a parent myself – albeit a step-parent.

Only two of his children attended his funeral; I and one of my sisters decided to stay away. In my case, I genuinely felt as though my father had already been dead for years. I did not consciously take a decision not to go to his funeral; it never occurred to me to do anything else. When his will was read, we found out that he had left almost everything to his second wife.

I have never had any regrets about not being reconciled with him. My sisters and I all know that the way my father behaved after our mother's death had a profound effect on us and contributed to the decisions we made in life and the difficulties we encountered. I have no doubt that I was more reckless than I might otherwise have been as a young man, partly because I felt cast aside from the life we had known and as a result I answered to no one. I was up for anything in my early twenties and prepared to take a chance without considering what the consequences of my actions might be. It took me a while to understand that and overcome my impulsive streak.

——————

During my decade of writing about sailing I continued to push anything I associated with my old career aside, avoiding the people and the places – especially the office, which I visited no more than five times in ten years – that might remind me of what had gone on before. Jeanna and the children put up with my desire for escape and for peace and quiet and we fled London for a remote part of rural Herefordshire for eight years. We made our home in a cottage in the middle of a field at the bottom of an unmade track complete with pigs, a fleet of dogs and a cat. My time in Herefordshire was divided 40:60 between writing about sailing and creating a garden out of three wild acres of Hereford clay.

The survival of my marriage is down as much to the treatment I was lucky to receive at Ticehurst as it is to Jeanna's preparedness to put up with me, and her patience and loving good nature. Dr Mills reminded me that we are cheating the general rule: 'With PTSD not many relationships survive so what you've got is something really special,' he said.

With the physical shrinking of the paper, the retirement of Ellen MacArthur after her remarkable ten years of achievement in sailing, and a feeling that I had exhausted my immediate interest in that sport, I was delighted to accept the offer to become the paper's Formula One writer. I knew a little bit about motor racing and its history but it didn't take long to get hooked on the excitement of Formula One and the poisonous intrigue of the paddock. My first visit to a Grand Prix was one summer's day at Silverstone in 2006. Tim Hallissey, the sports editor, had suggested that I pop along to check it out.

As I walked into the circuit after parking my car, I heard the rumbling and then the deafening shrieking and howling of a Formula One car at full throttle for the first time. The hairs stood up on the back of my neck. 'Sure,' I thought. 'I can do this. What a blast.' Indeed I enjoyed four action-packed years covering Bernie Ecclestone's circus and loved almost every minute of it, apart from the hundreds of hours spent every year in economy-class seats and increasingly shabby hotels.

With its constant travelling and faster pace, Formula One warmed me up for my eventual return to the office as deputy foreign editor in 2010. I had made it clear to the paper that I did not want to do another season of motorsport and Rick Beeston, the foreign editor, spotted the opportunity he had long predicted and hoped would come to pass. He called me one afternoon and asked me if I would like to be his deputy. After fourteen years in the backwaters, I knew it was time to return to my roots. I was delighted to be back working with Rick, a hugely experienced foreign correspondent and long-time friend who had joined the paper two years before me.

I was back where I had started but this time in an editing and commissioning role, something I had never envisaged. I had finally overcome my aversion to the part of journalism I had loved with a passion. It was my job, and privilege, to talk to our correspondents around the world, from Sydney to New York and from Mexico City to Moscow, discussing their stories, working out how we wanted to present them in the paper and then editing their copy.

It was also my job to talk to, and counsel, our reporters who were on the road in war zones, trying to weigh up the risks in places like Afghanistan, Iraq or, later, Libya. I had been there myself and knew what was involved. I had also made some big mistakes, after all. No wonder I tended to be cautious in my advice. 'There is a limit to what you need to do for a good story,' I heard myself telling someone down the phone one day. If only I had been given that advice back in 1985.

In the course of my duties I was required to attend a management training course dealing with trauma. I was impressed that the company was taking this issue so seriously. The Trauma Risk Management (TRiM) course was designed to help us identify colleagues – correspondents in my case – who might be in danger of suffering from some form of trauma or post-traumatic stress and then knowing what to do about it. Among my colleagues on that two-day programme was Marie Colvin, the celebrated foreign correspondent of *The Sunday Times,* who was killed not long afterwards at Homs in Syria in February 2012. Marie had struggled with her own issues as a result of years of travelling to war zones and completing some extraordinarily tough assignments. With her trademark patch over one eye and weather-beaten face, she was down to earth and fun and we enjoyed comparing notes on our shared love of the sea and sailing.

Not long after I joined the foreign desk I experienced the first of two relapses triggered by my return to my old stomping grounds. At the time, one of my responsibilities was dealing with *The Times* correspondent then on assignment in Afghanistan – the paper's veteran war reporter Anthony

Loyd who was embedded with the US 82nd Airborne Division in Kandahar province. Anthony was certainly in harm's way on that mission, risking his life and facing up to the daily threat of injury or death from improvised bombs to get stories back to the paper. All I was doing was sitting in a comfortable swivelling armchair in the newsroom talking to him about his story for the day, and joshing with him on the phone. But even that – no more than talking to Anthony – sent me on another journey to the black hole. I went home that night and sat down with Jeanna and we went through a practised routine of debriefing, as she allayed my fears that I might not be able to continue with my new job, and gradually my symptoms cleared.

Thereafter things were going well. I was enjoying helping to manage our foreign news coverage and was talking on a regular basis to Anthony and to Jerome Starkey, our Kabul-based correspondent, without any adverse effects. Three months into the job, I made my first overseas trip to Israel on a briefing tour. Again there were no adverse effects, though clearly there was a negligible threat and Israel had not been an area that I had reported on during my early days as a foreign correspondent.

I was feeling confident that I could handle my new role when, in late 2010, Rick suggested I might like to spend a week in Afghanistan on a NATO-organised junket for journalists. 'It is nothing special,' he said. The group would start by visiting Kabul for a few days, talk to the ambassador, other diplomats and senior military officers and then head down to Helmand, the centre of British military operations in the south. There was no prospect of seeing fighting; it would just be a routine trot round to get the lie of the land. 'Of course, I'd love to go,' I said, genuinely believing I could handle this.

Within minutes my body as much as my mind went into revolt. All the old ghosts that had dogged me for years came back, insidiously, misleadingly at first. By that evening

Jeanna had no doubt what was happening and was trying to persuade me to back out. But I felt I had to go. It was part of my new responsibilities and would be an invaluable opportunity to catch up on what had been going on in Afghanistan since my last, fateful trip in 1994. I soldiered on through the next day and even sent my passport off to get an Afghan visa.

But my condition got worse and worse and I began to realise this was hopeless. There was no way I could go back. The mere mention of Afghanistan had haunted me for years and I had only just managed to deal with Anthony Loyd. Now the prospect of going there was in danger of sending me into the depths and I had to remove the cause. It seems so straightforward in retrospect but at the time my addled brain and determination to fulfil my role made it a devilish decision. Surely things would improve once I settled down, I told myself? But I knew in my heart of hearts that they would not. I remembered what Dr Mills had told me: 'Don't go back to a war zone!'

I sat down at my computer and sent Rick a note.

Hi Rick

I don't think I can do this Afghan trip. I am beginning to realise that, even fifteen years after my PTSD episode, it remains the one place on this planet I can't seem to face going back to. As you probably know, it was events there back in 1985 that have caused me some problems ever since. I could take a risk but I feel concerned that a relapse would be bad for me and for my ability to do my job. It's incredibly frustrating because I'd love to go but my body/brain is already flashing up warning signs.

Jeanna is adamant that she does not want me to go and, I have to admit, the doctors who treated me in the first place always said it would not be a good idea to go there

again, especially if there is a war on. I apologise for
having indicated I would like to go – I thought I would –
but I was wrong.

I will tell the people at NATO.

Ed

Then I went to see the editor, the ebullient James Harding,
and told him I had come to the conclusion that Afghanistan was probably off-limits to me for the rest of my life and
that my wife was totally opposed to the trip. I would have to
back out. James was instantly understanding. 'Thank God
for your wife,' he joked. 'She and I are on the same page on
this.' He told me not to worry about it. The paper could
easily send someone else.

As I walked out of his office, almost immediately I felt the
heat, the fever and the preoccupation start to drain away and
my faculties return. It was a tangible feeling, the ghosts of
the past floating away, leaving me in peace. I could access my
normal personality again – within minutes – and waves of
relief swept over me as I returned to my chair, put my feet up
on the desk and called Jeanna to let her know the trip was off.

I left the paper – after twenty-five years – in 2013 following Rick's death at fifty of cancer and Harding's dismissal
by Rupert Murdoch, something I found difficult to accept.
Even before I left, in my final role as deputy head of news, I
somehow found the time to begin this manuscript, twenty-
eight years after the events that form its central core. It took
me longer to finish than I imagined but the process of finally
putting it all down, in order, explaining it, describing what
happened, has proved a remarkable therapy in its own right.

At last I can look back without fear.

POSTSCRIPT

When I returned to Kabul in 1994 and visited Zulmai's family I was told that Niazuldin was dead but there was uncertainty about exactly what had happened to him. As I have written, he was said to have got into a feud with a rival and been thrown down a well, where he died. Over the years, I have always wondered if that was true and when I finally started writing this book I decided to try and find out a bit more.

In my final months at the paper I phoned up one of *The Times'* reporters in Kabul, Nooruddin Bakhshi. I told him the story about Niazuldin, who he was, what sort of man he was, what he did during the now-distant Soviet war and the story about how he died. It was only when I had finished explaining it all to Noor that I realised that all these events, that still seem so immediate to me, were nearly twenty years old. This was ancient history in modern Kabul, now beset by a very different war between the Taleban and an international coalition led by NATO.

Noor very kindly took up the challenge to try and find out more. He took a taxi one day to Musei, then a risky place to be with Taleban fighters in the area, and spoke to village elders and the local police chief. They were all certain that Niazuldin had indeed been killed – one used the word *shaeed*. They hadn't heard the story of him being thrown down a well but said he had been ambushed by some Hazara fighters during the civil war which raged between 1992–96.

The elders said that Hazaras of the Islamic United Party

of Afghanistan had come to Musei to demand that Niazuldin either join them or hand over his weapons and allow
them to take control of the village. The Hazaras, hailing
from central Afghanistan, are the third-largest ethnic group
in the country and at the time were heavily involved in con-
testing the civil war around Kabul. True to form, Niazuldin
refused to obey the Hazaras and there seems to have been an
altercation during which he was shot and killed and one of
his brothers savagely beaten, leaving him with brain injuries.
Noor said he had been told that Niazuldin was almost certainly buried in Musei.

No one seems to know when this happened but it is likely
that Niazuldin died in either 1992 or 1993 when he would
have been thirty-nine or forty. I listened to Noor talking about
this man, who meant little to him, with a certain detachment. I had known for years that Niazuldin was dead but this
version of events seemed to carry the ring of truth with it.
I could easily imagine Niazuldin's outrage at being asked to
hand over control of Musei to outsiders after having fought
for the village throughout the Soviet war. In my mind's eye
I have an image of Niaz walking away from his killers and
being shot in cold blood from behind – I can't imagine any
other way that they could have extinguished his life force.

Having seen what men like Niazuldin went through in
the 1980s, it is difficult for someone in my position not to
conclude that the sacrifices they made then and the suffering
they endured have been wasted.

Their goal was to rid the country of the Soviet invaders and they achieved that in February 1989. But since then
Afghanistan has lurched from civil war to the rise of the
Taleban and the war against the coalition led by the United
States and Britain. As I write, the country remains fragile
and still buffeted by the threat of the Taleban with NATO
forces having largely left the scene.

Looking back over the whole period, it seems a tragedy

that one very debateable decision by an ailing Leonid Brezhnev in the winter of 1979 has had such a catastrophic long-term impact on what was a generally peaceful, tribal society. That decision caused one of the key fissures in the Soviet edifice and hastened its demise while in Afghanistan it triggered decades of war, hundreds of thousands of deaths and injuries, and the displacement of millions to refugee camps inside Afghanistan or in neighbouring Pakistan and Iran.

Just as war does anywhere, decades of conflict have hugely destabilised the nation, speeding up its development in a chaotic way, as modern technology, modern weapon systems, modern infrastructure, modern medicine and alien Western cultural norms have been foisted upon it, leaving a confused and disrupted – not to say traumatised – society.

In the process the Soviets, through their sheer brutality and destructive tactics, radicalised Afghanistan, leaving a poisoned legacy for the Afghans and the West to deal with. Prior to the 1979 invasion the mullah was an important figure in Afghan society – much like an Anglican priest in Britain today. But the Soviet war gave him a new platform and the peasants of rural Afghanistan, many of them still illiterate, gathered round the call from the mosque like never before as they committed themselves to Holy War.

In the refugee camps of Pakistan and Iran new genera-tions of Afghans, whose fathers were being killed or injured over the border, were growing up in miserable poverty, brain-washed by the ranting mullahs. These camps were the perfect breeding grounds for the Taleban – the more radical, second-generation version of the Mujahidin.

Even by 1985, the men that I spent time with in Afghani-stan were fairly extreme in their religious observance and more than happy to die as martyrs to the cause. By that stage fanatical Arab volunteers – one of whom was Osama Bin Laden – were already travelling to Afghanistan to fight and train and acquire skills that they would take back with them to the Middle East and North Africa. Eventually those early roots produced Al Qaeda and the abomination of 9/11.

It is a sad and depressing picture for anyone who learnt to love the people of a proud country whose medieval ways prior to 1979 have been lost forever. Afghanistan is a tenuous nation made up of a patchwork of ethnic groups between whom there has always been a degree of enmity, spurred on by the competing interests of its neighbouring states. It has always been regarded as a strategic crossroads, fought over by foreign powers, but in the later years of the twentieth century it had the misfortune to be situated under the belly of a slowly decaying superpower. In my view, it has largely been the victim – not the cause – of its own misery.

***

PTSD has now become a household term, but when I was diagnosed it was little known in Britain. I was lucky to find doctors who were able to join the dots and work it out, and even luckier to take part in Dr Turnbull's pioneering course at Ticehurst. Now we know far more about how the body and mind can respond to the stresses of modern warfare and other harrowing events in peacetime and about a condition that afflicted thousands of men after the trenches in the First World War and many others after the Second World War.

Every year more and more former soldiers who served in either Northern Ireland, the Balkans, Iraq or Afghanistan are presenting with PTSD and there is an urgent requirement for the government to come up with a proper strategy and funding to deal with it. There are big debates about how best to treat the condition and certainly there is no one-size-fits-all approach. However one thing I do know from personal experience is that PTSD is a jail cell for the mind – but with help, the keys to freedom can be found.

ACKNOWLEDGEMENTS

Many years ago I was attending a regatta in Scotland and over dinner one night at Tarbert, in Argyll, I explained to Nigel Bramwell a little bit about what had happened to me in Afghanistan. I remember him urging me to sit down and write about it in full. It took me many more years to do that but I am grateful to him for pouring a little water on the seed planted in my mind by Lawrence Walsh in the hills southeast of Kabul in the summer of 1985.

My thanks to David Luxton for his enthusiasm and determination to try and get this book published and to Georgina Simon for her refusal to let it lie on a shelf and for making the breakthrough with Arcadia. I would like to thank Gill Paul for her forensic editing and valuable advice on structure, Angeline Rothermundt for meticulously preparing my manuscript for printing, Joanne Curran for her work on the jacket design and Jonathan Harley for typesetting.

At Arcadia Piers Russell-Cobb and Joe Harper have been a joy to work with and their enthusiasm for this project has been instrumental in bringing it to life. I would like to thank Martin Lubikowski for his work on the maps, Florence Benton for her sketch of Niazuldin's camp and Lucy Dundas and Cassie Lawrence at Flint for their contribution to promoting the book.

My agent Mark Lucas has guided me and advised me through new waters, Bob Benton has always been wonderfully encouraging and Matthew Gwyther and Daniel Green have given me sound advice over the years. My thanks also to Helena Michell who has helped me to learn how to speak about my experiences in public.

My three sisters and their husbands – Jane and Peter Symonds, Kate and John Charlton-Jones and Fi and Simon Pearson – have always been supportive and loving and have taken turns to come to my aid when I returned injured or ill from somewhere, either in body or mind. I would like to thank Kate for her valuable comments on reading my manuscript and Fi for her edit of my first draft.

I would also like to take this opportunity to thank Celia and the late Howard Root and their family who offered me their home in Winchester when my own was no longer available.

My three step-children – Tilou Griffiths, Florence Benton and Marcus Turner – have lived with me for 21 years but only understood my background before I knew them when they read this manuscript. Their unquestioning love – both before and after they read it – has been an immeasurable source of support.

Finally I would like to thank my wife Jeanna who named this book and whose patient understanding and love has been critical to my recovery.

Walderton, West Sussex
March 2017